DISCOVERERS

OF

AMERICA

By the Same Author

DISCOVERERS

OF

AMERICA

CHARLES NORMAN

O my America, my new-found land!

—JOHN DONNE

Thomas Y. Crowell Company
NEW YORK
ESTABLISHED 1834

DESIGNED BY *Margaret F. Plympton*

MANUFACTURED IN THE UNITED STATES OF AMERICA

L.C. Card 68–27318

1 2 3 4 5 6 7 8 9 10

TO

The Indian Tribes

OF

North America

FOREWORD

✿

This book is about "men full of activity, stirrers abroad, and seekers of remote parts of the world," in Richard Hakluyt's noble phrase about the English discoverers of his time. It is applicable to all who first came to these shores on voyages of discovery—Frenchmen and Spaniards, Italians, Portuguese and Hollanders as well as Englishmen. On the whole, they managed pretty well with their crude or fanciful maps, a compass, astrolabe and sailing directions—when these were to be had. The maps, of course, improved fairly rapidly.

It is also about the garden that was America, whose fragrance was wafted far out to sea, where the discoverers tossing on their little ships smelled it and marveled, then gazed in rapture on the flowering land. It is about the greatest hunting and fishing grounds the world has ever known, now barren and desecrated, but still teeming with game and fish in the narratives that follow.

It is about the Indians, who suffered most from the coming of the white man; yet, with the exception of Florida, where slavers had come before the discoverers, they were everywhere friendly, and almost everywhere saved the white man from starvation. The civilization of the Indians, which the newcomers destroyed, seems to have been perfected to a harmony with nature and the seasons which gave them, in turn, the yield of the stream, the soil, and the forest; but it was not what Europeans left home to find.

Marc Lescarbot, who has been termed "the French Hakluyt," was almost alone in his views about colonization. "I attach little importance to mines," he said. "The true mine for the settler is waving wheat and grazing cattle." Later, the perilous voyages were made for furs, and it is curious to reflect that the clash of empires which followed was over millinery.

The rapidity with which maritime events were communicated may appear astonishing. A new profession came into being as a result—cartography. In Seville there was even a clearing house— Casa de Contratación (House of Trade)—which, while concerned chiefly with commerce between Spain and the New World, was also a training center for pilots, and where a master map was under constant revision. Brereton's *Brief and True Relation,* the earliest book relating to New England, inspired Captain John Smith to go with the Jamestown settlers, and Smith himself sent Henry Hudson a map he had drawn in Virginia to help the latter on his voyage of discovery.

Many odd facts emerge from the narratives of the discoverers and settlers. One of them is that the New Found Land had been known to British, Breton and Portuguese fishermen decades before the famed voyages—perhaps even as much as a century. Fish was needed in Europe, and fishermen from Europe went where fish were in abundance, dried them on the rocks, and brought them back. Communism was tried in Jamestown and New Plymouth; in the former, a new military governor ordered it abolished in 1619, in the latter it was quietly dropped in 1623. In the end, private initiative and private property sped the growth of the colonies.

Religious beliefs played an important role, but not always a happy one. There could not have been, of course, a greater contrast than that between revealed religion and the unenlightened pantheism of the natives. The Indians, says the narrator of Cartier's second voyage,

> "believe no whit in God, but in one they call Cudruaigni. They say that often he speaketh with them and telleth them what weather shall follow, whether good or bad. Moreover, they say that when he is angry with them he casteth dust into their eyes. They believe that when they die they go into the stars, and thence by little and little descend down into the horizon, even as the stars do, and that then they go into certain green fields full of goodly, fair and precious trees, flowers and fruits."

The French set them right:

> "After that they had given us these things to understand, we showed them their error, and told [them] that their Cudruaigni did but deceive them, for he is but a devil and an evil spirit, affirming unto them that there is but one only God, who is in heaven, and who giveth us all necessaries, being the Creator of all Himself, and that only we must believe in Him; moreover, that it is necessary for us to be baptized, otherwise we are damned into Hell."

The Spaniards brought with them a lengthy document to be read to the natives, preferably by the governor in the presence of a notary. It was authorized by the Council of the Indies, and was considered fair warning, although in Castilian. It called on the Indians to acknowledge Spain's sovereigns as their own, and to accept instruction in the Catholic faith; they would then be received "with love and charity." But if not, "I protest to you," the governor was ordered to proclaim, "I will enter with force, making war upon you from all directions and in every manner that I may be able, when I will subject you to obedience to the Church and the yoke of their Majesties." This was done, with or without a reading, and it is strange to consider the slaughters of the day followed by the trumpet call at vespers for the Ave Maria in the American wilderness.

The English also hoped to make converts, but first distributed shirts and breeches.

Negroes accompanied almost all of the early expeditions. One of them has the distinction of being the first man to cross the continent, enter Mexico, and return; the three white men with him on this memorable trek did not come back to the present confines of the United States.

I have used only firsthand, on-the-scene accounts to tell the story of the discoverers and settlers, the accounts they wrote themselves. Discovery, however, becomes geography, and geography quickly turns into history, and occasionally I have given events their essential environment. An effort has also been made to utilize contemporary illustrations.

It gives me great pleasure to thank all those who have helped me in the preparation of this book. I begin with the treasure house I have learned to know so well, the New York Public Library. In the Rare Book Division, I thank Mr. Lewis M. Stark, chief, Mrs. Maud D. Cole, first assistant, and Mrs. Philomena C. Houlihan; in the Map Division, Mr. Gerard L. Alexander, chief, and Mr. Norwood B. Vail, Mr. Edward M. Gardner and Mr. Russell Hendler; in the Prints Division, Miss Elizabeth E. Roth, and in the Arents Collections, Mr. Perry Hugh O'Neil.

I thank Dr. Helmut Nickel of the Metropolitan Museum of Art; Dr. Roman Drazniowsky, map curator of the American Geographical Society; the Museum of the American Indian, Museum of the City of New York, the Bancroft Library, University of California, Berkeley, the Hispanic Society of America, and The Montreal Museum of Fine Arts. I thank Mr. Thomas R. Adams, Librarian of The John Carter Brown Library, Brown University, Providence, R.I., and Miss Jeanette D. Black, of the Library Map Room; Miss Ellen Shaffer, Rare Book Department, The Free Library of Philadelphia; Mr. John L. Lochhead, of The Mariners Museum, Newport News, Va., and Mr. John Parker, curator, James Ford Bell Library, University of Minnesota.

I thank the National Portrait Gallery–Smithsonian Institution, Washington, D.C., the Public Record Office and the National Portrait Gallery, London, and the Walters Art Gallery, Baltimore. Special thanks are due to Mr. Martin Leifer, assistant curator, The New-York Historical Society; Mr. Vincent J. Mrazek, Acting Chief Park Ranger, Cape Hatteras National Seashore, National Park Service; Mrs. Mary M. Hirth, Academic Center Library, The University of Texas, and Mr. Henry D. Grunder, Rare Book Division, William and Mary College, Williamsburg, Va.

The reproductions of John White's watercolors are from the Page-Holgate facsimiles of the original paintings in the North Carolina Collection of the L. R. Wilson Memorial Library of the University of North Carolina, by permission of the University of North Carolina Press. I thank Mr. William S. Powell, of the University of North Carolina Library, and Mr. Lambert Davis, director, the University of North Carolina Press, for their unfailing courtesy and assistance.

Finally, I wish to thank Mr. Roger Butterfield, whose encouragement was decisive, and Professor James Rush Beeler of William and Mary College, whose labors in my behalf, including an extensive bibliography, helped to set me on my course in the fresh waters of early Americana.

C. N.

CONTENTS

*I*LLUSTRATIONS

PROLOGUE:
THE NEW WORLD

"Lumbre! Tierra!"—"Light! Land!"

With these two words, shouted at midnight October 11, 1492, off an island in the Bahamas, the story of the discoverers may be said to begin. They were uttered by Pedro Yzquierdo, a seaman on the *Santa María*; Columbus himself had seen a light some two hours earlier and was to claim, and receive, the royal annuity of 10,000 maravedis promised the first member of his expedition to sight land.

To this day, no one knows for certain what kind of light Columbus claimed to have seen. It could not have been what he thought it was like, "a wax candle rising and falling," or even a torch, for at ten o'clock the *Santa María* was still some thirty-five miles offshore. What Yzquierdo saw was probably a shaft of moonlight on a beach—the moon, in its third quarter, rose that night at eleven and was above and behind the fleet. One Rodrigo de Triana, a lookout on the *Pinta*, which was sailing ahead of the *Santa María*, actually saw land at 2 A.M., and a gun was fired as prearranged (he, too, was barred from the reward and is never heard of again). Sails were shortened, and the vessels hove to.

When daylight came—it was Friday, October 12—Columbus and the captains of the *Pinta* and *Niña* went ashore in an armed boat, watched by naked inhabitants,

COAT OF ARMS OF FERDINAND AND ISABELLA
From the title page of Caesar's *Commentaries* published in Toledo, 1498. Courtesy of the Hispanic Society of America.

"all of good stature, a very handsome people. Their hair is not curly, but loose and coarse, like horsehair. In all, the forehead is broad, more so than in any other people I have hitherto seen. Their eyes are very beautiful and not small, and themselves far from black, but the color of the Canarians [i.e., the Canary Islands]. Their legs are very straight, all in one line." (From Columbus's *Journal of the First Voyage*.)

Under their gaze, he planted royal standards in the luxuriant soil and took possession in the names of Don Ferdinand and Doña Isabella, "by the grace of God King and Queen of Castille, Leon, Aragon, Sicily, Granada, Toledo, Valencia, Galicia, Majorca, Seville, Sardinia, Cordova, Corsica, Murcia, Jaen, Algarbe, Algeciras, Gibraltar and the Canary Islands." The land claimed for them was an island called by the natives "Guanahani," which Columbus named

THE *Niña,* THE *Pinta* AND *Santa María* IN THE WEST INDIES
This is the first printed representation of the New World in the
Old, from a letter of Columbus to Gabriel Sanxis, treasurer of
Aragón, published in Basel, 1494. Extremely stylized, it shows
San Salvador, the first landfall, at right center; above it, His-
paniola (today's Haiti and the Dominican Republic); upper left
and center, two islands named for Ferdinand and Isabella (Long
Island and Crooked Island, respectively); and left center, the
first island encountered southwest of San Salvador, which Columbus named Santa María de la Concepción, now called Rum Cay.
Cuba, which he named Juana, does not appear in this woodcut.
Columbus wrote: "When I reached Juana, I followed its coast to
the westward, and I found it so long that I thought it must be
the mainland, the province of Cathay" (i.e., China). The artist's
imagination was also at work, hence castles where there were
only huts. Courtesy of the Rare Book Division, The New York
Public Library.

San Salvador: The son of a Genoese wool weaver had some titles of
his own to savor, exacted for himself and his sons and successors
from the monarchs he served—"Don Christopher Columbus, Admiral [afterward, Admiral of the Ocean Sea], Viceroy and Governor
of the Islands and Mainland That May Be Discovered."

Although Columbus's vision of the world was astonishingly modern—he placed it "within the sphere of the heavens, so that it
touches them upon no side, nor has aught of firmness to rest upon,
but is only earth and water globed by heat within the hollow vault
of the sky"—he did not know where he was on earth. He thought
he was at the gateway to the golden East—the Spice Islands, and

Cathay, the land of the Grand Cham, to whom he had a letter from his sovereigns; later, sailing southward, he coasted along the north shore of Cuba, which was to become "la joya más preciosa de la corona de España"—"the most precious jewel in the Spanish crown" —and believed it to be Japan, the "Cipango" of Marco Polo.

On his second voyage to the New World in 1493 he discovered Dominica, Puerto Rico, some of the Leeward Islands, Virgin Islands, and Jamaica, and explored the southern coast of Cuba. On his third voyage, in 1498, he discovered South America, which he thought was the mainland, and on his last, in 1502, Central America. He still believed that he had reached the East Indies, and "Las Indias" is the name he gave the entire region, whence "Indians" for the inhabitants.

Although he had judged correctly "that from whatever part of the ocean he should begin his passage, he could not fail to meet land," Columbus was unaware that another land mass existed between Europe and Asia. Yet fifty years before he sailed on his epochal voyage there was already a map in existence which showed—west of Iceland and Greenland—North America in lopsided island form. This map, dating from around 1400, and copiously annotated, bears an inscription which labels the continent "Vinland Island, discovered by Bjarni and Leif in company," thus bearing out the Norse sagas of the discovery of America in the eleventh century by Bjarni Herjolfsson and Leifr Eiriksson.

It remained for another Italian, also sailing under the banner of Spain, Amerigo—in Latin *Americus*—Vespucci, to give his name, in its feminine form, to the whole of the New World, literally getting it on the map before anyone else. It was Vespucci's view that South America, which he saw in 1499, was not a part of Asia, but a separate continent. It is probable that if Columbus had not persisted in his belief that he had reached the East Indies, North and South America would have been named for him.

The news he brought back was sensational enough. It launched fleets in the shipyards of Portugal, France and England as well as Spain. A skein of routes appeared in northern and southern waters, from Lisbon, Palos and Cadiz; from London, Plymouth and Bristol; from Dieppe and St. Malo. It twisted and stretched to the Azores and the Canaries; to the northern and southern coasts of North America; in and out of the Caribbean; to the South Atlantic, and past the Horn to the Pacific. Africa was rounded, the earth circumnavigated, the world remapped.

Although many were still to seek a northwest passage to India, the pre-Columbian notion that the land mass to the west of Europe

COSMOGRPHIAE

Capadociam/Pamphiliam/Lidiam/ Ciliciã/Arme
nias maiorē & minorē.Colchiden/Hircaniam/Hi⁄
beriam/Albania.et preterea mĺtas quas fingilatim
enumerare longa mora effet.Ita dicta ab eius nomi
nis regina.

Nũc ꝯo & hę partes funt latius luftratæ/& alia
quarta pars per Americũ Vefputiũ(vt in fequenti
bus audietur)inuenta eft/quã non video cur quis
iure vetet ab Americo inuentore fagacis ingenij vi

Ameri⁄ ro Amerigen quafi Americi terrã / fiue Americam
ca dicendã:cũ & Europa & Afia a mulieribus fua for
tita fint nomina.Eius fitũ & gentis mores ex bis bi
nis Americi nauigationibus quæ fequunĺ liquide
intelligi datur.

Hunc in modũ terra iam quadripartita cogno⁄
fcit:et funt tres primę partes cõtinentes/quarta eft
infula:cũ omni quacꝗ mari circũdata confpiciaĺ.Et
licet mare vnũ fit quĕadmodũ et ipfa tellus/multis
tamen finibus diftinctum / & innumeris replętum

Prifcia infulis varia fibi noĩa affumit :quę et in Cofmo gra
nus. phiæ tabulis cõfpiciunĺ/& Prifcianus in tralatio ne
Dionifij talibus enumerat verfibus.

Circuit Oceani gurges tamen vndiꝗ vaftus
Qui ꝗuis vnus fit plurima nominafumit.
Finibus Hefperijs Athlanticus ille vocatur
At Boreꝗqua gens furit Armiafpa fub armis
Diciĺ ille piger necnõ Satur,idē Mortuus eft alijs.

FIRST APPEARANCE OF "AMERICA"

From Martin Waldseemüller's *Cosmographiae Introductio,* 1507
(second paragraph and margin). He also put it on a map the
same year, but afterward concluded that Amerigo Vespucci was
not deserving of the honor, and dropped "America" from his
later work, without substituting another name—it probably
would have been "Columbia" if he had. Photograph courtesy
of the Rare Book Division, The New York Public Library

was Asia, or linked with it, was a thing of the past, as remote to the
new age of discoverers as the map which depicted the known
world in the form of a circle, its center Jerusalem as fixed by Holy
Writ: "Thus saith the Lord God; This is Jerusalem: I have set it
in the midst of the nations and countries that are round about her"
(Ezekiel 5:5). With it went the maps, global and rectangular, which
showed Europe and Africa on the right, Asia and Cipango on the
left, with a vast ocean between.

On March 5, 1496, one John Caboto, a Venetian citizen but a native
of Genoa like Columbus, applied for a patent from the English king
for a voyage of discovery in the eastern, western and northern seas;
the omission of southern seas would indicate that Cabot (as he was
afterward known) knew of the prior claims of Spain and Portugal.

The Spanish ambassador in England quite calmly informed Ferdinand and Isabella that "one like Columbus had come to engage the king in another enterprise like that of the Indies, yet without prejudice to Spain and Portugal," which by the Treaty of Tordesillas, 1494, had divided the as yet unexplored world with a meridian drawn about halfway between the Azores and the West Indies.

Sometime in May, 1497, Cabot, in a ship of about forty tons burden, manned by eighteen seamen, set forth from Bristol and appears to have steered north and then across the Atlantic, reaching Cape Breton Island and the North American coastline. Three months later, in August, he was back in Bristol. Like Columbus, he reported that he had reached the land of the Grand Cham (which indicates his familiarity with the great discoverer's accounts). Henry VII, like his famous granddaughter after him, was bountiful with displays of the royal pleasure but niggardly about cash awards. In the privy purse accounts, under August 10, there is this terse entry: "To hym that found the New Isle, £10." In December, however, Cabot was granted a pension of twenty pounds a year—not from the privy purse, but from Bristol customs receipts.

Unlike Columbus before him, and others later, Cabot did not leave written memorials of his own, and the accounts of his son Sebastian remain controversial; but there are glimpses of him in England in official records, like those given above, and in the correspondence of interested resident foreigners.

> "He is now at Bristol with his wife, who is also Venetian, and with his sons; he is styled the Great Admiral. Vast honor is paid him; he dresses in silk, and these English run after him like mad people, so that he can enlist as many of them as he pleases, and a number of our own rogues besides." (From a letter of Lorenzo Pasqualigo to his brothers Alvise and Francesco, "merchants in Venice," August 23, 1497.)

From the agent of the Duke of Milan in London, Raimondo de Soncino, December 18, 1497 (Soncino appears not only to have talked with Cabot, but with some of the mariners who accompanied him):

"Most Illustrious and Excellent My Lord:

"Perhaps among your Excellency's many occupations, it may not displease you to learn how his Majesty here has won a part of Asia without a stroke of the sword.

"There is in this kingdom a Venetian fellow, Master John Caboto by name, of fine mind, greatly skilled in navigation, who seeing that those most serene kings, first he of Portugal, and then the one of Spain, have occupied unknown islands, determined to make a like acquisition for his Majesty aforesaid. And having obtained royal grants that he should have the usufruct of all that he should discover, provided that the ownership of the same is reserved to the crown, with a small ship and eighteen persons he committed himself to fortune; and having set out from Bristol, a western port of this kingdom, and passed the western limits of Ireland, and then standing to the northward he began to sail toward the Oriental regions, leaving (after a few days) the North Star on his right hand; and, having wandered about considerably, at last he struck mainland, where, having planted the royal banner and taken possession on behalf of this King, and taken certain tokens, he has returned thence.

"The said Master John, as being foreign-born and poor, would not be believed if his comrades, who are almost all Englishmen and from Bristol, did not testify that what he says is true. This Master John has the description of the world in a chart, and also in a solid globe which he has made, and he shows where he landed, and that going toward the east he passed considerably beyond the country of the Tanais [perhaps Tana, mentioned by Marco Polo]. And they say that it is a very good and temperate country, and they think that Brazilwood and silk grow there; and they affirm that that sea is covered with fishes, which are caught not only with the net but with baskets, a stone being tied to them in order that the baskets may sink in the water. And this I heard the said Master John relate.

"And the aforesaid Englishmen, his comrades, say that they will bring so many fishes that this kingdom will no longer have need of Iceland, from which country there comes a very great store of fish which are called stockfish. But Master John has set his mind on something greater; for he expects to go farther on toward the East from that place already occupied, constantly hugging the shore, until he shall be over against an island, by him called Cipango, situated in the equinoctial region, where he thinks all the spices of the world, and also the precious stones, originate; and he says that in former times he was at Mecca, whither spices are brought by caravans from distant countries, and that those who brought them, on being asked where the said spices grow, answered that they do not know, but that other caravans come to their homes with this merchandise from distant countries, and these again say that they are brought to them from other remote regions. And he argues thus—that if the Orientals affirm to the Southerners that these things come from a distance from them, and so from hand to hand, presupposing the rotundity of the earth, it must be that the last ones get them at the North toward the West; and he said it in such a way, that, having nothing to gain or lose by it, I too believe it: and what is more, the King here, who is wise and not lavish, likewise puts some faith in him; for since his return he has made good provision for him, as the same Master John tells me. And it is said that, in the spring, his Majesty aforenamed will fit out some ships, and will besides give him all the convicts, and they will go to that country to make a colony, by means of which they hope to establish in London a greater emporium of spices than there is in Alexandria; and the chief men of the enterprise are of Bristol, great sailors, who, now that they know where to go, say that it is not a voyage of more than fifteen days, nor do they ever have storms after they get away from Hibernia."

Finally, there is a dispatch from Pedro de Ayala, Spain's junior ambassador at the English court, to Ferdinand and Isabella, July 25, 1498, which indicates that Cabot, like Columbus before him, and Magellan after him, had sought backing in Portugal as well as in Spain.

"I think your Majesties have already heard that the King of England has equipped a fleet in order to discover certain islands and mainland which he was informed some people from Bristol, who manned a few ships [sic] for the same purpose last year, had found. I have seen the map which the discoverer has made, who is another Genoese, like Columbus [,] who has been in Seville and in Lisbon, asking assistance for this discovery.

"The people of Bristol have, for the last seven years, sent out every year two, three or four light ships, in search of the island of Brazil and the Seven Cities [a legendary island in the Atlantic], according to the fancy of this Genoese. The king determined to send out, because, the year before, they brought certain news that they had found land. The fleet consisted of five vessels, which carried provisions for one year. It is said that one of them has returned to Ireland in great distress, the ship being much damaged. The Genoese continued his voyage.

"I, having seen the route which they took, and the distance

they sailed, find that what they have found, or what they are in search of, is what your Highnesses already possess since it is, in fine, what fell to your Highnesses by the treaty with Portugal. It is expected that they will be back in the month of September. I inform your Highnesses in regard to it.

"The King of England has often spoken to me on this subject. He hoped to derive great advantage from it. I think it is not farther than four hundred leagues [about 1200 miles]. I told him that, in my opinion, the land was already in the possession of your Majesties; but, though I gave him my reasons, he did not like it."

Cabot was granted a new patent in February, 1498, and sailed in early spring with five vessels. With the exception of the ship reported to have limped into an Irish port there is no record of a return voyage. If it is true, as some scholars believe, that Cabot traversed the coast as far as South Carolina, and perhaps farther, a royal injunction to Spanish officials to put a stop to English encroachment in southern waters may be ominous. However the information came to him, the portolan map or chart of Juan de la Cosa, himself an explorer of the northern shore of South America, shows the area of Cabot's discoveries as "sea discovered by the English." The map is dated 1500. The Cantino map, drawn in Lisbon in 1502, not only depicts Florida as a peninsula, but the coastline to the north of it. Someone had been there.

AMERICA NAMED

Waldseemüller's globe map, 1507, the first appearance of the name on a map. Reproduced with permission of the James Ford Bell Library, University of Minnesota.

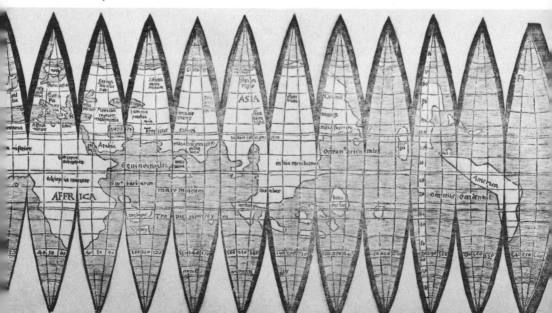

The remapping of the world was swift and dramatic. South America would have been discovered even if Columbus had never existed, and the bulge of Brazil was in fact discovered while he was yet alive. So was India. An exultant dispatch from King Emanuel of Portugal to Ferdinand and Isabella in 1499 reveals for the first time that the real Indies had been found, where there were "large cities, large edifices, and rivers, and great populations, among whom is carried on all the trade in spices and precious stones." The discoverers were Vasco da Gama, "a nobleman of our household, and his brother Paulo da Gama." They had brought back, in quantity, cinnamon, cloves, ginger, nutmeg and pepper; they also brought rubies and other precious stones. The contrast between their descriptions and those of Columbus must have been evident to the Spanish monarchs; perhaps they contributed to the difficulties he afterward faced.

The da Gama brothers had sailed along the coast of Africa with four ships in 1497; in 1500, thirteen set out under the command of Pedro Alvares Cabral, who although also bound for India first took a southwesterly course and reached the east coast of Brazil. After dispatching one of his ships to report his discovery, he recrossed the South Atlantic to continue the voyage to the East. King Emanuel let Ferdinand and Isabella know that the land discovered by Cabral "was very convenient and necessary for the voyage to India."

Portuguese mariners were also to be found in northern waters. The same year that Cabral reached Brazil, Gaspar Corte-Real discovered a "very cool" land filled with great woods, identified as the eastern shore of Newfoundland. The following year, 1501, sailing this time with three vessels, he made another voyage; two of the ships returned, but not the one he was on. It is believed that he reached the southern end of Greenland, sailed toward Labrador, and continued the exploration of Newfoundland. The two ships that made it back brought a number of captives whose description makes it appear that they were Eskimos.

In May, 1502, Miguel Corte-Real went with three ships to search for his brother; nothing more was heard of him. Their memorial appeared shortly on Portuguese maps, where Newfoundland and the adjacent mainland now bore the legend, "Land of the Corte-Reals."

The Pacific Ocean is notably absent from the maps of the period. Vasco Nuñez de Balboa, at the head of an expedition in the Isthmus of Panama, was told by a native of "another sea where they sail with ships as big as yours"—whose, can only be conjectured; perhaps Portuguese. On September 1, 1513, he set out to find it. As he

BALBOA FINDS THE SOUTH SEA, 1513
The climax of his march across the Isthmus of Panama, as imagined by a
Spanish artist. From the title page of Herrera's *Historia General.* Courtesy
of the Rare Book Division, The New York Public Library.

afterward related it in letters, on the morning of September 25 he
reached the peak from which he saw the other sea, and fell to his
knees to give thanks to God and all the heavenly host. The descent
from the mountains began. On the shore of a bay which he named
San Miguel, he awaited the rising tide; then, in full view of his
men, he rushed into the water, flashing his sword in the brilliant
sunlight, and took possession for Spain. He called it the "South
Sea."

The exaltation and frenzy of the discoverers were magnificent,
their exertions daring and patriotic. There was, in addition, something else that drove them; it was a three-letter word: *oro*—in English a yellow, nonrusting, malleable, ductile metal of high specific
gravity. For this they endured incredible hardships, fought battles
in which they were outnumbered on unknown terrain in landscapes
of mystery and fear, and inflicting as they passed, on once friendly
natives, cruelties unmatched in the annals of man. The theme of
oro runs through all the narratives of the Spanish discoverers in
America, beginning with those of Columbus, who saw precious little
of this commodity, but hoped for a great deal; Balboa himself set
out to find the other sea because he had also been told that there
was a region to the south "flowing with gold."

It will be seen, presently, that once the natives understood the white man and his quest, they were eager to give directions where gold was to be found, always out of their own lands and far away— toward the sea, toward the sun or toward the sunset, over mountains, over rivers—speeding his departure with presents and porters. One man alone sought something else, and became the first Spanish leader to explore a part of the present United States.

Juan Ponce de León had come over with Columbus in 1493. Based on Hispaniola, he showed himself a natural leader by his courage and tactics in the Indian war at the eastern end of the island. His appointment as provincial governor followed. He afterward conquered Puerto Rico and became its governor. In 1513 he set out to find the island of Bimini, not only because it had not yet been colonized, not only because there might be gold and slaves, but because there was an Indian tradition of a spring that restored youth to the aged—the "Fountain of Youth."

After touching at San Salvador on his passage through the Bahamas, he found himself off the shore of what he supposed to be an island, following the coastline until nightfall. It was Pascua Florida, the Easter season, and seeing the luxuriant foliage of the new land, he named it Florida. Not finding a harbor, he turned about and followed the coast southward, rounded the peninsula, and continued up the west coast. His explorations ceased on May 23, when he retraced his course. On June 14 he steered for Puerto Rico, still keeping a watch for Bimini.

It was not until 1521 that he was able to set out again, this time to determine whether Florida was in fact an island, and to establish a colony. He did not find the Fountain of Youth. Instead, on the west coast of Florida, in a battle with Indians, he lost many of his men and was himself critically wounded. A reference to the disaster occurs in the Third Dispatch of the conquistador Hernando Cortez to Charles V, which tells of the conquest of Mexico and a setback of his own: "By this time, those who had been wounded in our rout were already recovered, and a ship had arrived at Villa Rica, belonging to Juan Ponce de León, who had been routed in the country or island of Florida." This was one of two ships; on the other, Ponce de León returned to Cuba, where he died. Villa Rica de la Vera Cruz, the first European settlement on the North American continent, was three years old when Cortez wrote the above, in 1522.

The year Ponce de León died, Vespucci's view—that South America was a continent—was proved dramatically when Ferdinand Magellan, a Portuguese in the employ of Spain, passed through the

PONCE DE LEÓN'S LANDING OPPOSED

Florida Indians in the act of driving off the Spaniards, 1521. Insets: Aztec sacrifices. From title page of Herrera's *Historia General*. Courtesy of the Rare Book Division, The New York Public Library.

strait that bears his name on the voyage which stands first in the history of navigation, ancient or modern.

Magellan had come to the Spanish court at Valladolid, bringing with him "a well-painted globe in which the whole world was depicted, and on it he indicated the route he proposed to take." He convinced Charles V that the Spice Islands lay within the Spanish western division of the demarcation line. As a result, he received a patent for the voyage of discovery. Unlike later explorations, this one was financed by the crown; Magellan was to be given five ships with supplies for two years, provided he did not go beyond "the limits which belong to us in the ocean within the bounds of our demarcation." Portugal, hearing of the plan, protested—to no avail.

On Tuesday, September 20, 1519, the *San Antonio, Trinidad, Concepción, Victoria* and *Santiago,* ranging from 75 to 150 tons burden, left the harbor of San Lucar de Barrameda. On board were a polyglot crew which, besides Spaniards and Portuguese, included Genoese, Sicilians, French, Flemings, Germans, Greeks, Neapolitans, Corfiotes, Negroes and Malays. There was even one Englishman, a Master Andrew of Bristol. The fleet reached the coast of Brazil in the neighborhood of Pernambuco and continued south-

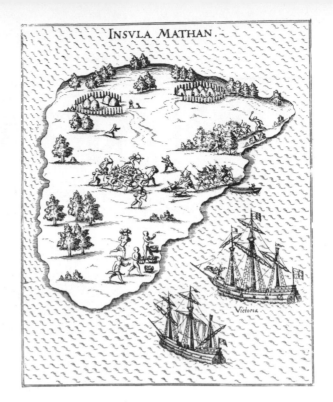

INSVLA MATHAN.

Victoria.

WHERE MAGELLAN DIED

The island of Matan, in the Philippines, where the commander of the first ship to circumnavigate the globe fell in battle with the natives. The *Victoria* is seen offshore, together with a sister ship, either the *Concepción* or the *Trinidad*. Only the *Victoria* got back to Spain, under the command of Sebastian del Cano. Drawing from Hulsius, *Voyages*, 1603. Courtesy of the Rare Book Division, The New York Public Library.

ward into higher latitudes. In the desolate region of St. Julian, latitude 49 degrees south, Magellan decided to take up winter quarters. It was now March of 1520, the intervening time having been spent charting each bay and inlet along the route. Less resolute, perhaps less ambitious than Magellan, other officers preferred to return to Spain.

At nightfall, April 1, armed men led by Captain Quesada of the *Concepción* boarded the *San Antonio* and put its captain in irons. Captain Mendoza of the *Victoria* went over to the mutineers. Magellan awoke on the *Santiago* to find that a longboat from the *San Antonio* had brought him terms. He now proved himself a skillful commander as well as navigator. He sent the longboat to the *Victoria* with a judicial official bearing a written order to Mendoza to report to him at once; with the official went five men, all six carrying concealed weapons and certain instructions. When Mendoza refused to comply, he was stabbed and left for dead. At the same moment, the ship was boarded and seized by men of the *Trinidad;* the *Santiago,* meanwhile, had taken up a position which blocked exit from the harbor. The *Trinidad* now opened fire on the *San Antonio,* which was then boarded by her men and men from the *Victoria.* The *Concepción* surrendered.

The entire action took place in the night. In the morning the body of Mendoza was quartered. Forty mutineers were condemned to death, but all were pardoned save ringleaders. Captain Quesada was beheaded; Juan de Cartagena and a priest named Sanchez were put ashore when the fleet left the bay, August 24. On October 21 the Antarctic passage to the western ocean was found, but while in the forbidding strait the *San Antonio* slipped away to return to Spain.

For thirty-eight days the remaining ships battered their way through dark and windy seas bordered by precipices and snow-topped mountains, to emerge upon the calm and glitter of "Mare Pacificum"—the peaceful sea—as Magellan termed it with thanks-giving. Supplies had long given out—biscuits that remained were only worm-ridden crumbs, the water yellow and thick. Those who

FOREVER "AMERICA"

The first map naming North and South America. By Gerard Mercator, 1538. From the original in the Rare Book Division, The New York Public Library.

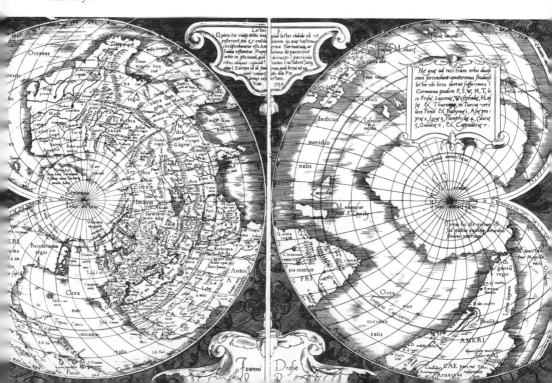

caught rats, and did not eat them themselves, sold them for a ducat apiece. Oxhides covering the main yard were soaked in brine and broiled. It was not until March 6, 1521, that an island was reached, and ten days later the Philippines. A Malay on board Magellan's ship was able to converse with some of the islanders. A month later, the great navigator fell in a battle with natives on the island of Matan, and the circumnavigation of the world was completed by Sebastian del Cano.

Only one ship made it back to Spain, the *Victoria,* which reached San Lucar on September 7, 1522, with twenty-six tons of cloves from the Moluccas. The thirty-one men who had rounded the globe were received by Charles; del Cano was rewarded with five hundred ducats and a coat of arms showing a globe and the proud legend, "Primus Circumdedisti Me" (First thou didst encompass me). It has been estimated that the value of the cargo brought back by the *Victoria* exceeded the cost of the entire expedition.

A globe with Magellan's and del Cano's route, drawn in 1523, shows North and South America massive between Europe and Cathay. The peninsula explored by Ponce de León is plainly delineated, with the name he gave it, as is the isthmus traversed by Balboa, which bears the immortal place name of Darien.

I

ᴀ́TLANTIC ᴄoAST HEARTLAND

On July 8, 1524, safe once more in the port of Dieppe, the captain of a sturdy ship well named the *Dolphin* sat down to write a letter to his most serene Majesty, Francis I, King of France. He wrote in Italian, for he was a Florentine; his name, Giovanni da Verrazano.

Four ships had set out under his command in wintry weather some six months before. Two were lost almost at once; the others, the *Dolphin* and the *Normandy,* had "put into Britanny in distress," he now wrote. Repaired, they set out again; but after cruising together along the coast of Spain, as in his privateering days under the French flag, Verrazano decided to proceed alone, his intention being "to reach Cathay, on the extreme coast of Asia." He had fifty men on board, provisions for eight months, and a store of arms and ammunition.

Verrazano did not reach Cathay; instead, he saw the entire coastal heartland of the original United States, from the Carolinas, or below, to Maine. At various points, including the harbor of New York and the site of Newport, Rhode Island, he went ashore to reconnoiter.

The voyage of discovery began on January 7, when the *Dolphin* sailed westward from a point near the island of Madeira. On February 24 it encountered a hurricane; Verrazano ascribed his survival to "divine assistance and goodness," but also had praise for the "glorious and fortunate name of our good ship." Proceeding on a more northward course, the *Dolphin* twenty-four days later, reached "a new country, which had never before been seen by anyone, either in ancient or modern times." It was the Carolina coast. Indian fires were burning up and down the shore. The shoreline "stretched to the south," and the *Dolphin* continued along it, with lookouts peering in vain for a harbor. In this manner the ship proceeded some 150 miles, when Verrazano decided to change his course and stand to the northward; again a harbor eluded him, and he saw that

DISCOVERER OF NEW YORK HARBOR
Glazed terra-cotta bust of Giovanni da Verrazano by an unidentified Italian artist. Courtesy of The New-York Historical Society, New York City.

his only recourse was to draw closer to the land and send a boat ashore. Some Indians who saw the boat approaching fled, then stopped to look back. The sailors made friendly signs, and a few came to meet them, marveling at their dress and complexion. The Indians showed where the boat could be better secured, and offered them food. In Verrazano's words:

"That your Majesty may know all that we learned, while on shore, of their manners and customs of life, I will relate what we saw as briefly as possible. They go entirely naked, except that about the loins they wear skins of small animals like martens fastened by a girdle of plaited grass, to which they tie, all round the body, the tails of other animals hanging down to the knees; all other parts of the body and the head are naked. Some wear garlands similar to birds' feathers.

"The complexion of these people is black, not much different from that of the Ethiopians; their hair is black and thick, and not very long, worn tied back upon the head in the form of a little tail. In person they are of good proportions, of middle stature, a little above our own, broad across the breast, strong in the arms, and well formed in the legs and other parts of the body; the only exception to their good looks is that they have broad faces, but not all, however, as we saw many that had sharp ones, with large black eyes and a fixed expression."

Verrazano, like Columbus, had some preconceptions. He thought the Indians he saw resembled "the people of the East, especially those the most remote." From this he deduced he had reached the East. "As the East stretches around this country, I think it cannot be devoid of the same medicinal and aromatic drugs, and various riches of gold and the like, as is denoted by the color of the ground." He also noted "beautiful fields and broad plains, covered with immense forests of trees, more or less dense, too various in colors, and too delightful and charming in appearance to be described." Deer, stags, and hares abounded, and there were many varieties of birds. The air was "salubrious, pure and temperate, and free from the extremes of both heat and cold." The fragrance of the forests reached him on board the *Dolphin*, which now continued northward, close to the coast. "The inhabitants being numerous, we saw everywhere a multitude of fires."

Verrazano appears next to have rounded Cape Hatteras, since he plainly states that he found the coast "stretching out," and that he was in "an open roadstead." But perhaps it was Chesapeake Bay, his narrative being filled with obscurities. It was while he was at anchor "on this coast" that he sent the ship's boat with twenty-five men to obtain water. There was a high sea, and they found it impossible to land. Indians on the shore tried to help.

"One of their noble deeds of friendship deserves to be known to your Majesty. A young sailor was attempting to swim ashore through the surf to carry them some knickknacks, as little bells, looking glasses, and other like trifles; when he came near three or four of them he tossed the things to them, and turned about to get back to the boat, but he was thrown over by the waves, and so dashed by them that he lay as it were dead upon the beach. When these people saw him in this situation, they ran and took him up by the head, legs and arms, and carried him to a distance from the surf; the young man, finding himself borne off in this way, uttered very loud shrieks in fear and dismay, while they answered as they could in their language, showing him that he had no cause for fear."

The Indians warmed him by a fire, hugged him affectionately, and accompanied him to the shore; then, for further reassurance, they withdrew to a little hill, and watched him until he was safely back in the boat. Again the *Dolphin* proceeded northward, and came to

"another land, which appeared very beautiful and full of the largest forests. We approached it, and going ashore with twenty men, we went back from the coast about two leagues, and found that the people had fled and hid themselves in the woods for fear."

This is how Verrazano's men repaid the kindness of the Indians thus far encountered.

"By searching around we discovered in the grass a very old woman and a young girl of about eighteen or twenty, who had concealed themselves for the same reason; the old woman carried two infants on her shoulders, and behind her neck a little boy eight years of age. When we came up to them they began to shriek and make signs to the men who had fled to the woods. We gave them a part of our provisions, which they accepted with delight, but the girl would not touch any; everything we offered to her being thrown down in great anger. We took the little boy from the old woman to carry with us to France, and would have taken the girl also, who was very beautiful and very tall, but it was impossible because of the loud shrieks she uttered as we attempted to lead her away; having to pass some woods, and being far from the ship, we determined to leave her and take the boy only."

With this sentence the boy vanished from history.

The incident took place about 150 miles north of the spot where the Indians rescued the French sailor. Of the new Indians, Verrazano says:

"We found them fairer than the others, and wearing a covering made of certain plants, which hung down from the branches of the trees, tying them together with threads of wild hemp;

their heads are without covering and of the same shape as the others. Their food is a kind of pulse [peas or beans] which there abounds, different in color and size from ours, and of a very delicious flavor. Besides, they take birds and fish for food, using snares and bows made of hardwood, with reeds for arrows, in the ends of which they put the bones of fish and other animals."

He noted grapevines, wild roses, violets, lilies "and many sorts of plants and fragrant flowers different from our own."

Sailing only by day, and anchoring at night, the *Dolphin* came to "a very pleasant situation among some steep hills, through which a very large river, deep at its mouth, forced its way to the sea; from the sea to the estuary of the river, any ship heavily laden might pass, with the help of the tide, which rises eight feet."

VERRAZANO's *"Dolphin"*
Model of the Mediterranean type of carrack which explored New York Harbor in 1524. Courtesy of the Museum of the City of New York.

Verrazano's description seems apt for the Palisades, the Hudson, and the Narrows, now spanned by the bridge bearing his name. He did not venture to take the *Dolphin* up the river; he went, instead, in the ship's boat, finding its banks "well peopled, the inhabitants not differing much from the others, being dressed out with the feathers of birds of various colors. They came toward us with evident delight, raising loud shouts of admiration, and showing us where we could most securely land our boat."

A sudden storm made him return to the ship, and he left the island of Manhattan and "this region which seemed so commodious and delightful" with regret. Scudding northward still, the *Dolphin* passed an island "of a triangular form, about ten leagues from the mainland, in size about equal to the island of Rhodes, having many hills covered with trees, and well peopled, judging from the great number of fires which we saw all around its shores; we gave it the name of your Majesty's illustrious mother." This was Block Island; the Queen Mother's name was Louise.

Verrazano's next port of call was Narragansett Bay and the site of the future city of Newport. He found the region

"situated in the parallel of Rome, being 41° 40′ of north latitude, but much colder.

"It looks toward the south, on which side the harbor is half a league broad; afterward, upon entering it, the extent between the coast and north is twelve leagues, and then enlarging itself it forms a very large bay, twenty leagues in circumference, in which are five small islands, of great fertility and beauty, covered with large and lofty trees. Among these islands any fleet, however large, might ride safely, without fear of tempests or other dangers."

The *Dolphin* stayed fifteen days, during which time Verrazano had ample opportunity to observe the Narragansett Indians, whom he thought "the finest-looking tribe, and the handsomest in their costumes, that we have found on our voyage." He was particularly impressed by two chiefs, whom he termed "kings," and who were

"more beautiful in form and stature than can possibly be described. One was about forty years old, the other about twenty-four, and they were dressed in the following manner. The oldest had a deer's skin around his body, artificially wrought in damask figures; his head was without covering, his hair was tied back in various knots, [and] around his neck he wore a large chain ornamented with many stones of different colors. The young man was similar in his general appearance."

Verrazano found that these Indians exceeded his sailors in size, and that their complexion was lighter than that of the tribes to the south. The women were

> "graceful, of fine countenances and pleasing appearance in manners and modesty. They wear no clothing except a deer-skin, ornamented like those worn by the men. Some wear very rich lynx skins upon their arms, and various ornaments upon their heads, composed of braids of hair, which also hang down upon their breasts on each side."

Their dwellings were circular, made of split logs, with roofs of straw "nicely put on."

The countryside, which he explored, was "as pleasant as is possible to conceive, adapted to cultivation of every kind, whether of corn, wine or oil; there are open plains twenty-five or thirty leagues in extent, entirely free from trees or other hindrances, and of so great fertility, that whatever is sown there will yield an excellent crop." He notes apples, plums, nuts, as well as various fruits, unspecified. Among the animals observed were stags, deer and lynxes.

Loaded with fresh stores, the *Dolphin* proceeded northward, "keeping so close to the coast as never to lose it from sight"; in this manner Verrazano came to "a more elevated country, full of very thick woods of fir trees, cypresses and the like, indicative of a cold climate." The natives were unfriendly—they had met white men before. Loud war cries and a volley of arrows greeted Verrazano's crew when they ventured inland; the land he found "sterile and unfit for growing of fruit or grain of any kind."

Off the mainland Verrazano saw a cluster of small islands, and "after sailing between east and north the distance of 150 leagues more, and finding our provisions and naval stores nearly exhausted, we took in wood and water and determined to return to France." Now, bringing his narrative to a close, he hoped that with his Majesty's aid more discoveries would follow and signed himself his Majesty's humble servant. There is no record to show that he ever returned to the North American continent.

Some of the regions traversed by him were explored by Spaniards the following year. The area of New England and New York on Ribeiro's map of 1529 is inscribed: "Land of Stephen Gomez, who discovered it by his Majesty's command in 1525. Trees and fruits like those of Spain abound, and turbot, salmon, and pike. They found no gold." But farther south he made some slave raids. Gomez was the pilot-commander who deserted Magellan in the *San Antonio*. In 1526 an expedition under Lucas Vásquez de Ayllón left Santo Domingo in three ships carrying some five hundred adventurers and slaves, three Dominican friars, and eighty-nine horses. An attempt to establish a colony in the region of Cape Fear River ended in failure, two of the causes being Indian hostility and inept leadership. Ayllon himself died of fever, and was buried at sea. About 150 survivors made it back to Santo Domingo.

II

CANADA

The French flag was brought back ten years later by a Frenchman. He was Jacques Cartier, a Breton navigator who, casting about for a way to follow up Verrazano's explorations, addressed a letter to Philippe de Chabot, Sieur de Brion, the High Admiral of France, proposing a new voyage of discovery. The king's approval was obtained, and on April 20, 1534, Cartier sailed from St. Malo, his birthplace, with two vessels of sixty tons burden, each carrying sixty-one "well-appointed men" sworn, in a ceremony before sailing, "to behave themselves truly and faithfully in the service of the most Christian King of France," Francis I.

Cartier rounded Newfoundland from the north, entered the Strait of Belle Isle, and explored almost the entire Gulf of St. Lawrence. In his detailed and vivid narrative, which winds in and out like his ships among the numerous capes, bays and islands of the strait and gulf we get, perhaps for the first time, an indelible image of the white man's wooden swans with sails drifting past primeval shores.

Cartier reached Newfoundland on May 10 after a fair-weather crossing. For ten days, because of ice along the coast, he remained in haven about fifteen miles southeast of Bonavista, where "we mended and dressed our boats." On May 21, proceeding north by east, he came upon Funk Island, which he called "Isle of Birds," the nesting place of the great auk, "whereof there is such plenty, that unless a man did see them, he would think it an incredible thing." (They are now extinct.) As they could not fly, their short wings being suitable only for waddling and paddling, "in less than half an hour we filled two boats full of them, as if they had been with stones; so that besides them which we did eat fresh, each ship did powder [flour] and salt five or six barrels of them." Besides the great auk, Cartier observed two other species which rose at the approach of his longboats—razorbills and gannets; the latter attacked the intruders, "biting even as dogs."

There were other raiders—polar bears, swimming from the mainland to feast on eggs and fowls. One, "as great as any cow and as white as any swan," the sailors pursued in longboats and killed; its flesh was "as good to be eaten as the flesh of a calf of two years." It happened while the ships were under way, on Whitsun Monday, May 25; on May 27 they entered the Strait of Belle Isle. There was ice everywhere, the weather was bad, and Cartier put into a harbor, Quirpon, where he stayed until June 9 "because we would not come out of it."

Another Isle of Birds: on this one, besides numerous razorbills, Cartier observed "crows with red beaks and red feet"—puffins, another ducklike sea bird with a triangular red bill. Later, he also came upon the islands still known as Bird Rocks, "as full of birds as any field or meadow is of grass." These were great auks, razorbills and gannets. On the smallest island, his men killed "above a thousand." The longboats were quickly laden down: "in less than one hour we might have filled thirty such boats of them." They also made a great haul of salmon in a river which he named the St. James. The Frenchman's emphasis on good things to eat is not unexpected. He makes little enough of what must have been a dramatic encounter on the river: "We saw a ship of La' Rochelle," a fishing vessel. "We with our boats approached near unto it, and did direct it to another port one league more to the west than the said river of St. James, which I take to be one of the best in all the world, and therefore we named it Jacques Cartier Sound"—now Cumberland Bay.

As for the land, Cartier found it disappointing at first: "stones and wild crags, and a place fit for wild beasts." The few inhabitants he encountered were

"men of an indifferent good stature and bigness, but wild and unruly; they wear their hair tied on the top like a wreath of

AN OLD MAP OF NEW FRANCE

"La Nueva Francia" in "Terra de Nurumbega," the old name of the New England coast. To the right is Cape Breton Island; further to the right is "Bacalaos" (from a Basque word meaning codfish), the old name for Newfoundland. The fact that the ships (lower left and right) are adorned with the lilies of France shows that the voyage, which resulted in this map, was not a private undertaking, but sponsored by the crown. From Ramusio, *Delle navigationi,* the Rare Book Division, The New York Public Library.

hay, and put a wooden pin within it, and with them they bind certain birds' feathers. They are clothed with beasts' skins, as well the men as women, but that the women go somewhat straiter and closer in their garments than the men do, with their waists girded. They paint themselves with certain roan colors. Their boats are made of the bark of birch trees, with the which they fish and take great store of seals, and as far as we could understand since our coming thither, that is not their habitation, but they come from the mainland out of hotter countries to catch the said seals." They are thought to have been Beothucks, a vanished tribe.

Cartier was now passing down the northwestern coast of Newfoundland, making soundings all the way, and noting in detail dis-

tances and navigation hazards. The number of islands amazed him
—"so many that it was not possible they might be told" (i.e.,
counted). South of Bonne Bay he came upon the Bay of Islands
"full of round islands like dove houses, and therefore we named
them The Dove Houses." Near Cape St. George "we sounded and
found twenty fathom of water, and there is the greatest fishing of
cod that possibly may be; for staying for our company, in less than
an hour we took above a hundred of them."

The expedition now came to an island "full of goodly trees,
meadows, fields full of wild corn and peas bloomed as thick, as
rank, and as fair as any can be seen in Britanny, so that they seemed
to have been plowed and sowed. There was also a great store of
gooseberries, strawberries, damask roses, parsley, with other very
sweet and pleasant herbs." He named it Brion Island, for his patron,
the Sieur de Brion, High Admiral of France.

It was here that he had his first sight of walrus—"beasts as great
as oxen, which have two great teeth in their mouths like unto ele-
phants' teeth." His men tried to capture one, which was asleep on
the shore; but as soon as they approached, it slithered into the
water. Continuing across the Great Gulf, Cartier's ships coasted past
Prince Edward Island.

Finding no harbor, the men went ashore in longboats in several
places; at one, they entered a river which Cartier named "The River
of Boats" because they saw boats "full of wild men that were crossing." This was The Narrows in Malpeque Bay.

On July 1 the ships encountered fog and storm. Sails were struck
until 2 P.M., when the weather cleared, and they reached North
Point; Cartier noted that there was "a very dangerous shelf and
bank of stones" on the north side. Again the longboats were put out
and the men went ashore in four places "to see the goodly and
sweet-smelling trees that were there" and whose fragrance had
reached them on the water. They found cedars, yews, pines, white
elms, ash, willow, "with many other sorts of trees to us unknown."
In the meadows there were peas, white and red gooseberries, strawberries, blackberries and wild corn. Also noted were "many thrushes,
stockdoves, and other birds." Cartier's conclusion: "there wanteth
nothing but good harbors."

On July 2 they passed the Strait of Northumberland, which Cartier thought a bay. He correctly describes Miramichi—"fashioned
trianglewise, very deep."

"All that night the weather was very ill, and great winds, so
that we were constrained to bear a small sail until the next

morning, being the third of July, when the wind came from the west, and we sailed northward to have a sight of the land that we had left on the northeast side, above the lowlands, among which high and low lands there is a gulf or breach in some places fifty-five fathoms deep and fifteen leagues in breadth."

This was Chaleur Bay. Because of its breadth and depth he hoped to find in it a passage to China. He traversed it by longboat and under sail, without result. The fertility of the land impressed him:

"The ground that lieth on the south side of the said gulf is as good and easy to be manured, and full of as goodly fields and meadows, as any that ever we have seen, as plain and smooth as any die; and that which lieth on the north is a country altogether hilly, full of woods, and very high and great trees of sundry sorts; among the rest there are as goodly cedars and fir trees as possibly can be seen, able to make masts for ships of three hundred tons."

On July 4, unable to find a harbor, his ships entered a creek, and despite the fact that they found "no succor against the wind," they stayed there until July 12. While the ships were at anchor, one of the longboats set out to explore a point of land about twenty miles distant and had almost reached it when two flotillas, comprising about forty or fifty boats filled with Indians, were sighted. Although the French were armed, it was enough to suggest a change of plans, even though the first Indians to land beckoned them to the shore. As an enticement, they held up skins of animals; perhaps they had already traded with other white men. They were Micmacs, as the offer of friendship in their language, which Cartier jotted down phonetically, reveals: "Napou tou daman asurtat," also written "Napeu tondamen assurtah."

The men in the longboat were not to be lured, and, turning about, set off for the other side of the cape, from which there now came five Indian boats to meet them, while two followed them from the original landing place. The French signaled to them to go back, but the boats kept coming at a great speed, and suddenly they were surrounded.

"And because they would not away from us by any signs that we could make, we shot off two pieces among them, which did so terrify them, that they put themselves to flight toward the said point, making a great noise; and having stayed a while, they began anew, even as at the first to come to us again, and being come near our boat we struck at them with two lances, which thing was so great a terror unto them, that with great haste they began to flee, and would no more follow us."

The marvel is that the Micmacs persisted in their proffers of friendship, for the very next day they came to the entrance of the creek where the French ships were at anchor. This time there were nine boats. At their approach the French launched both their long-boats and rowed against them, and the Indians again made signs that they wished only to trade. The French were thus forced to indicate that they were not enemies, and to settle the matter, two sailors went ashore with knives, "other iron wares," and a red hat to give to the Micmac chief. The Indians thereupon also landed, laughing and dancing, and gave the Frenchmen everything they had, even to the skins they wore, "so that they were constrained to go back again naked." After additional friendly contacts Cartier concluded: "We perceived that this people might very easily be converted to our religion."

He had different views about the next "wild men" he encountered, probably Hurons, on the Gaspé peninsula. He had taken shelter from a storm by entering a river; the Indians, who had been fishing for mackerel with nets, he thought "truly wild, because there is no poorer people in the world. For I think all that they had together, besides their boats and nets, was not worth five sous. They go altogether naked saving their privities, which are covered with a little skin, and certain odd skins that they cast upon them."

Cartier knew them to be different from the Micmacs.

"Neither in nature nor in language do they any whit agree with them which we found first. Their heads be altogether shaven, except one bush of hair which they suffer to grow upon the top of their crown as long as a horsetail, and then with certain leather strings bind it in a knot upon their heads. They have no other dwelling but their boats, which they turn upside down, and under them they lay themselves all along upon the bare ground. They eat their flesh almost raw, save only that they heat it a little upon embers of coals, so do they their fish."

When the French went among them the Indians welcomed them by singing and dancing in groups; nevertheless, they had sent all their young women into the woods except two or three, to whom the sailors gave combs and little tin bells. That brought the others out, and being given presents, they also began to sing and dance.

Cartier observed a well-known Huron characteristic: "They are very great thieves, for they will filch and steal whatsoever they can lay hold of, and all is fish that commeth to net."

In their presence, on the shore of Gaspé Bay, a cross thirty feet high was constructed, carved at the top with the words "Vive le Roy de France" and with a shield in the middle bearing three fleur-de-lys. As soon as the cross was raised Cartier and his men knelt in prayer, then returned to their ships. They were followed by a single canoe in which were a Huron chief, clad in a bear's skin; his three sons, and the chief's brother. From the canoe the chief harangued the white men, pointing to the cross, and making gestures which took in the entire countryside. The land, he thus informed them, was not theirs to claim; it was his. All five were seized by sailors in a longboat and forced on board where it was explained that the cross has been set up merely to mark the place, since the French intended to return there shortly, bringing much ironware for the Indians. Presumably on the spur of the moment, it was decided to take with them two of the chief's sons, Taignoagny and Domagaia, with a promise to bring them back with the ironware. They were stripped and given shirts, colored coats and red caps to wear. A copper chain apiece, hatchets and knives, were presented to the others, who departed apparently pleased, taking along the discarded apparel of the Huron boys. That afternoon boatloads of Hurons came to the ships to bid farewell to the chief's sons, bringing fish as an offering. This was on July 24; on the 25th the French ships left.

Sailing east-northeast, Cartier missed the broad mouth of the St. Lawrence River. Two days later his ships reached Anticosti Island, "the fairest and most without woods that we have seen, with goodly green fields and meadows." Rounding the island on the east, they proceeded northwest, and on August 1 came in sight of the Labrador coast, "very high and craggy," probing the strait for five days in adverse weather. The St. Lawrence was missed a second time, even though Cartier reached the northwestern point of Anticosti. Once, after reconnoitering on land, he returned to find the ships "fallen more than four leagues to leeward from the place where we had left them."

Cartier assembled his captains, master seamen and mariners, "to have their advice and opinion what was best to be done"—to winter there, or return to France. The decision was unanimous: to go home. The ships proceeded up the Labrador coast past the Strait of Belle Isle, and set their course for St. Malo. The account ends on a note of triumph:

"With a happy and prosperous weather we came into the middle of the sea that is between Newfoundland and Brittany, in which place we were tossed and turmoiled three days long with great storms and windy tempests coming from the east, which with the aid and assistance of God we suffered; then had we fair weather, and upon the fifth of September we came to the port of St. Malo."

What his Huron captives thought of all this we are not told. They were brought back on Cartier's second voyage to "the land newly discovered, called New France" the following year, when three ships left St. Malo under his command, May 19, 1535. This time he hoped to find a northwest passage to China. Once again the French replenished their larder at the Isle of Birds (Funk Island), filling two boatloads with slaughtered fowl: "and yet for the great number that there is, it would not seem that any were taken away." Again the ships transited the Strait of Belle Isle; but now the two Indians on board showed the way to the great river of Hochelaga—the St. Lawrence.

Stadacona, the present site of Quebec, is described—

"as goodly a plot of ground as possibly may be seen, and therewithal very fruitful, full of goodly trees even as in France, as oaks, elms, ashes, walnut trees, maple trees, cedars, vines, and white thorns [hawthorns], that bring forth fruit as big as any damsons, and many other sorts of trees, under which groweth as fair tall hemp as any in France, without any seed or any man's work or labor at all."

Later, they came to Hochelaga, a palisaded village next to a mountain which Cartier named Mount Royal, whence Montreal. From the top the view extended to the Laurentian Hills, the Adirondacks in northern New York, and the Green Mountains of Vermont.

"Amongst and between them," says the narrator of the second voyage, "the country is as fair and as pleasant as possibly can be seen, being level, smooth, and very plain, fit to be husbanded and tilled; and in the midst of those fields we saw the river further up a great way than where we had left our boats, where was the greatest and the swiftest fall of water that anywhere hath been seen."

This was the Lachine Rapids, which marked the end of the search for a northwest passage to China (Lachine: China).

Cartier's ships had been left on the St. Charles River. There was now a fort on the shore, and it was decided to spend the winter there. While trading with the Indians, the French heard dire news:

"In the month of December we understood that the pestilence was come among the people of Stadacona, in such sort that, before we knew of it, according to their confession, there were dead above fifty; whereupon we charged them neither to come near our fort, nor about our ships or us. And albeit we had driven them from us, the said unknown sickness began to spread itself amongst us after the strangest sort that ever was either heard of or seen, insomuch that some did lose all their strength, and could not stand on their feet; then did their legs swell, their sinews shrink as black as any coal. Others also had all their skins spotted with spots of blood of a purple color, then did it ascend up to their ankles, knees, thighs, shoulders, arms and neck. Their mouth became stinking, their gums so rotten, that all the flesh did fall off, even to the roots of the teeth, which did also almost all fall out."

The pestilence was scurvy, brought about by deficiency in diet (it was before the English introduced citrus fruits as part of sailors' rations—whence "Limey" for Englishman) and before knowledge of vitamins. Of the 110 men in Cartier's expedition, eight were now dead, with fifty so sick as to be thought past recovery. Those who were able to walk prayed in procession before an image of Christ. A young man named Phillip Rougemont died—he was twenty-two —and it was decided to examine his body.

"He was found to have his heart white, but rotten, and more than a quart of red water about it. His liver was indifferent fair, but his lungs black and mortified. His blood was altogether shrunk about the heart, so that when he was opened a great quantity of rotten blood issued out from about his heart. His milt [spleen] toward the back was somewhat perished, rough as if it had been rubbed against a stone. Moreover, because one of his thighs was very black without, it was opened, but within it was whole and sound. That done, as well as we could he was buried."

This is the first record of an autopsy performed in the New World. Twenty-five were now dead. The ships were locked in the ice. Over the ice came Indians from Stadacona, among them Domagaia, whom Cartier had seen only two weeks before sick of the disease—"his knees swollen as big as a child of two years old, all his sinews shrunk together, his teeth spoiled, his gums rotten and stinking." And there he was—"whole and sound." Asked what had cured him, "he answered that he had taken the juice and sap of the leaves of a certain tree, and therewith had healed himself."

Cartier asked him if that kind of tree grew thereabouts—"one" of his men had been stricken. Domagaia sent two squaws, who returned with a dozen branches. The recipe was as follows: "take the bark and leaves of the said tree, and boil them together, then to drink of the said decoction every other day." The French thought the tree was the sassafras, which will reappear in this narrative, more than once; but it may have been hemlock or white pine, the bark of the latter being an antiscorbutic.

The afflicted sipped with trepidation, overcame the taste, and drank as prescribed. They not only recovered, but claimed they were cured of everything else that ailed them, including the French pox—syphilis—"of four or five years."

> "After this medicine was found and proved to be true, there was such strife about it, who should be first to take it, that they were ready to kill one another, so that a tree as big as any oak in France was spoiled and lopped bare, and occupied all in five or six days; and it wrought so well, that if all the physicians of Montpellier and Louvain had been there, with all the drugs of Alexandria, they would not have done so much in one year as that tree did in six days."

Returning to France in the spring of 1536, Cartier set his course from St. Pierre, an island off the southern coast of Newfoundland, where he again encountered French fishermen—this time, "many ships." One such was to figure in an English voyage of exploration in that region and in the same year.

There lived in London "a man of goodly stature and of great courage, and given to the study of cosmography," whose name was Robert Hore. Hore persuaded some of his friends to join him in outfitting an expedition of discovery "upon the northwest parts of America," he having the approval of the king, Henry VIII. One of those who went along was a London merchant named Oliver Dawbeney (as it is spelled; perhaps for Danby or Dabney), whose recollections are the basis for the present narrative.

Two ships set out from Gravesend, on the right bank of the

Thames below London, at the end of April, 1536. They were the
Trinity and *Minion,* the first a ship of 140 tons. Aboard them were
about thirty gentlemen and ninety sailors. The voyage appears to
have been ill-fated from the start, for it took the *Trinity* and *Minion*
more than two months to cross the Atlantic, and food was in short
supply when they came to Funk Island, Cartier's Isle of Birds,
"whereon they went and found it full of great fowls white and gray,
as big as geese, and they saw infinite numbers of their eggs." The
slaughter began; they found the meat "very good and nourishing."
They also killed some bears, both black and white, "and took them
for no bad food."

This was the high point of the expedition, which accomplished
nothing and seemingly did not even reach the mainland. One day,
Dawbeney, who was on the *Minion,* and was taking his constitu-
tional on the hatches, saw a boat full of Indians paddling toward
the English ships. It is anybody's guess where this was; Dawbeney
says that it happened after their arrival in Newfoundland, and that
the Indians were "rowing down the bay toward them."

A boat was launched and started out to meet the Indians, who
turned and fled "unto an island that lay up in the bay or river there,
and our men pursued them into the island, and the savages fled
and escaped; but our men found a fire, and the side of a bear on a
wooden spit." This, it will soon be seen, was useful, although there
were a lot of mouths to feed. They also found a leather boot decorated with a tassel, and a mitten, presumably also of European
make. These ominous trophies were brought back.

In that bay, somewhere in Newfoundland, in a region of firs and
pines, their supplies ran out. It is hard for us to imagine why the
gentlemen, who were armed, did not hunt, and the sailors fish, for
never again would the world see such hunting and fishing grounds,
which kept entire Indian tribes in food as season followed season,
century after century. It can only be supposed that something had
paralyzed their collective will to survive—with some exceptions—
for Dawbeney makes it clear that the men were slowly starving. A
few found relief by robbing an osprey's nest of fish brought there
hourly by the parent bird. Men began to wander off to gather herbs
and roots, and some did not return; but while a few died of starvation, others disappeared mysteriously.

"By this means," Dawbeney related, "the company decreased,
and the officers knew not what was become of them. And it
fortuned that one of the company driven with hunger to seek
abroad for relief found out in the fields the savor of broiled

flesh, and fell out with one for that he would suffer him and his fellows to starve, enjoying plenty as he thought. And this matter growing to cruel speeches, he that had the broiled meat burst out into these words:

" 'If thou wouldst needs know, the broiled meat that I had was a piece of such a man's buttock.'

"The report of this was brought to the ship, the captain found what became of those that were missing, and was persuaded that some of them were neither devoured by wild beasts, nor yet destroyed by savages."

The captain, thoroughly horrified, exhorted the men to repent and pray; at the same time "they agreed among themselves rather than all should perish, to cast lots who should be killed." But "such was the mercy of God, that the same night there arrived a French ship, well furnished with victuals," which the English seized by a stratagem. "They became masters of the same, and changing ships and victualing them, they set sail to come into England."

Swept northward at their setting out, they watched with awe as "mighty islands of ice" drifted past; on some of them birds roosted. They reached St. Ives, on the Cornwall coast, about the end of October.

Such was the story told, with all its horrors, by Oliver Dawbeney, merchant, to Richard Hakluyt of the Middle Temple, London, who was, like the expedition's leader, Hore, a student of cosmography. Many years later, Hakluyt's cousin, also named Richard, interviewed the last survivor—Thomas Butts, son of Sir William Butts, physician to Henry VIII and one of the founders of the College of Physicians. When Butts came to his home in Norfolk, he was so changed in appearance that his father and mother did not recognize him, and would have spurned him for an imposter, had they not been shown "a secret mark which was a wart upon one of his knees, as he told me, Richard Hakluyt of Oxford, himself, to whom I rode 200 miles only to learn the whole truth of this voyage from his own mouth, as being the only man now alive that was in this discovery."

Hakluyt's interest was understandable—he was compiling his monumental work, *Principal Navigations, Voyages and Discoveries of the English Nation,* which is the source of this and the preceding narrative about Cartier in an Elizabethan translation.

As for the French fishermen whose ship had been taken, they came to England and complained to the king who, "causing the matter to be examined, and finding the great distress of his subjects,

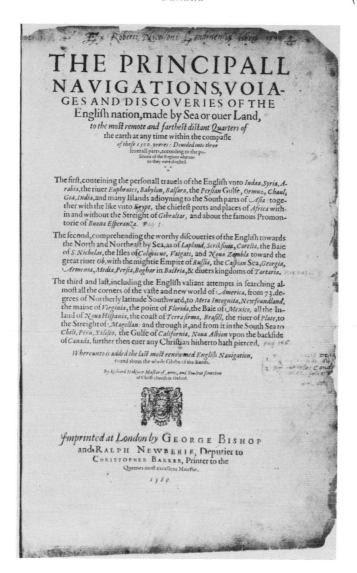

THE FOUNTAINHEAD

Title page of the first edition of Hakluyt's great work, inspired, in part, by Psalm 107: "They that go down to the sea in ships, that do business in great waters." From the Rare Book Division, The New York Public Library.

and the causes of the dealing so with the French, was so moved with pity, that he punished not his subjects, but of his own purse made full and royal recompence unto the French."

III

$\mathcal{F}$LORIDA OF THE

$\mathcal{I}$NDIES

A tall, long-faced, one-eyed and red-bearded veteran of Cuba and Mexico led a mighty expedition of soldiers and colonists to an even greater disaster than that which overtook Vásquez de Ayllón. He was Pánfilo de Narváez who, on June 17, 1527, sailed from the Spanish port of San Lucar de Barrameda, at the mouth of the Guadalquivir, with five ships in which were six hundred men, soldiers and colonists, some of whom were accompanied by their wives. In addition, some of the officers and hidalgos brought along their slaves; one of these, named Estévan (Stephen), a Negro from Morocco, was among the four survivors.

Narváez' mission was to conquer and colonize certain "provinces of the Main"—roughly, the Gulf Coast from Mexico to the Florida cape. Although he had been in Mexico, and had in fact lost his eye in battle against Cortez, whom he had sought to overthrow, Narváez had no real knowledge of the geography of that land. The vision that led him was the glitter of gold. His Sacred Catholic Caesarian Majesty, the Emperor Charles V of Spain, shared his vision, and Narváez set forth with an army, an armada, and the title of governor.

With him in command were Cabeza de Vaca, treasurer and high sheriff; Alonzo Enríquez, comptroller; Alonzo de Solis, assessor and

COAT OF ARMS OF CHARLES V OVER FLORIDA

Detail from map of the world by Giovanni Vespucci, Seville, 1526, with Spanish ships of the sixteenth century. Courtesy of The Hispanic Society of America, New York.

distributor of the treasures to be found; and Juan Xuarez, a Franciscan friar, commissary, with a staff of four friars of the same order.

Alvar Nuñez Cabeza de Vaca was a native of the province of Cadiz. His father was Francisco de Vera, son of that Pedro de Vera who conquered Grand Canary in 1483. His mother was Teresa Cabeza de Vaca, literally "cow's head," descended from a shepherd so named by the King of Navarre whose army he had guided through a pass marked by him with the skull of a cow in July, 1212, which led to the defeat of the Moors. Although the names of both his parents were honored ones, de Vaca seemingly preferred that of his mother. It is to him that we are indebted for an account of the Narváez expedition and its survivors who nine years later reached a Spanish outpost in Mexico.

Arriving at Santo Domingo, the fleet commanded by Narváez tarried about a month and a half for refitting, provisioning and the purchase of arms, horses, and an additional ship. Some 140 men deserted, lured by present comforts and the promises of riches held out by settlers. More equipment and men were taken on at Santiago, Cuba. The fleet, which now consisted of six ships, set out for a place called Trinidad, on the southern coast of the island, where Narváez had been offered additional provisions by Vasco Porcallo, a gentleman trader and slaver. Halfway there, Narváez paused at Cabo Cruz, and two ships went ahead to pick up the supplies. One of them was commanded by de Vaca, who went ashore and headed for the town as a tropical storm commenced.

"All the houses and churches fell, and it was necessary in order to move upright that we should go seven or eight holding on to each other that the wind might not blow us away."

When he returned to the harbor there was no sign of the ships.

"The buoys belonging to them were floating on the water; whence we knew the ships were lost, and we walked along the shore to see if anything could be found of them. As nothing was discovered, we struck into the woods, and having traveled about a quarter of a league in water, we found the little boat of a ship lodged upon some trees. Ten leagues thence, along the coast, two bodies were found, belonging to my ship, and some lids of boxes; but the persons were so disfigured by beating against the rocks that they could not be recognized. A cloak, too, was seen, also a coverlet rent in pieces, and nothing more. Sixty persons were lost in the ships, and twenty horses."

De Vaca and the men with him lived wretchedly until November 5, when Narváez arrived with the four remaining ships; these, too, had been buffeted, but had found a haven. Those on board, as well as those on shore, now feared to venture into the unknown during the winter season, and it was decided that the fleet should put in at Xagua, the present Jagua at the entrance to the bay of Cienfuegos, some thirty miles distant, with de Vaca in command; Narváez himself remained behind, in order to transact more business, which included the purchase of a brigantine in Trinidad and another ship in Havana.

On February 20 he arrived at Xagua in the brigantine; with him was one Miruelo, who claimed to be "a thorough pilot for all the coast of the north," but was nothing of the sort; he did not even get the fleet out of Xagua without running it aground on one of the keys between Xagua Bank and the Isle of Pines. It was not until a storm two weeks later swept them off that the ships were able to proceed.

Narváez' plan was to round Cape St. Antonio, the westernmost

HIS SACRED CATHOLIC CAESARIAN MAJESTY
Charles V on horseback, by Titian, sometimes called the greatest portrait in the world. The original is in the Prado, Madrid. Courtesy of the Prints Division, The New York Public Library, Astor, Lenox and Tilden Foundations.

point of Cuba, to Havana, to pick up the other ship, on which forty additional foot soldiers and twelve of cavalry waited to join the expedition. But just as he was about to enter the harbor a storm drove ships and brigantine toward Florida, where a landfall was made April 12, 1528; on April 14 the fleet anchored on the west side of Tampa Bay near an Indian settlement. The next day, which was Good Friday, the Spaniards debarked; the Indians, who were Timucuans, had fled during the night in their canoes. Flags were raised, and Narváez took possession of the country for Charles V and Spain.

On a march inland four Indians were seized, who led them to a spot where there were wooden packing cases which had contained Spanish merchandise; in each of them was a dead Spaniard covered by painted deerskins. These were from a wrecked ship, as the Indians explained by signs—whose, has never been ascertained; perhaps one of those which had set out from Cuba for the capture of Indian slaves. Friar Xuarez ordered the bodies burned. There were also bits of canvas, broadcloth, iron, and some "traces of gold," in unspecified form. Asked where the gold came from, the Indians "motioned to us that very far from there was a province called Apalache, where was much gold."

It was now that Narváez committed his greatest blunder; but perhaps he was secretly emulating his old opponent, Cortez, who had burned his ships to bind his men to a common purpose and fate. He ordered his ships, with the colonists on board, to proceed along the coast "toward Mexico," and finding a harbor, await him there; at the same time the brigantine was to sail to Havana and return with the ship which had been purchased and outfitted, and join the others. De Vaca protested, in vain.

Ships and expedition never saw each other again. Narváez marched to the north and the doom of his men. These numbered 260 foot soldiers and 40 horsemen, including the leaders. The horses were lean and weak from their long confinement in the ships. Provisions were low. Operating without a base, the men had to carry everything with them, besides arms and the clothes and armor on their backs. Their arms included flintlock arquebuses, supported in firing on a tripod or forked rest; windlass or stirrup crossbows; swords; daggers—there were even left-handed ones; halberds, a combination of spear and ax; and some battle-axes. The horsemen carried lances as well as side arms; the great spurs on their boots were of finely wrought steel, with foliate and other varieties of rowels, designed for show as well as utility. The horses themselves were a weapon against Indians who had never seen them and who, fleeing terrified, could be run down and slain or captured.

The march began May 1, a Saturday. Each man was given rations consisting of two pounds of biscuit and half a pound of bacon. Incredible as it may seem, they went fifteen days without finding anything but palmettos, the dwarf fan palm, to add to their diet; perhaps the clang and clamor of the marching men drove beasts and birds into hiding. It also kept the Indians at a distance, for de Vaca says they did not see one during this time.

It was after a crossing of the Withlacoochee River, some of the men swimming, the rest going across on rafts, that more Timicuans were encountered, about two hundred strong. Five or six were seized; these led the Spaniards to their village, where corn ripe enough to eat was found in "large quantity." It was quickly devoured. With the captive Indians for guides, the expedition started out once more for the country of the Apalachens. We are not told what rations were carried—probably corn. Indians were glimpsed occasionally, but these did not stay for the arrival of the invaders.

FLORIDA INDIAN ART
Pre-Columbian open-work jar, found in Washington County, Florida. Height: 8⅜ inches. Photograph, courtesy of Museum of the American Indian, Heye Foundation.

On June 17 there was an unusual encounter. To the sound of flutes an Indian procession met Narváez and his men (eleven years later, in the same region, Hernando de Soto was also met by Indians playing flutes made of reed). The chief, who wore a painted deerskin, was borne on the back of a brave and surrounded by attendants. He was carried to where Narváez stood, and the two leaders conversed; perhaps the only word both knew was "Apalachen." Narváez gave the chief some beads and hawk bells, and the chief gave Narváez his painted deerskin. When the Indian procession wound back, the Spaniards followed.

That night they came to the Suwannee river, which was wide and deep at that point and had a rapid current; to cross it, it was necessary to build a boat, probably flat-bottomed, and the expedition spent a whole day getting over. One horseman, becoming impatient, steered his mount into the river, and was swept to his death, together with his horse. He was the first man lost on the march. The horse was recovered and eaten.

The following day the Spaniards arrived at the chief's village, and were given corn to eat; but that night, as one of the men was fetching water, he was shot at. It was probably a warning shot; in the morning not a single Indian was to be seen—all had fled. The march recommenced, this time through thick forest, and on June 24 they saw in the distance the town of Apalache, not far from the present-day Tallahassee.

It may be that Narváez had visions of another Aztec capital full of treasures. De Vaca says: "We gave many thanks to God, at seeing ourselves so near, believing true what had been told us of the land." What they found was otherwise—there were about forty small thatched houses surrounded by dense woods and lakes— ground and water strewn together with fallen trees. By Narváez' order, de Vaca and de Solis, the assessor of the expedition, led a detachment of cavalry consisting of nine men, followed by fifty foot soldiers, into the town, which they found occupied only by women and children; the braves, however, returned and discharged their arrows, killing de Solis' horse, then withdrew. The Spaniards found corn "fit for plucking, and much dry that was housed; also many deerskins, and among them some mantelets of thread, small and poor, with which the women partially cover their persons. There were numerous mortars for cracking maize."

The Spaniards stayed twenty-five days, taking over the houses and subsisting on the Indians' provisions. Like other adventurers before and after them, they were unable to live off the land; yet de Vaca states "there are deer of three kinds, rabbits, hares, bears, [mountain] lions, and other wild beasts. Among them we saw an animal with a pocket on its belly, in which it carries its young"— the first mention of the opossum in the literature of the discoverers. As for birds, there were "geese in great numbers. Ducks, mallards, royal ducks, flycatchers, night herons and partridges abound. We saw many falcons, gerfalcons, sparrow hawks, merlins and numerous other fowl."

They were in a land of sand and "stiff earth," encompassed by immense and luxuriant trees—walnut, laurel, liquidambar (the sweet gum), cedars, savins (tree or shrub yielding a medicinal oil), evergreen oaks, pines, red oaks "and palmettos like those of Spain" —and continually harassed and ambushed; once, the houses they were in were set on fire. When the Spaniards issued forth the Indians had disappeared. Armed patrols were sent forth to survey the land, and captives were tortured and questioned about the nature of the country, until it became clear that in all that region nothing better was to be found than Apalache itself.

There was one glimmer of hope. They learned that toward the south, a journey of nine days, there was a town called Aute, which had much corn, beans and pumpkins, and being near the sea, fish. The Spaniards decided to march there, leaving their dead, and burdened by wounded, both men and horses. They took along a captive to serve as guide. On the second day of their march they came to a lake which they crossed breast-deep in water, and were ambushed while in the middle; in the ensuing confusion the guide got away. Many of the soldiers were wounded, despite their armor, such was the power of the Indian bows and bowmen.

"The Indians we had so far seen in Florida are all archers. They go naked, are large of body, and appear at a distance like giants. They are of admirable proportions, very spare and of great activity and strength. The bows they use are as thick as the arm, of eleven or twelve palms in length, which they will discharge at 200 paces with so great precision that they miss nothing."

About three miles from Aute they were ambushed again; when they arrived, they found the town deserted. Corn, beans and pumpkins being ripe enough for gathering, the hungry and weary army feasted on them and rested.

Aute was situated at the head of St. Marks Bay, into which the river of that name flows. Narváez now had hopes that the sea was near, and sent de Vaca with mounted and foot soldiers to find it. They were lucky; for while they feasted on oysters at the mouth of the bay, the main body of troops was under attack.

De Vaca now relates the next to final agony of the once mighty expedition:

"The next morning [August 3, 1528] we left Aute, and traveled all day before coming to the place I had visited. The journey was extremely arduous. There were not horses enough to carry the sick, who went on increasing in numbers day by day, and we knew of no cure. It was piteous and painful to witness our perplexity and distress. We saw on our arrival how small were the means for advancing farther. There was not anywhere to go; and if there had been, the people were unable to move forward, the greater part being ill, and those were few who could be on duty."

Among those who were ill was Narváez himself. To him came, singly, the officers and gentlemen to discuss ways and means to save the expedition. A plan of great imagination, but disastrous consequences, came into being: to build a fleet of boats, although "this appeared impossible to everyone; we knew not how to construct, nor were there tools, nor iron, nor forge, nor tow, nor resin, nor rigging." Above all, de Vaca says, "there was nothing to eat, while building, for those who should labor."

But it was not easy to drop so promising a plan, which in itself brought some relief and hope. One of the soldiers said he could make pipes out of wood which, with deerskins, would provide the bellows needed. From stirrups, spurs, crossbows and other iron implements, nails, saws and axes were fashioned. The work of sawing began on September 4; by the 20th, five boats about thirty feet in length each were ready for caulking, which was done with palmetto fiber and pitch made from pine resin. Ropes and rigging were made from the husk of the palmettos and the tails and manes of horses. The sails were stitched from shirts, and oars made from the low-growing savins.

To get food, four sorties were made into Aute, each time with the men and horses able to go; the raiders brought back, in all, 640 bushels of corn. In addition, every third day a horse was killed, and divided among the laborers and the sick. (The horses were first flayed, the skin of the legs being taken off whole to make containers for water.) Shellfish were also gathered in the coves and creeks; but the Indians attacked twice, killing ten men in full view of the camp. Forty more men died of sickness and hunger before the expedition embarked. A single horse remained; de Vaca says they called the place Bahia de Caballos—"Bay of Horses."

The embarkation took place on September 22. The manner of embarking was as follows:

Narváez took 49 men—they were, of course, the most fit;

Alonzo Enríquez and Friar Xuarez, another 49;
Captain Alonzo del Castillo and Captain Andrés Dorantes, 48;
Captain Tellez and Captain Peñalosa, 47;
Cabeza de Vaca and Alonzo de Solis, 49.
No mention is made of the remaining horse; perhaps it was now
slaughtered for food.

"After the provisions [chiefly ears of corn] and clothes had
been taken in, not over a span of the gunwales remained above
water; and more than this, the boats were so crowded that we
could not move: so much can necessity do, which drove us to
hazard our lives in this manner, running into a turbulent sea,
not a single one who went having a knowledge of navigation."

Despite their straits, room was made for the gewgaws with which
to dazzle braves and squaws they hoped still to meet in provinces
richer than those they were leaving—hawk bells and cheap beads,
whence the word *tawdry*, from St. Audrey's fair, where such beads
were sold in honor of that saint.

For seven days the boats, shipping water to the men's waists,
proceeded along desolate shores; suddenly an island loomed, and
from it came five canoes. De Vaca's boat was in the lead and he
started in pursuit. The Indians turned and fled, beaching their
canoes, which the Spaniards seized and afterward put to good use;
meanwhile, the other boats reached the island and the men went
ashore, where they found abandoned houses stocked with dried
mullet and roes. The canoes were used to make waist-boards for
the boats, so that, as de Vaca recounts, "the sides rose two palms
above the water." This was comforting; but it was offset by growing
hunger and thirst, the water bottles made from the hides of horses
having rotted. Some of the men began to swallow salt water, became crazed, and fell dead.

Incredibly, in their waterlogged boats the Spaniards reached
Pensacola Bay, where Indians, probably Choctaws, permitted them
to land and even gave them water and fish; but in the middle of the
night attacked them with great fury, using stones as well as arrows.
De Vaca says not one escaped injury; he himself was wounded in
the face. The men betook themselves to the boats, leaving a rear
guard led by the three captains—Dorantes, Peñalosa and Tellez—
which ambushed the Indians in the final onslaught and drove them
off. This was on October 27. On the 28th, holding the shore against
further attack, the Spaniards broke up thirty canoes with which
they built bonfires; a cold north wind was blowing, and they were
unable to put off because of a rough sea.

At last they embarked, and were on the water three or four days, when they came to a place in the Gulf of Mexico where a river poured into it "in freshet." It was the mighty Mississippi, now seen by white men for the first time, fourteen years before de Soto "discovered" it. De Vaca says: "We came together there and took fresh water from the sea." After drinking their fill, they tried to reach land to roast some of their corn which, he relates, they had eaten raw for two days; but so great was the current of the river, so strong the wind from the shore, that the boats scudded before both into the Gulf. Two were swept out of sight—de Vaca says of his:

"Keeping my course until the hour of vespers, I observed two boats, and drawing near I found that the first I observed was that of the Governor. He asked me what I thought we should do. I told him we ought to join the boat which went in advance, and by no means to leave her; and, the three being together, we must keep on our way to where God should be pleased to lead.

"He answered saying that could not be done, because the boat was far to sea and he wished to reach the shore; that if I wished to follow him, I should order the persons of my boat to take the oars and work, as it was only by strength of arm that the land could be gained.

"Discovering his will I took my oar, and so did everyone his, in my boat, to obey it. We rowed until near sunset; but the Governor having in his boat the healthiest of all the men, we could not by any means hold with or follow her. Seeing this, I asked him to give me a rope from his boat, that I might be enabled to keep up with him; but he answered me that he would do much, if they, as they were, should be able to reach the land that night.

"I said to him, that since he saw the feeble strength we had to follow him, and do what he ordered, he must tell me how he would that I should act.

"He answered that it was no longer a time in which one should command another; but that each should do what he thought best to save his own life; that he intended so to act; and saying this, he departed with his boat."

As de Vaca could not follow Narváez, he steered for the other boat, which he found to be the one commanded by the captains Peñalosa and Tellez. Their fate was pitiful. Separated four days later from de Vaca by a storm, they and the men with them were all killed by Indians on the Texas coast, having arrived in such feeble condition that they could offer no resistance; de Vaca afterward saw their clothes and rusting arms, and was told where their stranded boat still lay.

The fate of two other boatloads is soon told. Somewhere in the Mississippi delta the boat carrying the comptroller Enríquez and Friar Xuarez overturned, and it was necessary to ferry the men, in Narváez' boat, to a point on the bay which he had made his base. Enríquez was stripped of his commission and it was given to a captain of crossbowmen, one Juan Pantoja, who had been with Narváez in Mexico. Whether Narváez feared for his life, or from

some other cause, he stayed that night in his boat, where his page lay ill; with them was another member of his crew. There was neither food nor water; the anchor was a stone. A wind in the night swept the boat from its mooring, and it was never seen again. As for the hundred or so men, left leaderless except for Pantoja, now termed lieutenant governor, they trudged along the coast, and one by one succumbed to arrows, hunger and cold, some of the dead being eaten by the living.

Of the remaining boats, that of de Vaca also drifted toward the Texas coast. His men subsisted on a ration of half a handful of raw corn a day; only five were able to stand or feebly row. On November 6 they heard the sound of breakers; then a huge wave lifted their craft and tossed it on an island somewhere between Galveston and Matagorda. The Spaniards called it Malhadado Island—"Isle of Misfortune."

One of the castaways, sturdier than the rest, was sent by de Vaca to spy out the land. A mile or so away he came across some huts without inhabitants. From them he took an earthen pot, some mullets, and "a little dog." By the time he returned, he was being followed—at first by three Indians with bows and arrows; then, behind them, came a hundred, all armed. Their aspect was fierce—their ornaments were lengths of cane thrust through their ears, lips and breasts.

De Vaca and de Solis walked toward them, displaying beads and hawk bells to the three leaders, who gave each of them an arrow in return as a sign of friendship. They also signified that they would return in the morning with food. They kept their word, bringing quantities of fish and "certain roots, some a little larger than walnuts." These they dug up in shoal water, and had been at this occupation when their huts were pilfered. With friendly relations established, the Indians sent their women and children to gaze at the strangers; they "went back rich with hawk bells and beads." More provisions were brought that evening.

Refreshed and strengthened, the Spaniards decided to launch their boat and continue. Despite the cold, they stripped to facilitate their labors, placing their clothes aboard with their other gear. About a hundred yards from the shore a wave drenched them, and the oars fell from their numbed hands. A second wave capsized the boat. Three drowned under it, among them Alonzo de Solis, assessor of treasures never found. The rest were carried back by the surf, and clambered ashore "naked as they were born." When the Indians returned with food they were confounded by the sight that met their eyes and started to retire; but de Vaca ran to them and explained by signs the calamity that had befallen. Two of the bodies had been washed ashore; seeing these, the Indians sat down and began a loud lament which continued for half an hour. When it was over, de Vaca asked them to take the Spaniards into their houses. They agreed to do so, and even showed delight.

Thirty Indians loaded themselves with wood and started for the huts. The Spaniards were escorted by the rest a short time later. On the way they found four or five large fires, built at intervals, at which they warmed themselves; between the fires everyone ran—"so swiftly," says de Vaca, "that they hardly let us touch our feet to the ground." When they got to the huts they found that the Indians had put up a shelter for them in which there were many fires. Their guests being safe and warm, the hosts began to dance outside, which led some of the Spaniards to believe they were going to be sacrificed. The dancing continued all night. In the morning the Indians shared their fish and roots.

It was on this day that de Vaca saw "an article of traffic" which he had not given the Indians. He was told by signs that men like himself were also on the island. They were, in fact, the men from the boat commanded by Castillo and Dorantes, cast ashore on November 5. They, too, had now been told that other white men were on the island, and were on the way to learn who they were. The reunion was joyful—and sad: "Having come up, they were surprised at seeing us in the condition we were in, and very much pained at having nothing to give us, as they had brought no other clothes than what they had on," de Vaca wrote.

A new attempt was made to get away, those setting forth being the strongest and most determined. The second boat sank by the shore. Later, four men who were "excellent swimmers" were sent to the mainland to walk to New Spain and send help back. They perished on the way.

As the winter wore on, rations diminished. Wind and cold prevented the Indians from pulling up roots. The Spaniards, quartered with them in small and scattered groups, began to die. Five, in a hut on the coast, turned cannibal: "the body of the last one only was found unconsumed." De Vaca gives their names, and adds: "This produced great commotion among the Indians." Finally: "Of eighty men who arrived in the two instances, fifteen only remained alive."

Following their food supply, the Indians crossed to the mainland, taking the Spaniards in two separate groups. Those with de Vaca "went to the seashore, where we ate blackberries all the month"— April, 1529. The other group "went to the opposite shore of the main to eat oysters." Whether because of the cannibalism or their diminished numbers, the Spaniards were no longer guests, but slaves; de Vaca himself was made to dig roots under water, as well as the sprouts between stands of cane on the shore. His fingers were so worn, he says, "that did a straw but touch them they would bleed."

He decided to escape.

De Vaca wrote that he spent six years wandering from tribe to tribe "trafficking" in cones, conches, sea snails and "a bean of the highest value among them, which they use as a medicine and employ in their dances and festivities." For these he received in exchange skins, ocher, shafts of canes for arrows, flint, and tassels made from the hair of deer. "The Indians would beg me to go from one quarter to another for things of which they have need; for in consequence of incessant hostilities, they cannot traverse the country."

One day, arriving with Indians at a place where they lived for two months of the year off walnuts, he learned of the presence nearby of Castillo, Dorantes and Estévan. This was in the year 1533; the day of their reunion, de Vaca says, "was a day to us of the greatest pleasure we had enjoyed in life." They planned to escape together when the two tribes they were with came together again in cactus country to live off prickly pears.

"We had thirst all the time we ate the pears, which we quenched with their juice. We caught it in a hole made in the earth, and when it was full we drank until satisfied. It is sweet, and the color of must. In this manner they collect it for lack of vessels."

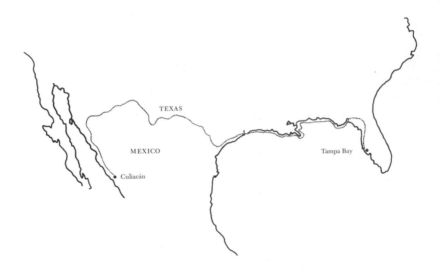

CROSSING AMERICA, 1528–1537
Cabeza de Vaca's conjectured route, from the landing of the Narváez expedition at Tampa Bay to his arrival in Culiacan, Mexico, nine years later. Drawn for this book.

From somewhere in the region between the Trinity and Brazos rivers, or the Brazos and Colorado (Texas), the four men made their way across the Lone Star State to where the Pecos joins the Rio Grande, thence across Mexico through Chihuahua and Sonora to the Gulf of California—one of the most astonishing treks in history. They traded, they cured the sick by making the sign of the cross and reciting litanies and prayers, and were everywhere welcome. Their fame as healers preceded them; at a place which de Vaca afterward called Pueblo de los Corazones—"Town of Hearts"—near present-day Ures, they were given several hundred hearts of deer.

CABEZA DE VACA TELLS HIS STORY
Title page of the first edition of the narrative which tells of the disaster that befell Narváez and of Cabeza de Vaca's astonishing journey across the United States into Mexico. From the original in The John Carter Brown Library, Brown University.

Many Indians now accompanied them. But the closer they came to where their countrymen held sway the more signs appeared of their inhuman deeds. De Vaca wrote:

"We passed through many territories and found them all vacant; their inhabitants wandered fleeing among the mountains, without daring to have houses or till the earth for fear of

Christians. The sight was one of infinite pain to us, a land very fertile and beautiful, abounding in springs and streams, the hamlets deserted and burned, the people thin and weak, all fleeing or in concealment. As they did not plant, they appeased their keen hunger by eating roots and the barks of trees. We bore a share in the famine along the whole way; for poorly could these unfortunates provide for us, themselves being so reduced they looked as though they would willingly die."

In the spring of 1536, at an outpost on the Rio Sinaloa, in Sinaloa province, de Vaca and his companions encountered a cavalry detachment hunting Indians. Soon after, they were welcomed by Melchior Diaz, the chief magistrate and captain of the province of Culiacán. Diaz was a tough soldier; nevertheless, "he wept with us, giving praises to God our Lord for having extended over us so great care."

The wanderers were escorted to Compostela where the governor of the northern provinces received them. He was Nuño de Guzmán, perhaps the most cruel of the conquistadors; but this is a moot point. From Compostela the wanderers were sent on to Mexico City, where the viceroy, Antonio de Mendoza, and Cortez, now Marquis of the Valley of Oaxaca and Captain General of New Spain and of the Main (de la Costa del Sur), entertained them lavishly. On the Day of St. James the Apostle—July 25, 1536—there was a celebration, including a bullfight, in their honor.

A year later, Cabeza de Vaca was back in Spain. In Mexico, in Cuba, where he stopped en route, and in Spain itself, he learned what had happened to the ships sent by Narváez to seek a harbor in Mexico, in the wrong direction.

"After we left," he wrote, "the vessels made sail, taking their course onward; but not finding the harbor, they returned. Five leagues below the place at which we debarked, they found the port, the same we discovered when we saw the Spanish cases containing dead bodies, which were of Christians. Into this haven and along this coast, the three ships passed with the other ship that came from Cuba, and the brigantine, looking for us nearly a year, and not finding us, they went to New Spain.

"The port of which we speak is the best in the world. At the entrance are six fathoms of water and five near the shore. It runs up into the land seven or eight leagues. The bottom is fine white sand. No sea breaks upon it nor boisterous storm, and it can contain many vessels. Fish is in great plenty. There are a hundred leagues to Havana, a town of Christians in Cuba, with which it bears north and south. The northeast wind ever prevails and vessels go from one to the other, returning in a few days, for the reason that they sail either way with it on the quarter."

The port was Tampa Bay.

It is curious to reflect that, after all the hardships he and his companions had endured, Cabeza de Vaca wished to return to Florida —this time as the commander of his own expedition. He brought his narrative to court, and had some private interviews with the emperor. But he was too late; the assignment had already been given to Hernando de Soto, a veteran of Peru, who had come back from the land of the Incas so wealthy that Charles V himself had borrowed money from him. De Soto tried to enlist de Vaca, who was understandably reluctant to set out again under another's standard, while hinting, as occasion offered, that he alone knew where gold was to be found, and precious stones as well.

The fascination of Florida for Spain and the conquistadors lay in this: it comprised, for them, not only the entire eastern half of the United States, but all the unexplored coastal territories from Mexico to Newfoundland. It was not something to be given up because of the failure of an expedition or two; besides, left there for the first comers, it might fall into the hands of the English or French.

The year was 1537. De Soto, thirty-eight years old, was now Don Hernando de Soto, Governor of Cuba and Adelantado of Florida, with the promise of a marquisate of conquered territories. He has been aptly described as "an inflexible man, and dry of word." This was in the field; in Seville, no hidalgo lived in higher style. De Soto's retinue included a superintendent of his household, a chamberlain, ushers, pages, footmen and an equerry. Whenever he ventured forth, he was surrounded by adjutants who had been his comrades in arms in the conquest of Peru and were almost as rich as himself. On the first muster of his men these officers and their followers, in contrast to others who appeared in polished armor, turned out "very showily, in silk over silk, pinked and slashed." The description is from the most authoritative account of the expedition, written by a Portuguese who accompanied de

Soto, and who signed himself modestly "A Gentleman of Elvas," a town in eastern Portugal near the Spanish border.

Noblemen and gentlemen, as well as soldiers, sought to go with the expedition, and money and influence, as well as proved ability, kinship with de Soto or with personages close to Charles V, swelled the councils of the Adelantado. The post of chief castellan, or chatelain, went to Baltazar de Gallegos, a kinsman of Cabeza de Vaca; that of factor to Antonio de Biedma; of comptroller to Juan de Añasco, and of treasurer to Juan Gaytan, a nephew of the Cardinal of Ciguenza. Notable in the ranks of commanders was Luis de Moscoso, a veteran of Peru, who took along two brothers. There were also several priests and friars.

In the ranks there were, in addition to disciplined fighting men, the usual adventurers of "low degree" who, armed themselves, are never so heroic or efficient in slaughter as when unarmed men and women are at their mercy.

On a Sunday in April, 1538, to the sound of trumpets and cannonading, de Soto sailed from San Lucar de Barrameda with a fleet of seven ships and six hundred men, many of the gentlemen having their wives aboard, including the governor. She was Doña Isabel de Bobadilla, daughter of Pedro Arias Davila, Count of Punorostro and onetime governor in New Spain, who had put Balboa to death.

The fleet was bound for Havana. Because of a calm, fifteen days after sailing the ships had got no farther than one of the Canary Islands—Gomera—where they put in on Easter Sunday. Their reception, as recounted by the gentleman of Elvas, was diverting:

> "The governor of the island was appareled all in white—cloak, jerkin [jacket, often of leather], hose, shoes, and cap, so that he looked like a governor of gypsies. He received the Adelantado with much pleasure, lodging him well and the rest with him gratuitously. To Doña Isabel he gave a natural daughter of his to be her maid-in-waiting."

During the voyage to Cuba, one Nuño de Tobár, a captain general, made love to the governor's daughter, and was deprived of his rank. In order to remain with de Soto, Tobár married her in Havana, she being with child by him, and thus enabled her, as his wife, to remain with the ladies when the expedition sailed.

Meanwhile, de Soto inspected the island and, like Narváez before him, negotiated with Vasco Porcallo for provisions. These included loads of cassava bread; pigs, which were afterward bred on the march; and bloodhounds. Porcallo impressed de Soto sufficiently to be offered the post of lieutenant general—perhaps his vast holdings of slaves, granaries, and other stores, appealed to a commander with foresight; perhaps it was his knowledge of the natives and his harsh discipline. On Porcallo's part, it must have appeared that he had nothing to lose. If gold was found, he would share in it; if not gold, slaves, since Indians were numerous on the mainland.

The work of outfitting and provisioning went on for almost a year; at last, on May 18, 1539, a Sunday, de Soto left Havana with five ships, two caravels and two brigantines, bound for Tampa Bay. Landfall was made on the 25th, but because they rode low in the water the ships anchored some distance from the shore. Soldiers and mariners alike, staring out, saw the entire coast plumed by smoke signals. The Indians were abandoning their towns.

On the 30th, the soldiers began to disembark. With them went 213 horses. As men and horses left, the ships, drawing less water each day, at length came close to the spot where camp had been pitched. Porcallo, losing no time, mustered seven horsemen to hunt down Indians to serve as guides. He came upon six, who defended themselves with bows and arrows. Two were killed, and the others faded into the swamps, where the horses could not follow.

The next day, de Soto led three squadrons of horsemen to a deserted Indian town about six miles off. It consisted of houses built of timber, and thatched with palm leaves. Here he made his base, taking over the chief's house for himself, Porcallo, and Luis de Moscoso, who was master of the camp. All the other buildings were destroyed and the woods around the town felled the distance of a crossbow-shot to provide a field of fire in case of an attack. Sentinels were set up, and horsemen constantly made the rounds of their posts.

Thus secure, de Soto sent two forces to seize Indians for questioning. The first consisted of forty horsemen and eighty foot soldiers; the second numbered fifty infantrymen, some of whom were armed with swords and shields, the rest with crossbows and guns. The infantry came upon some huts near a river; at once the inhabitants plunged into the water, but four women were seized.

The haul that the other force made was more impressive. Arriving in open country, the horsemen swooped down on ten or eleven Indians, wounding and capturing some, while the rest fled into the woods. In the pause that followed they heard one of the Indians cry out:

"Do not kill me, cavalier—I am a Christian! Do not slay these people—they have given me my life!"

The horsemen stared. Naked, sunburned and tattooed like the

rest, this one spoke the purest Castilian, and was in fact a noble-man of Seville, by name Juan Ortiz. He called to the others to come out of hiding, and mounted behind the horsemen, all rode back to the base camp, where the astonished Adelantado heard his story.

Ortiz had been a member of the Narváez expedition who returned to Cuba with the ships. At the command or request of Narváez' wife, he had gone back to the Florida coast in a brigantine to seek her husband. Arriving at Tampa Bay he saw in the sand a cleft stick holding what appeared to be a letter. Accompanied by another Spaniard, Ortiz went ashore; Indians sprang upon them, and his companion was killed. The brigantine sailed away. Ortiz was carried to the town now occupied by de Soto, where the chief ordered him put to death. He was bound hand and foot to four stakes on a scaffold to be burned alive, when the chief's daughter interceded for him; according to Ortiz, her argument was, "Though one Christian might do no good, certainly he could do no harm, and it would be an honor to have one for a captive."

Another chief, to whose tribe Ortiz escaped three years later, thought so, too. He made Ortiz swear that he would not leave him for another master; in return, he would treat him well, and promised that if at any time Christians came to that land, he would let him go to them. Nine years passed; the ships of de Soto were spotted, and the chief sent Ortiz to the coast with an escort, with the result already told.

It was clear to de Soto that he had found a prize. Ortiz knew the interior of the country up to a distance of fifty or sixty miles, and spoke several of the Indian tongues like a native. He was given apparel suited to his station, good armor and a good horse. This event may have raised de Soto's confidence and hopes, for he now decided that the ships should go to Cuba for additional provisions, with orders to return at a specified time. Porcallo seized this opportunity to go with the ships. The gentleman of Elvas wrote:

> "As the principal object of Vasco Porcallo de Figueroa in coming to Florida had been to get slaves for his plantation and mines, finding, after some incursions, that no seizures could be made, because of dense forest and extensive bogs, he determined to go back to Cuba; and in consequence of that resolution, there grew up such a difference between him and [de] Soto, that neither of them treated nor spoke to the other kindly. Still, with words of courtesy, he asked permission of him to return, and took his leave."

The caravels and pinnaces remained at Tampa Bay, close to the

base camp, from which detachments of cavalry and infantry probed
the countryside for Indians, gold, or corn, now a staple of the soldiers' diet. On one of these foraging expeditions an infantryman
named Juan Munoz was seized by Indians and carried off.

It was now only a matter of time when the great conquistador
would go inland himself and, as in the case of Narváez, the mere
rumor of gold proved decisive. He received, one day, a dispatch
from de Gallegos, who had taken prisoners. From them he had
learned that:

> "toward the sunset there was a province called Cale, the in-
> habitants of which were at war with those of territories where
> the greater portion of the year was summer, and where there
> was so much gold, that when the people came to make war
> upon those of Cale, they wore golden hats like helmets."

Leaving thirty cavalry and seventy infantry with provisions for
two years under a captain named Calderón, de Soto marched to
join de Gallegos, who awaited him in the territory of a chief named
Paracoxi. The combined force reached Cale, only to find it deserted,
though plentifully surrounded by fields of corn. De Soto ordered
the ripe ears picked, enough for a three months' supply; this was
contested by Indians who suddenly appeared and discharged their
arrows. Three men fell dead. In the counterattack, twenty-eight
prisoners were taken, and one of them, in the now common formula,
declared that "seven days' journey distant was a large province,
abounding in maize, called Apalache."

History was repeating itself.

On August 11, 1539, de Soto moved out of Cale with fifty cavalry
and sixty infantry, leaving de Moscoso in command. With him, as a
prisoner, went an Indian chief who had come to parley and was
seized. Six days later de Soto reached a place called Caliquen,
where other prisoners described the advance of Narváez to Apalache
and how he had embarked there because, as they told de Soto, "no
road was to be found over which to go forward, and of there
being no other town, and that water was on all sides."

> "Every mind was depressed at this information," wrote the
> gentleman of Elvas, "and all counseled the governor to go back
> to the port, that they might not be lost, as Narváez had been,
> and to leave the land of Florida; that, should they go further,
> they might not be able to get back, as the little maize that was
> yet left [growing] the Indians would secure."

But de Soto remained unconvinced. He advised the horsemen to be ready for the saddle, and sent couriers to Moscoso to advance from Cale. Certain that they would have to return that way, Moscoso buried iron implements there. The march to Caliquen was made on short rations, the land over which de Soto had passed having been laid waste.

The two forces having come together again, a bridge was thrown over a river near the Indian town. The crossing was made on September 10; thereafter, every day, Indians appeared playing flutes, a sign of peace. Their repeated requests to de Soto to free their chief brought only excuses or rebuffs. It was only the presence of Juan Ortiz that saved the expedition from destruction or rout. The following is from the eyewitness account of the gentleman of Elvas:

"We marched five days, passing through some small towns, and arrived at Napetaca on the fifteenth day of September, where we found fourteen or fifteen Indians who begged for the release of the cacique [chief] of Caliquen, to whom the governor declared that their lord was no prisoner, his attendance being wished only as far as Uzachil.

"Having learned from Juan Ortiz, to whom a native made it known, that the Indians had determined to assemble and fall upon the Christians for the recovery of their chief, the Governor, on the day for which the attack was concerted, commanded his men to be in readiness, the cavalry to be armed and on horseback, each one so disposed of in his lodge as not to be seen of the Indians, that they might come to the town without reserve.

"Four hundred warriors, with bows and arrows, appeared in sight of the camp; and, going into a thicket, they sent two of their number to demand the cacique. The Governor [on horseback], with six men on foot, taking the chief by the hand, conversing with him the while to assure the Indians, went toward the place where they were, when, finding the moment propitious, he ordered a trumpet to be sounded. Directly, they

who were in the houses, foot as well as horse, set upon the
natives, who, assailed unexpectedly, thought only of their
safety. Of two horses killed, one was that of the Governor, who
was mounted instantly on another.

"From thirty to forty natives fell by the lance; the rest
escaped into two very large ponds, situated some way apart,
wherein they swam about; and, being surrounded by the Christians, they were shot at with crossbow and arquebus, although
to no purpose, because of the long distance they were off.

"At night, one of the lakes was ordered to be guarded, the
people [the Christians] not being able to encircle both. The
Indians, in attempting to escape in the dark, would come swimming noiselessly to the shore, with a leaf of water lily on the
head, that they might pass unobserved; when those [who were]
mounted, at sight of any ruffle on the surface, would dash into
the water up to the breasts of the horses, and the natives would
again retire.

"Juan Ortiz told them that, as escape was impossible, they
would do well to give up; which they did, driven by extreme
chillness of the water; and one after another, as cold overpowered, called out to him, asking not to be killed—that he
was coming straightway to put himself in the hands of the
Governor. At four o'clock in the morning, they had all surrendered, save twelve of the principal men, who, as of more
distinction and more valiant than the rest, preferred to die
rather than yield. Then the Indians of Paracoxi, who were going about unshackled, went in after them, swimming, and
pulled them out by the hair. They were all put in chains, and,
on the day following, were divided among the Christians for
their service.

"While captive, these men determined to rebel, and gave the
lead to an interpreter, one reputed brave, that when the Governor might come near to speak with him, he should strangle
him; but no sooner was the occasion presented, and before his
hands could be thrown about the neck of [de] Soto, his purpose
was discovered, and he received so heavy a blow from him in
the nostrils, that they gushed with blood.

"The Indians all rose together. He who could only catch up
a pestle from a mortar, as well as he who could grasp a weapon,
equally exerted himself to kill his master, or the first one he
met; and he whose fortune it was to light on a lance, or a
sword, handled it in a manner as though he had been accustomed to use it all his days. One Indian, in the public yard of

the town, with blade in hand, fought like a bull in the arena, until the halberdiers of the Governor, arriving, put an end to him. Another got up, with a lance, into a maize crib, made of cane, and defended the entrance with the uproar of ten men, until he was stricken down with a battle-ax.

"They who were subdued may have been in all two hundred men. Some of the youngest the Governor gave to those who had good chains and were vigilant. All the rest were ordered to execution, and, being bound to a post in the middle of the town yard, they were shot to death with arrows by the people of Paracoxi."

One of those spared was a young brave who stated that he came from afar, "in the direction of the sun's rising, from which he had been a long time absent visiting other lands; that its name was Yupaha, and was governed by a woman, the town she lived in being of astonishing size, and many neighboring lords her tributaries, some of whom gave her clothing, others gold in quantity." He was given to Juan Gaytán, treasurer of the expedition, after he had told "how the metal was taken from the earth, melted, and refined, exactly as though he had seen it all done." He fared better than the other captives, though chained like them.

Word of the slaughter reached the Indian settlements. When the expedition came to Uzachil, the town was deserted. But food was there in great plenty—not only corn, but beans and pumpkins. "The pumpkins are better and more savory than those of Spain," commented the gentleman of Elvas. From Uzachil detachments of cavalry and foot were sent out in opposite directions to capture Indians, and returned with a hundred braves and squaws, all of them in chains, some with iron collars around their necks. They were put to work grinding corn, and afterward made to carry luggage.

Up to this time, in order to make flour, the soldiers had ground the corn themselves in mortars hollowed from logs, then sifted it through their shirts of mail. Some found this laborious or wasteful, and had eaten the corn roasted or raw. The only mention of venison thus far occurs after the slaughter at Napetaca, when two Indians brought de Soto a deer. It may have been an act of propitiation; it may also have been intended to delay the march of the white men. Like many other such gestures, it proved unavailing.

Swollen with captives, the Spanish columns reached Apalache on October 26, and found it deserted. Here, de Soto decided to set up winter quarters. Raiding parties brought back not only more

Indians, but plentiful provisions—now added to the diet were dried persimmons, which the invaders thought plums. "These plums are better than those of Spain, and come from trees that grow in the fields without being planted." Persimmon, the American date-plum, softens and sweetens with frost.

More somber was the news brought back from a reconnaissance of the coast. Horses' skulls were found, and other traces as well, which left no doubt where the boats had been built that carried Narváez and his men to their doom. It was Bahia de Caballos—the "Bay of Horses."

The gentleman of Elvas had sufficient opportunity to observe de Soto. His characterization may now be given more fully of this "inflexible man, and dry of word, who although he liked to know what the others all thought and had to say, after he once said a thing he did not like to be opposed, and as he ever acted as he thought best, all bent to his will." De Soto's decision was to send thirty cavalry under the command of Juan de Añasco to Tampa Bay with orders to Captain Calderón to abandon the base camp and march to Apalache with the cavalry and some crossbowmen on foot; de Añasco, meanwhile, was to dispatch the caravels to Havana and bring back the foot soldiers in the brigantines. On the caravels went twenty young Indian women in chains, a gift to Doña Isabel.

Like Narváez' wife, she was to wait in vain for her husband's return. But while Narváez and his men marched to oblivion, de Soto's army marched to renown and legend through Florida, Georgia, North and South Carolina, Tennessee, Alabama, Mississippi, Arkansas, Texas, and the Indian Territory of the Old West. His bones, like those of Alexander the Great, lie in the bed of a mighty river after a secret burial.

For all that, he is not an attractive hero.

As soon as Captain Calderón arrived, de Soto ordered planks and spikes to be carried to the Bay of Horses for the construction of a two-masted barge (piragua) in which thirty armed men would guard the shore for Añasco's brigantines. War canoes were on the estuary, warriors in the thickets around the camp. In late November, on a day of high wind, an Indian slipped past the sentries and set fire to the town.

And now, once more, history repeated itself. When the brigantines came, de Soto sent Francisco Maldonado, a captain of infantry, "to run the coast to the westward with fifty men, and look for an entrance, proposing to go himself in that direction by land." Maldonado had better luck than Narváez' pilot; he found a sheltered port —Pensacola Bay—sixty leagues from Apalache, and brought back with him a captive who said the name of his country was Ochuse.

"The Governor was highly pleased, hoping to find a good country ahead; and he sent Maldonado to Havana for provisions, with which to meet him at that port of his discovery, to which he would himself come by land; but should he not reach there that summer, then he directed him to go back to Havana and return there the next season to await him, as he would make it his express object to march in quest of Ochuse."

This he never did, although Maldonado waited for him there.

On March 3, 1540, a Wednesday, de Soto set out to find Yupaha, the town or province governed by a woman to whom gold was given in tribute. The winter, lack of food, and hard usage had killed most of the captives, who worked "naked and in chains," with the result that rations for a march of sixty leagues were carried by the men, in addition to their arms and other gear. The rations consisted of corn; de Soto's pigs, multiplied to three hundred from the original thirteen sows, were not to be touched.

"There was such want of meat and salt," wrote the gentleman of Elvas, "that oftentimes, in many places, a sick man had nothing for his nourishment, and was wasting away to bone, of some ail[ment] that elsewhere might have found a remedy; and would die of pure debility, saying: 'Now, if I had but a slice of meat, or only a few lumps of salt, I should not thus die.'

"Such was the craving for meat," he goes on, "that when the 600 men who followed [de] Soto arrived at a town, and found there twenty or thirty dogs, he who could get sight of one and kill him, thought he had done no little; and he who proved himself so active, if his captain knew of it, and he forgot to send him a quarter, [the captain] would show his displeasure, and make him feel it in the watches, or in any matter of labor that came along."

Yet—to quote the gentleman of Elvas again—

"the Indians never lacked meat. With arrows they get abundance of deer, turkeys, rabbits, and other wild animals, being very skillful in killing game, which the Christians were not; and even if they had been, there was not the opportunity for it, they being on the march the greater part of their time, nor did they, besides, ever dare to straggle off."

How de Soto's pigs were tended and driven, one can only guess; their presence, however, may account for the fact that there is no mention of snakes in the narrative of the expedition. How they were taken across the streams and rivers of the southern states is another subject for conjecture. To cross the Flint (Fayette County, Georgia), a piragua, hollowed out from a single tree trunk, was used for the men, and probably the pigs; the horses swam across, drawn alongside a cable by a windlass. To pass over a stream beyond the Ocmulgee River, a small bridge was constructed.

Towns deserted, towns burning, marked the route as the Indians fled to the woods before the white man's approach. But some hung on the flanks, discharged their arrows, wheeled and disappeared. Of five men who sought to find mortars for their corn in a deserted town, one was killed, three wounded; the fifth had fled, crying "To arms!" When he returned with help, the Indians were gone.

Thus, marching, resting, and fighting, the expedition came to Toalli, a town with houses

"different from those behind, which were covered with dry grass, thenceforward they were roofed with cane, after the fashion of tile. They are kept very clean; some have their sides so made of clay as to look like tapia [mud walls]. Throughout the cold country every Indian has a winter house, plastered inside and out, with a very small door, which is closed at dark, and a fire being made within, it remains heated like an oven, so that clothing is not needed during the nighttime. He has likewise a house for summer, and near it a kitchen, where fire is made and bread baked. Maize is kept in a barbacoa, which is a house with wooden sides, like a room, raised aloft on four posts, and has a floor of cane [the American corn crib is a copy of this]."

The expedition was now in Creek territory. No Indians were seen until the Spaniards reached a town on a river, into which the inhabitants plunged pell-mell at the approach of the columns; "nevertheless, some men and women were taken, among whom was found one who understood the youth, the guide to Yupaha." The chief was sent for, and is reported to have spoken as follows:

"Very High, Powerful, and Good Master. The things that seldom happen bring astonishment. Think, then, what must be the effect on me and mine, of the sight of you and your people, whom we have at no time seen, astride the fierce brutes, your horses, entering with such speed and fury into my country, that we had no tidings of your coming—things so altogether new, as to strike awe and terror to our hearts, which it was not nature to resist, so that we should receive you with the sobriety due to so kingly and famous a lord. Trusting to your greatness and personal qualities, I hope no fault will be found in me, and that I shall rather receive favors, of which one is that with my person, my country, and my vassals, you will do as with your own things; and another, that you tell me who you are, whence you come, whither you go, and what it is you seek, that I may the better serve you."

When allowance has been made for romantic, or at the least, flowery translation, while bearing in mind that chiefs were often great orators, this speech, and similar ones in the narrative, may be accepted as expressing what was said. De Soto, through his inter-preter, replied that "he was the child of the Sun, coming from its abode, and that he was going about the country, seeking for the greatest prince there, and the richest province," which was candid. The chief offered him a guide to the territory called Ocute, and the captives were released; before departing, the Spaniards set up a cross, and explained as best they could the suffering of Christ, "who was God and man."

Ten days later, while approaching Ocute, de Soto was met by two thousand Indians bearing gifts: "many rabbits and partridges, maize bread, many dogs." The reputation of the Spaniards as dog-eaters had preceded them. The columns rested two days; on leav-ing, the chief gave de Soto four hundred tamemes (porters). More chiefs appeared along his route and declaimed as above; from one, he received corn for four days' rations and seven hundred tamemes to carry it. Led by their guide to Yupaha the columns forded the Great Ohoopee and Cannouchee rivers, then the Ogeechee; Yupaha itself remained distant.

"The Governor menaced the youth, motioning that he would throw him to the dogs [i.e., the bloodhounds] for having lied to him in saying that it was four days' journey, whereas they had traveled nine, each day of seven or eight leagues; and that the men and horses had become very thin, because of the sharp economy practiced with the maize. The youth declared that he knew not where he was. Fortunately for him, at the time, there was not another whom Juan Ortiz understood, or he would have been cast to the dogs."

De Soto was becoming impatient, but he was still inflexible. He sent horsemen on reconnaissance—Baltazar de Gallegos ascending by the river, Juan de Añasco going down it, Alfonso Romo and Juan Rodríguez Lobillo "striking into the country."

Añasco brought back a squaw and a youth, and the news that he had found a small town "twelve or thirteen leagues off"—which suggests hard riding. "The governor and his people were as much delighted as though they had been raised from death to life," wrote the Portuguese narrator.

The time had come to do more than look with longing on the great herd of swine, and de Soto ordered a sufficient number killed daily to provide each man with half a pound of pork. This, with

"THE GENTLEMAN OF ELVAS" AS AUTHOR
Title page of the first edition of the narrative of the Portuguese fidalgo who accompanied the expedition of de Soto. From the original in The John Carter Brown Library, Brown University.

boiled greens, was now the diet; but, first, the tamemes were dismissed so they would not have to be fed.

Somewhat strengthened, but fuller of hope than meat, the Spaniards marched to the town discovered by Añasco, and found it deserted. It was full, however, of untouched stores of dried corn and flour. Four luckless Indians were brought in, "not one of whom would say anything else than that he knew of no other town." De Soto ordered one burned alive in the presence of the others, who revealed that "two days' journey from there was a province called Cofitachequi" (Creek for Dogwood Town).

Although he did not know it, de Soto was now in the region where a woman reigned as cacica (chieftainess). Arriving on the banks of the Savannah River, near present-day Augusta, the Spaniards saw four canoes approaching; in one was an Indian princess who addressed de Soto as follows:

> "Excellent Lord. My sister sends me to salute you, and to say, that the reason why she has not come in person is, that she has thought to serve you better by remaining to give orders on the other shore; and that, in a short time, her canoes will all be here, in readiness to conduct you thither, where you may take your repose and be obeyed."

She was followed by the cacica herself; her name, unfortunately, is nowhere given. She came in a canoe with an awning, seated on cushions; around her swarmed other canoes laden with presents. Again we get, in translation, a formal address:

> "Excellent Lord. Be this comnig to these your shores most happy. My ability can in no way equal my wishes, nor my services become the merits of so great a prince; nevertheless, good wishes are to be valued more than all the treasures of the earth without them. With sincerest and purest good will I tender you my person, my lands, my people, and make you these small gifts."

She now took from around her neck a large string of pearls and placed it around de Soto's; meanwhile, from the canoes, her attendants brought shawls and skins of the finest workmanship to lay at the conquistador's feet.

The cacica's lands were on both sides of the Savannah, in South Carolina as well as Georgia; true to her word, canoes were furnished for the crossing to Cofitachequi, where turkeys were supplied the famished soldiery. The gentleman of Elvas wrote:

> "The cacica, observing that the Christians valued the pearls, told the Governor that, if he should order some sepulchers that were in the town to be searched, he would find many; and if

he chose to send to those that were in the uninhabited towns, he might load all his horses with them."

There was a scramble for the graves. From those in Cofitachequi alone, 350 pounds of pearls were extracted. Some were on strings, some stitched together in decorative patterns, while some were in the form of birds and other figures. The manner in which the barrows sacred to the Indian dead were desecrated may have given the cacica her first intimation of things to come. The treasure hunt was followed by general looting and raping; even a tough campaigner like the gentleman of Elvas was shocked by "the outrages committed upon the inhabitants, there never failing to be men of low degree among the many, who will put the lives of themselves and others in jeopardy for some mean interest." Among the objects found by the soldiers were a dirk, rosaries and beads which had belonged to Ayllón's ill-fated expedition.

There was no gold in Yupaha.

"The natives were asked if they had knowledge of any great lord farther on, to which they answered, that twelve days' travel thence was a province called Chiaha, subject to a chief of Coça.

"The Governor then resolved at once to go in quest of that country."

It was May. He asked the cacica for guides and tamemes for the march. The princess was a heroine—she refused to provide either because of the treatment her people had received. De Soto placed her under guard and forced her to come along, on foot, attended by some of her women, one of whom carried a box full of unbored pearls, "of which those who had the most knowledge of their value said they were very precious." It was de Soto's plan to ask them of the cacica when the time came to dismiss her, in order to send them to Cuba to induce others to come to the land of Florida. The cacica, as it turned out, had other plans.

From Cofitachequi the bedrabbled army, with captives in chains and captive tamemes, the cacica and her women, Negro slaves and droves of pigs, marched in a northwesterly direction across South Carolina. To protect the horses, detachments of arquebusiers and crossbowmen were in the vanguard. The army reached mountainous country of "very rough and lofty ridges"—the Great Smokies at the southern end of the Blue Ridge Mountains—and came to the town of Xualla—Cherokee, Qualla—near the junction of the Tuckaseigee and Oconna-Luftee rivers in Swain County, North Carolina. Beyond that town was another—Guaxule, on the outermost limits of the cacica's territories, and beyond Guaxule "the province called Chiaha," de Soto's goal.

The presence of the cacica along the route was a boon to the Spaniards, for everywhere they went they were received peacefully and given food—seven hundred turkeys in one town alone. She was also able to order Indians into the ranks as tamemes. One day, on the march to Guaxule, she left the road "with an excuse of going into a thicket." Her women went with her, including the one who carried the box of pearls. The search for them was unavailing. Three slaves fled at the same time, following the women to Xualla, where a horseman named Alimamos, left behind to recover from a fever, saw them. He persuaded two of the slaves to go back with him; the third remained with the cacica. Alimamos told de Soto that they were returning to Cofitachequi and that "it was very sure they lived together as man and wife."

From Guaxule, which had little in the way of provisions, de Soto sent word to the cacique of Chiaha to provide sufficient stores of corn for a brief sojourn. The men were weary from the march, the horses so lean that they could not carry the horsemen. They were met on the way by twenty Indians, each bearing a basket of mulberries. A few days later, fifteen Indians appeared with baskets of corn and a welcome message: the cacique waited for them with twenty barbacoas full. On June or July 5—the different dates are those of the gentleman of Elvas and de Soto's secretary, respectively —the expedition came to Chiaha, an island at the junction of the Little Tennessee and Tennessee rivers in Loudon County, Tennessee. The waters were fordable. The cacique made the usual formal speech of welcome and obeisance, and de Soto replied in the usual formula, "that his gifts and his kindness pleased him greatly, and that he should ever consider him to be his brother."

The sojourn stretched to thirty days. The horses fattened in the lush grass. The men began to molest the Indian women. This was passed over; but when de Soto, at "the importunity of some who wanted more than was in reason," asked for thirty women to take along, the chief replied that he would have to confer with the elders of his tribe. The answer came in unexpected form. The Spaniards awoke one morning to find the Indians gone—men, women and children.

De Soto's reaction does not improve his image, but it was a necessary one to insure supplies along his route, which could only come

from submissiveness. He ordered the Indians hunted down, and led
the hunters himself with thirty of cavalry and thirty foot soldiers:

> "Passing by the towns of some of the chiefs who had gone off,
> he cut down and destroyed the great maize fields; and going
> along up the stream where the natives were, on an islet, to
> which the cavalry could not go, he sent word to them, by an
> Indian, that they should put away all their fears, and returning
> to their abodes, give him tamemes, as had been done all the
> way along, since he did not wish to have women, finding how
> very dear they were to them. The Indians judged it well to
> come and make their excuses to him, so they all went back to
> the town."

De Soto left Chiaha with the present of some Indian women for
himself; his destination was Coça, on the Alabama River, to which
the cacique of Chiaha was subject, as were numerous chiefs along
his route. The cacique of Coça came out to receive him, "borne in
a litter on the shoulders of his principal men, seated on a cushion,
and covered with a mantle of marten skins, of the size and shape
of a woman's shawl. On his head he wore a diadem of plumes, and
he was surrounded by many attendants playing upon flutes and
singing." The oration over, "the Governor gave him thanks, and
with mutual satisfaction they walked on toward the place, confer-
ring, the Indians giving up their habitations by order of their
cacique, and in which the general and his men took lodging."

It was full summer in a fat land. The Indians were friendly—at
first. But as it was a settled policy of the Spanish leaders to keep
the native chiefs under guard, in order to exact services before they
were released, the inhabitants not only of Coça but of the surrounding towns became uneasy and slipped silently away. Cavalry and
infantry went after them, bringing back many men and women in
chains. The rest followed.

> "Seeing how much harm they received, and how little they
> gained by going off, they came in, declaring that they desired
> to serve in all that was possible. Of the prisoners, some of the
> chiefs, whom the cacique interceded for, were let go; of the
> rest, each one took away with him as slaves those he had in
> chains, none returning to their country save some whose for-
> tune it was to escape, laboring diligently to file off their irons
> at night; or, while on the march, could slip out of the way,
> observing the carelessness of those who had them in charge,

sometimes taking off with them in their chains the burdens and the clothing with which they were laden."

The Indian youth who had led de Soto to the lands of the cacica was older. He declared that he wished to become a Christian, and was baptized and given the name Pedro. It was only then that his chains were struck off.

The Spaniards remained in Coça twenty-five days, horses, pigs and men basking in the sun and battening in the lush land. The usual interrogations were made, and de Soto learned there was a large province to the south called Tascaluça—the modern Tuscaloosa, the name meaning Black Warrior Town, on the Black Warrior River in Alabama. Setting out, he took the cacique of Coça with him and passed with his columns through Tallimuchase, "a great town without inhabitants."

Farther along the route there were Indians enough, in battle array—prepared, as de Soto afterward learned, to rescue their chief should he call for help. He did not call, but continued to smooth the passage of the white men from town to town, where women were given them for concubines or slaves, and new tamemes took the place of the old. He was dismissed after an envoy from Tascaluça arrived with a message of "service and obedience, friendship and peace."

Two leagues from Tascaluça the army halted, and Moscoso, master of the camp, with fifteen horsemen, went to inform the "grand cacique" of de Soto's approach (in part, of course, it was also a reconnaissance). They found him sitting in state.

"The cacique was at home, in a piazza. His appearance was full of dignity. He was tall of person, muscular, lean, and symmetrical. He was the suzerain of many territories, and of a numerous people, being equally feared by his vassals and the neighboring nations.

"The Master of the Camp, after he had spoken to him, advanced with his company, their steeds leaping from side to side, and at times toward the chief, when he, with great gravity, and seemingly with indifference, now and then would raise his eyes, and look on as in contempt."

He did not rise for de Soto; but that crafty leader took him by the hand and led him out of the circle of warriors. It was then that the chief made his oration, which ended on these words: "See in what you will command me."

One of the first commands he heard was to come along under guard when the march was resumed. In addition to this settled policy, of taking chiefs with him while passing through their territories, de Soto had another: to repay, with death or mutilation, natives who dared to lay hands on one of his men or on any of his stores. At a river crossing a soldier pursued a captive Indian woman who had gotten away; when he did not return, de Soto told the chief he would never be released if the Spaniard were not found. On the pretext of ordering a search, the chief of Tascaluça sent word to the chief of Mavila, toward which the army was advancing, to prepare for battle.

Mavila—given also as Mauilla and Mabila—was located near the junction of the Alabama and Tombigbee rivers. Although reconnaissance showed that warriors were massing, de Soto pressed on. Moscoso said, "Since the Indians were so evil disposed, it would be better to stop in the woods," but de Soto replied that "he was impatient of sleeping out, and that he would lodge in the town." They were met by Indians singing and playing flutes, and received by the chief with declarations of friendship and gifts—cloaks made of marten skins.

Mavila was a palisaded town. While the main force remained at a distance, de Soto entered with his bodyguard on foot. Accompanying him were a priest, a friar and servants carrying an altar, ornaments and vestments; these, with five soldiers, set off to seek a suitable house to convert into a chapel. The captives, meanwhile, brought their burdens as far as the palisade: food, clothing and armor, the pearls taken from Indian graves, and the great heaps of skins and shawls. In addition, many of them carried their masters' weapons.

In the presence of his vassals the chief of Tascaluça asked to be allowed to remain with his people, having walked enough. It was not a time for inflexibility; but de Soto was unable to differentiate between the pride and dignity of a great chief and insubordination. He refused. The chief left him and entered a house full of armed Indians. All the other houses were similarly garrisoned. The conquistador and his handful of men suddenly found themselves alone in an open space inside the palisade.

De Soto decided to let the chief know that he could stay, in exchange for a guide and tamemes. To this end, he addressed a warrior who happened to be passing, who not only made it clear

he would not listen—but continued walking. At this, Baltazar de
Gallegos attempted to seize him. War cries rent the air, followed
by the twang of bowstrings as Indians issued out of their houses.
All of the Spaniards, including de Soto, were wounded. Running
and stumbling, they made their way outside; there, they quickly
mounted and returned, lancing some Indians, and running others
down, before they wheeled to gallop back.

In the town itself, the five soldiers were all dead. The priest, friar
and servants had barricaded themselves behind a door. One of the
servants had a sword, the priest and friar snatched up clubs, and
they slashed and thwacked mightily as Indians attempted to enter.
Other Indians had rushed to the palisade where, taking the loads
from the captives, they brought them into the town and knocked
off their chains. The men were given bows and arrows; those who
had been carrying swords and halberds prepared to use them.

It was decided to assault the town. The order of battle was as
follows:

The cavalry to surround it, to prevent escape.

Four squadrons of foot soldiers to attack from four sides, in each
a soldier carrying a torch to fire the houses.

The men being deployed, de Soto ordered an arquebus to be shot
off, the signal to commence the assault. The squadrons surged forward. Some of the soldiers reached the house where the priest and
friar were and rescued them. The following account of the battle
is by the gentleman of Elvas:

"The Indians fought with so great spirit that they many times
drove our people back out of the town. The struggle lasted so
long that many Christians, weary and very thirsty, went to
drink at a pond near by, tinged with the blood of the killed,
and returned to the combat.

"The Governor, witnessing this, with those who followed

him in the returning charge of the footmen, entered the town on horseback, which gave opportunity to fire the dwellings; then, breaking in upon the Indians and beating them down, they fled out of the place, the cavalry and infantry driving them back through the gates, where, losing the hope of escape, they fought valiantly; and the Christians getting among them with cutlasses, they found themselves met on all sides by their strokes, when many, dashing headlong into the flaming houses, were smothered, and heaped one upon another, burned to death. [The cutlass, a short sword with a wide, slightly curved blade, could lay a man's torso open at a single stroke.]

"They who perished there were in all 2,500, a few more or less. Of the Christians there fell eighteen, among whom was Don Carlos, brother-in-law of the Governor; one Juan de Gamez, a nephew; Mem. Rodriguez, a Portuguese; and Juan Vázquez, of Villanueva de Barcarota, men of condition and courage; the rest were infantry.

"Of the living, 150 Christians had received 700 wounds from the arrow; and God was pleased that they should be healed in little time of very dangerous injuries. Twelve horses died, and 70 were hurt. The clothing the Christians carried with them, the ornaments for saying mass, and the pearls, were all burned there, they having set the fire themselves, because they considered the loss less than the injury they might receive of the Indians from within the houses, where they had brought the things together."

Thus far, de Soto had lost 102 men, the greater number from sickness, the rest in battle or picked off, one by one.

After the burning of Mavila the army camped in the open, levying tribute of food from other Creek towns and villages. Great care was necessary to enable the wounded men and horses to recover; some of the survivors had emerged bristling with as many as twenty arrows which had passed through the folds in their armor. It was during this period that de Soto learned through his Spanish interpreter—who learned it from the Indians—that Francisco Maldonado was waiting for him in the port of Ochuse (Pensacola Bay), six days distant; but, says the gentleman of Elvas, "he caused Juan Ortiz to keep the news secret, that he might not be interrupted in his purpose; because the pearls he wished to send to Cuba for show, that their fame might raise the desire of coming to Florida, had been lost."

The narrative of the expedition reflects, from time to time, the longings of the men to cease their wandering, to remain in one place or another and so prosper, and let who would journey endlessly in the quest for gold, which most had begun to believe did not exist. But de Soto remained inflexible.

A month after the burning of Mavila, in mid-November, he moved on once more, this time into the territory of the Chickasaws, who were related to the Creeks, and who opposed him at river crossings or harried his flanks on the march. On December 17 his army reached Chicaça, a town of twenty houses not far from the present-day Redland, in Pontotoc County, Mississippi. It was deserted. But, says the gentleman of Elvas: "The land was thickly inhabited, the people living about over it as they do in Mavila; and as it was fertile, the greater part being under cultivation, there was plenty of maize. So much grain was brought together as was needed for getting through with the season." Here, de Soto set up his winter quarters.

Snow had begun to fall; nevertheless, horsemen went out to hunt Indians, one of whom was sent to the chief with offers of friendship. The chief came and made his submission; several days later he returned with two other chiefs, who brought 150 rabbits in addition to the usual shawls and skins. It was an uneasy truce; the army was on constant alert, with sentries posted and horsemen making the rounds. To improve their relations, de Soto invited the chiefs to a pork dinner. They found it delicious.

The pigs, now numbering about four hundred, occupied several houses "a crossbow shot off from the camp." Following the dinner there were nightly raids on the pig-houses. A watch was set, and three Indians were caught in the act. De Soto ordered two shot to death with arrows; the third had his hands cut off, and thus mutilated was sent to his chief.

The abode of the chief of Chicaça was a mile or so from the Spanish encampment. Four cavalrymen, wandering in the open country between the camps, entered the Indian village and took some skins and shawls which caught their fancy. Their names were Francisco Osorio, a kinsman of the Marquis of Astorga, and one Reynoso; and Fuentes and Ribera, de Soto's chamberlain and page. There was an immediate commotion, and the Indians began to abandon their houses.

The four men were placed under arrest. De Soto condemned Osorio and Fuentes to death. Priests, friars and captains pleaded for them in vain; the conquistador was implacable. As they were about to be led out to be beheaded, Indians arrived with the formal complaint of their chief. Baltazar de Gallegos begged Juan Ortiz to change their words.

It was a terrifying moment. As the Indians looked on, Ortiz told de Soto that their chief "understood those Christians had been arrested on his account; that they were in no fault, having offended him in nothing, and that if he would do him a favor, to let them go free." To the Indians he said that "the Governor had the persons in custody, and would visit them with such punishment as should be an example to the rest."

De Soto ordered the men to be released. It did not pass unnoticed. Those who had pleaded for Osorio and Fuentes, and those who connived to save them, may have had second thoughts in a short time.

It was March. De Soto, preparing to leave Chicaça, asked the chief for two hundred tamemes. The reply came after midnight on the eighth, when Indians attacked the town from all sides, yelling and beating drums, and setting fires to the houses. The confusion was so great that only two men were able to mount—de Soto himself, and one Tapia; de Soto, thrusting his lance at an Indian, went over with his saddle.

All the rest, having had no time to snatch up arms and armor, "ran in all directions, bewildered by the noise, blinded by the smoke and the brightness of the flame, knowing not whither they were going, nor were able to find their arms, or put saddles on their steeds." Eleven fell dead, bristling with arrows like quills; three were badly burned, one dying several days later. Most of the horses broke their halters and plunged, neighing and snorting, among the attacking hordes, who, in the darkness, thought them cavalry and turned and ran; but fifty burned to death in their stalls.

Abandoning Chicaça, de Soto marched to the Indian town a mile away. Observed from a distance, it was a show of force; up close, however, it was different. For want of saddles, there were many riderless horses. The wounded, and the three badly burned men, were carried on litters on the shoulders of captive Indians. Some arquebusiers and crossbowmen were weaponless.

Eight days were spent on refurbishing arms and armor. On a forge hastily set up the swords burned in the conflagration were retempered. The bellows were made from a bearskin, with gun barrels for nozzles. The wood of the close-grained ash went into saddles, ash and birch into lances—the latter "as good as those made in Biscay." Skins were stretched over charred shields. On the ninth day, at four in the morning, three war parties of Indians approached the camp. This time, the watch beat the call to arms.

De Soto mustered his men in three squadrons and sallied forth. The speed with which he attacked, the terrible horses and horsemen in the van, scattered the Indians, who left the open field strewn with their dead. More might have been slain but for the shouts of a friar —"To the camp! To the camp!"—which made the squadrons wheel and return. It was a false alarm.

The next battle was less decisive, and brought grumblings from some of the officers and men.

From prisoners brought back, information was gained about the territory which lay ahead. De Soto had two reasons for asking about populated areas—in a large and settled community he would be sure to find food, and might hear of mines. The scarcity of food made it imperative to move again, and on April 25 the army left the region of Chicaça for a town called Alimamu, which turned out to be small and to have little corn. Three captains, with cavalry and foot soldiers, were sent to outlying towns to gather provisions; one of them, Juan de Añasco, with fifteen horsemen and forty of foot, reached a river (perhaps the Tallahatchie, in the neighborhood of New Albany, Union County, Mississippi). What he saw there was not a town, but a staked fort, with armed Indians waiting for them, "their bodies, legs and arms painted and ochered, red, black, white, yellow, and vermilion in stripes, so that they appeared to have on stockings and doublet. Some wore feathers, and others horns on the head, the face blackened, and the eyes encircled with vermilion, to heighten their fierce aspect."

When they saw the Spaniards, they began to beat on drums— then, yelling wildly, they sallied forth to meet them. Juan de Añasco deemed it wiser to withdraw "the distance of a crossbow shot," with the arquebusiers, crossbowmen and targeteers (the men with shields) forming a protective ring around the horses. They were now in an open space; in plain view the Indians built a fire, seized a brave by the head and feet, and pretended to pummel him and cast him into the flames, the pantomime signifying what they would do to the Spaniards. Three horsemen were dispatched to inform de Soto.

As usual, he decided to attack.

"He said that if this was not done they would be emboldened to make an attack at some other time, when they might do him more harm." The horsemen were ordered to dismount. Four squadrons were formed which, at a signal, charged toward the fort. The Indians resisted until the Spaniards reached the stakes. Then, leaving three dead: "they fled through that part near which passed a stream, sending back some arrows from the other bank; and because at the moment no place was found where the horses might ford, they had time to make their escape." Many Spaniards were wounded, some severely. "Everyone thought the Governor committed a great fault in not sending to examine the state of the ground on the opposite shore, and discover the crossing place before making the attack."

It is unlikely that they told the governor what they thought.

Again, de Soto pressed on—food was in short supply. For seven days the men marched through the wilderness—"pondy places, with thick forests, all fordable, however, on horseback, except some basins or lakes that were swum." Fifteen of the wounded died on the way. On May 8 the army arrived at a river town called Quizquiz; all the inhabitants were taken without a struggle, among them the chief's mother. De Soto offered to release them if the chief came, but the chief returned word that he would come only when they were released.

For once de Soto bowed to the exigencies of the moment. His men were weary from the march, the horses lean. He had found little corn. He let the Indians stream out and waited. The chief did not come; instead, warriors menaced the encampment, but withdrew when the horsemen drew up in formation to oppose them. De Soto pondered how to cross the river.

> "The distance was near half a league. A man standing on the shore could not be told whether he were a man or something else from the other side. The stream was swift, and very deep; the water, always flowing turbidly, brought along from above many trees and much timber, driven onward by its force."

This is the earliest description of the Mississippi by a white man. It is still like that in flood. The place where de Soto saw it may have been near Lower Chickasaw Bluffs.

> "He went to look at the river, and saw that near it there was much timber of which piraguas might be made, and a good situation in which the camp might be placed. He directly moved, built houses, and settled on a plain a crossbow-shot from the water, bringing together there all the maize of the towns behind, that at once they might go to work and cut down trees for sawing out planks to build barges."

Four were completed in a month's time. On June 8, before daybreak, they were carried half a mile upstream in order to land with the current opposite the camp. In three of them went twelve horse-

men—four in each—together with crossbowmen to cover their landing, and oarsmen to row. In the fourth were oarsmen to bring the
boats back. De Soto's orders were: "Secure the passage or die." The
piraguas descended without incident, and before the boats were
beached the horsemen spurred their horses through the shallow
water to hard, sandy ground. The landing place was secured. Two
hours after sunrise the entire expedition had been ferried across.

The piraguas were dismantled, the spikes and other metal parts
being salvaged for future use. Although de Soto did not know it,
it was not to be the last time that he would see the river. Nor did
he know that in less than a year the Mississippi would be his
monument.

Arkansas, 1541: "All the trees, the year round, were as green as
if they stood in orchards, and the woods were open."

Few places described in the narrative can be said with certainty
to belong to this or that locality. "He came to a small river, over
which a bridge was made, whereby he crossed. All that day, until
sunset, he marched through water, in places coming to the knees;
in others, as high as the waist." This may have been Fifteen-Mile
Bayou. The pigs went along. The gentleman of Elvas mentions
them when they are eaten, housed, stolen or destroyed, but never
tells how they were driven or transported, which is to be regretted.
Even with numerous tamemes carrying one pig apiece it must have
been an extraordinary feat as well as an extraordinary sight. For the
pigs were there—seven hundred of them—when de Soto died.

The first towns were deserted. But the relentless hunt continued.
Thirty Indians were seen on a plain: "The cavalry pursued, killed
ten, and captured fifteen." Pressing on, the Spaniards came to a
town which had not yet heard of them. "Many men and women
were taken, much clothing, blankets, and skins; such they likewise
took in another town in sight of the first, half a league off in the
field, whither the horsemen had run."

De Soto, learning of a great chief in a town called Casqui, sent
word to him that he was coming as a friend and as a brother. The
chief replied by presents on the road; thereafter, all the towns on
the march were found inhabited, the occupants coming out to offer
skins, shawls and fish. Near Casqui, the chief himself came out to
greet de Soto with a flowery oration and an invitation to lodge in
his town. De Soto declined, "using much courtesy."

FROM DE SOTO COUNTRY

Pre-Columbian jar from Mississippi County, Arkansas. Height: 5 inches. Photograph courtesy of the Museum of the American Indian, Heye Foundation.

Because of the heat, camp was pitched under trees half a mile or so away; here, a curious incident took place. The chief brought two blind men to de Soto. "He said, that inasmuch as the Governor was son of the Sun, he begged him to restore sight to those Indians." De Soto replied by pointing to the sky, the abode of Jesus who had suffered on the cross, "what of man there was of Him dying, what of divinity being immortal; and that, having ascended into heaven, He was there with open arms to receive all that would be converted to Him."

Here, as at Achese in the east, a tall cross made from two pine trees was erected on a mound, and around it the army first knelt, then marched in procession, priests in deerskin chasubles and friars chanting the litanies, soldiers the responses. Many of the Indians knelt with the Spaniards.

One day's journey from Casqui was the province of Pacaha. It lay beyond a river "of great depth and swiftness of current" (perhaps the Tyronza), and was a natural boundary between the two

neighboring chiefs. So eager was the chief of Casqui to see the white
men out of his domain that he offered to build a bridge over the
river; de Soto accepted his offer, and also took him along.

"The cacique of Casqui having come with his people, the
Governor sent word by an Indian to the cacique of Pacaha, that
though he might be at enmity with him of Casqui, and that
chief be present, he should receive neither injury nor insult,
provided that he attended in peace and desired his friendship,
for as a brother would he treat him. The Indian went as he
was bid, and returned, stating that the cacique took no notice
of the message, but that he fled out of the town, from the back
part, with all his people.

"Then the Governor entered there, and with the cavalry
charged in the direction the Indians were running, and at another town, a quarter of a league off, many were taken. As fast
as they were captured, the horsemen delivered them to the
Indians of Casqui who, from being their enemies, brought them
with great heed and pleasure to the town where the Christians
were, greatly regretting that they had not the liberty to kill
them.

"Many shawls, deer skins, lion and bear skins, and many cat
skins, were found in the town. Numbers who had been a long
time badly covered there clothed themselves. Of the shawls
they made mantles and cassocks; some made gowns and lined
them with cat skins, as they also did the cassocks. Of the deer
skins were made jerkins [jackets], shirts, stockings, and shoes;
and from the bear skins they made very good cloaks, such as no
water could get through. They found shields of raw cowhide
out of which armor was made for the horses."

The "cowhide" was, of course, buffalo hide; what the cats were
is more difficult to ascertain, but probably puma or cougar.

Pacaha was a large town, with towers and a palisade. It was
located, some think, in Mississippi County, Arkansas. There was not
only a great store of dried corn, but also a new stand in the fields.
Most remarkable of all was the chief's fish pond, fed by a canal
from the Mississippi. The fish that entered surprised the Spaniards:

"There was a fish called bagre, the third part of which was
head, with gills from end to end, and along the sides were
great spines, like very sharp awls [the Mississippi catfish].
Those of this sort that lived in the lake were as big as pike;
in the river were some that weighed from one hundred to one

hundred and fifty pounds. Many were taken with the hook.

"There was one in the shape of barbel [a large European fresh-water fish with fleshy filaments hanging from the mouth]; another like the bream, with the head of a hake, having a color between red and brown, and was the most esteemed. There was likewise a kind called peel-fish, the snout a cubit in length, the upper lip being shaped like a shovel [the spadefish; cubit: 18 inches]."

It was June's end. Pacaha was an ideal spot. The army remained there forty days.

There were incidents.

De Soto had sent word to the chief of Pacaha to come, and he had not come. A joint expedition by Casqui Indians and Spaniards set out to find him. He was discovered on an island, from which he fled in a canoe; his people, "in terror and confusion, plunging into the river to swim, many, mostly women and infants, got drowned."

The clothes and other possessions of these unfortunate Indians had been placed on rafts when they sought to escape; when the rafts were carried downstream by the current, the Indians from Casqui filled their canoes with the spoil and returned to their own territory. Seeing this, de Soto offered an alliance to the chief of Pacaha against the chief of Casqui. The chief of Pacaha made his appearance and obeisance, bringing gifts. Word was also sent to Casqui in the usual form, and that chief returned with gifts, an apology, and his daughter, telling de Soto that "his greatest desire was to unite his blood with that of so great a lord as he was, begging that he would take her to wife."

The chief of Pacaha, not to be outdone, gave de Soto two of his sisters.

"The name of one was Macanoche, that of the other Mochila. They were symmetrical, tall, and full. Macanoche bore a pleasant expression; in her manners and features appeared the lady. The other was robust."

The time had come to move on. The women went along. With guides and tamemes provided by the chief of Casqui, the army crossed the St. Francis River and marched on Quiguate, whose chief had left presents on the road for de Soto, but did not stay to greet him.

"That town was the largest seen in Florida. One-half of it was occupied by the Governor and his people; and, after a few days, discovering that the Indians were dealing in falsehoods, he ordered the other part to be burned, that it might not afford them cover should they attack him at night, nor be an embarrassment to his cavalry in a movement to repel them."

A prisoner led de Soto with twenty cavalry and fifty foot soldiers to the hiding place of the chief, who was seized, after being slashed with a cutlass, together with 140 of his subjects. The usual interrogations followed, and the usual answers were received—that to the south there were large towns, wide territories and numerous people, and to the northwest there was yet another province, called Coligoa, which was near some mountains. It was decided to go there first; mountains suggested a difference in the soil, and perhaps gold or silver would be found.

They crossed the L'Anguille River, Big Creek, Bayou de Vue and Cache River, living mainly on fish: "Fish were so plentiful in them that they were killed with blows of cudgels; and as the Indians traveled in chains, they disturbed the mud at the bottom, by which the fish, becoming stupefied, would swim to the surface, when as many were taken as were desired." On the seventh day the expedition reached high ground; before them the Indians scattered and fled, and were pursued by the horsemen.

Coligoa was in the valley of Little Red River. "The soil was rich, yielding maize in such profusion that the old was thrown out of store to make room for the new grain. Beans and pumpkins were likewise in great plenty; both were larger and better than those of Spain. The pumpkins, when roasted, have nearly the taste of chestnuts."

De Soto was now among the Quapaw Indians of the Plains; only a short distance to the north ranged the great herds of buffalo which could have provisioned his army; but even when he was shown buffalo skins he could not be sidetracked. Perhaps the presence of the multiplying pigs was, as he supposed, a sufficient safeguard against starvation; so were the Indian harvests along the route. A month was spent in a place called Cayas, in northwestern Arkansas. The horses fattened on corn, the men rejoiced at a salt spring, from which they made a quantity of salt to carry with them.

Strengthened and renewed, the Spaniards fanned out, on horseback and on foot, to capture more luckless Indians. Several were sent to their chief, to bid him come if he desired de Soto's friendship. The chief thought it better to remain where he was, with his people, and the Spaniards took him captive, together with a hundred and fifty braves and squaws. He told de Soto that there was a province to the southward, called Tulla, a journey of a day and a half, where there was a large population, but while he could provide a guide, he could not provide an interpreter—"the tongue of that country was different from his, and he and his ancestors had ever been at war with its chiefs."

De Soto fared no better—on approaching Tulla with his cavalry and fifty foot soldiers he was attacked by small groups with bows and arrows. In the town itself the Indians shot their arrows from the rooftops. "Fifteen were slain, and forty women and boys made prisoners." The Spaniards lost a horse, with several others wounded.

De Soto returned to Cayas to regroup his forces for an assault on the town. At his second approach he found Tulla abandoned, and occupied it; but in the dark middle of the night the Indians attacked from two directions. The alarm was sounded, cavalry and infantry responded, and the attackers were routed. Many were killed, and many taken. Of the latter, de Soto took six and ordered their right hands and noses cut off, and thus mutilated he sent them to their chief with the following message:

"That, if he did not come to him to apologize and render obedience, he would go in pursuit, and to him, and as many of his as he might find, would he do as he had done to those he sent. He allowed him three days in which to appear, making himself understood by signs, in the best manner possible, for want of an interpreter. At the end of that time an Indian, bearing a backload of cowskins from the cacique, arrived, weeping with great sobs, and coming to where the Governor was, threw himself at his feet."

The cacique himself came with eighty of his followers, all weeping, "the token of obedience and the repentance of a past error, according to the usage of that country. He brought a present of cowskins, which were found very useful; the country being cold, they were taken for bedcovers, as they were very soft and the wool like that of sheep."

The third winter in the strange new world had come. Marching, fighting and looting, the expedition passed over the Boston Mountains, seeking a province called Autiamque where, de Soto was told, there was maize to sustain him and his men in winter quarters. There was another reason for going there: the Indians had signified that near Autiamque there was a large body of water, which might be the sea. A plan was evolving in de Soto's mind.

Autiamque was on the south side of the Arkansas River, not far from the present-day Fort Smith. It was found deserted; but as the surrounding country was populous, de Soto ordered a stockade to be built, each Spaniard being allotted a share of the construction by the number of captives he possessed. It was completed in three days, being made of high trees trimmed and sunk deep in the ground. One night de Soto sent a soldier to beat the alarm, and having found some men slow to respond, continued the drills.

Autiamque was well stored with corn, beans, walnuts and dried persimmons. Two kinds of rabbits abounded in the countryside: "one of them like that of Spain, the other of the color, form, and size of the great hare, though longer even, and having bigger loins"—the jackrabbit. The Spaniards were taught how to snare them. "The contrivance is a strong spring that lifts the animal off its feet, a noose being made of a stiff cord to run about the neck, passing through rings of cane that it may not be gnawed. Many of them were taken in the maize fields, usually when it was freezing or snowing."

It was in Autiamque, after almost three years among his own people, that Juan Ortiz died. The baptized Indian, Pedro, was no substitute as an interpreter; "what would have been rendered in four words, it became necessary now to have the whole day, and oftener than otherwise the very opposite was understood of what was asked."

On Monday, March 6, 1542, de Soto decided to seek the sea. He had lost 250 men and 150 horses; the gentleman of Elvas estimates the force as "not over 300 efficient men, nor more than 40 horses. Some of the beasts were lame, and useful only in making out the show of a troop of cavalry; and, from the lack of iron, they had all gone a year without shoes."

De Soto's plan was to build two brigantines, sending one to Cuba, the other to Mexico, so that the arrival of one or the other would be tidings of him and his expedition; in Cuba he hoped to recruit a new force to enable him to continue westward, into the lands Cabeza de Vaca had reached, and where he had hinted there was gold.

The fateful march was resumed. It was not toward the sea, but to the banks of the Mississippi. Some of the severity visited upon Indian towns on his route suggest that de Soto was suffering from the illness that would shortly end his life. At Nilco, "the cries of the women and children were such as to deafen those who pursued them." As for the men, a hundred were killed but "many were allowed to get away badly wounded, that they might strike terror into those who were absent."

From Guachoya, a palisaded town on the river (perhaps near Arkansas City), horsemen under Juan de Añasco went to search for the sea, and were gone eight days; they traveled no more than fourteen or fifteen leagues "on account of the great bogs that came out of the river, the canebrakes and thick scrubs there were along the margin." Worse, they had found no inhabited spot. Despondent, and consumed by fever, probably typhus, de Soto doffed his armor and lay down on a pallet covered with buffalo robes. He then called his captains together.

"He asked that they would relieve him of the charge he held over them, as well of the indebtedness he was under to them all, as to forgive him any wrongs they might have received at his hands. To prevent any divisions that might arise, as to who should command, he asked that they would be pleased to elect a principal and able person to be governor, one with whom they should all be satisfied, and being chosen, they would swear before him to obey; that this would greatly satisfy him, abate somewhat the pains he suffered, and moderate the anxiety of leaving them in a country, they knew not where.

"Baltazar de Gallegos responded in behalf of all, consoling him with remarks on the shortness of the life of this world, attended as it was by so many toils and afflictions, saying that whom God earliest called away, He showed particular favor; with many other things appropriate to such an occasion. And, finally, since it pleased the Almighty to take him to Himself, amid the deep sorrow they not unreasonably felt, it was necessary and becoming in him, as in them, to conform to the Divine Will.

"'That, as respected the election of a governor, which he ordered, whomsoever his Excellency should name to the command, him would they obey. Thereupon the Governor nominated Luis Moscoso de Alvarado to be his captain general; when by all those present was he straightway chosen and sworn Governor.

"The next day, the twenty-first of May, departed this life the magnanimous, the virtuous, the intrepid captain, Don Hernando de Soto, Governor of Cuba and Adelantado of Florida."

His body was transferred secretly to another house where it remained for three days while de Alvarado and his officers pondered how to dispose of it without letting the Indians know their leader was dead. On the third night the body was taken to a grave dug inside the palisade, and horsemen rode back and forth over the spot—to no avail. "The cacique of Guachoya asked for him, saying: 'What has been done with my brother and lord, the Governor?'"

Once more in the middle of the night, the body was removed from its resting place. Shrouded in Indian shawls, it was placed in a canoe weighted with sand and committed to the Mississippi in midstream.

The property of the dead leader was sold at auction:

"two male and three female slaves, three horses, and 700 swine. For each slave, or horse, was given two or three thousand cruzados, to be paid at the first melting of gold or silver, or division of vassals and territory, with the obligation that should there be nothing found in the country, the payment should be made at the end of a year, those having no property to pledge to give their bond; a hog bought in the same way, trusted, two hundred cruzados. Those who had left anything at home bought more sparingly, and took less than others."

After the sale, almost everyone owned and raised hogs, says the gentleman of Elvas. More: "they lived on pork." And having a steady supply of meat, they now resumed observance of holidays, having in the past eaten meat when they got hold of it, even on Fridays.

The Narváez expedition, and in particular its survivors, with their tales of the vast territories they had traversed, aroused great excitement in Mexico as well as in Spain. Cabeza de Vaca, we have seen, returned to the mother country, and the new expedition to Florida he had hoped to lead had been entrusted to de Soto; later, he served in South America. Alonzo del Castillo went to Spain with him, but returned to Mexico, married there, and lived on a grant of rents from the Indian town of Tehuacan. Andrés Dorantes served under the viceroy, Antonio de Mendoza, in the conquest of Jalisco, married a widow, Doña Maria de la Torre, and had several sons, one of whom became king's treasurer of Vera Cruz.

The fourth man to reach Mexico with them was Estévan, the Negro from Morocco, who had entered the viceregal service with his master, Dorantes, but was now the slave of Mendoza. Such is the designation given him by some writers; it is more probable that his position was less that of slave than factotum. His appearance was impressive. He was bearded like a Spaniard, powerfully built, full of knowledge of the Indians he had encountered, having been a medicine man among them, and like them endowed with cunning as well as endurance—on all counts a useful servant in any future northward extension of New Spain. His chance came when Mendoza decided to use him to investigate the truth or falsity of reports concerning the "Seven Cities of Cibola."

This—as it turned out—mythical place, was born of a fusion of European legend with an Aztec tradition about Chicomoztoc, the Seven Caves, and further mingled with accounts of a people north of New Galicia, the northernmost province of New Spain, who wore clothes of cotton and wool, possessed turquoises, and lived in houses having many stories. The subject was pondered by many who dreamed of another empire like that of Mexico and Peru, not least Mendoza; another was Friar Marcos de Niza, a Franciscan who had been with Pizarro.

Mendoza, although ambitious, was nevertheless of a different stamp from de Guzmán, who had laid waste the Indian lands of northern Mexico. He was a friend of Friar Bartolomeo de Las Casas, that great Catholic pleader who had been appalled by the behavior of his countrymen, and who advised preaching Christ to the natives, instead of using force of arms. But the things of this world are not always so simple as such a saintly character might wish; Mendoza was human, and while he desired "good treatment of the natives of the province" [of New Galicia] when he sent Friar Marcos thither, he also wished to learn how the new governor went about his duties. "And if, through the favor of God our Lord and the grace of the Holy Ghost, you should find a road on which to proceed onward and penetrate farther inland, you shall take along with you Estévan of Dorantes as a guide."

On March 7, 1539, while de Soto was provisioning his ships in Havana, Friar Marcos and Estévan left Culiacán in the northwest part of New Galicia, accompanied by other friars and a number of Sonoran Pima Indians; these had assisted, then accompanied Cabeza de Vaca to Mexico, only to be enslaved. They had learned Spanish, had been converted, and now had been purchased and freed by Mendoza to act as guides and interpreters for Friar Marcos, whose mission was—to a certain extent—a scientific one, perhaps the first of its kind in the New World:

"To note the kind of people, if they are numerous or not, and if they are dispersed or live together; the quality and fertility of the land, its climate, the trees and plants, domestic or savage animals, the aspect of the country, whether rugged or level, the streams, if large or small, and the rocks and metals. And of whatever objects it may be possible to bring or send samples, bring or send them, in order that his Majesty be informed of everything."

Should a populous settlement be found, Friar Marcos was to advise Mendoza if it was suitable for the erection of a monastery, to which churchmen, "fitted for the work of conversion," could go. For souls were important; but, then, so were rocks and metals. So was the surveillance of the new governor of the province of New Galicia.

He was Don Francisco Vásquez de Coronado, a gentleman from Salamanca, who had married in Mexico the daughter of Alonso de Estrada who, it was reported, was the natural son of his Catholic Majesty Don Ferdinand.

Friar Marcos was well received in the north, great numbers of Indians coming to hear him preach, the word having spread that there was to be no more slave hunting. "These Indians," he reported modestly, "I instructed to the best of my ability, by means of the interpreters, with the contents of my instructions, that is, in the knowledge of our Lord who is in heaven, and of his Majesty who is on earth." They also rejoiced at seeing Estévan again, whom they considered a friend, and who was quite as adept with the medicine man's rattle as with the cross.

Marcos also went about the viceroy's business, as directed. Making his headquarters at Vacapa (perhaps today's Matapa), he dispatched two parties, one to the coast, to learn how far off it was, and the other, with Estévan as guide, to the north. Estévan's instructions were to proceed no farther than fifty or sixty leagues, and there await the friar; meanwhile, however, he was to send back tidings by a simple code utilizing the cross of Christ. A cross the size of a hand would indicate "but a mean thing" found; a cross of two hand spans would indicate some "great matter," perhaps a large city or town. But "if it were a country greater and better than New Spain, he should send me a great cross."

On Passion Sunday, the fifth Sunday in Lent, Estévan left Friar Marcos at Vacapa and set out on the mission from which he never returned. He was accompanied by several Franciscans and scores of friendly natives. Only four days had passed when an Indian courier arrived at Vacapa bearing in his hands a cross the height of a man and an urgent message to Marcos, that he "should forthwith come away" and follow Estévan. Two days after Easter, the good friar did so. For with the messenger bearing the cross had come

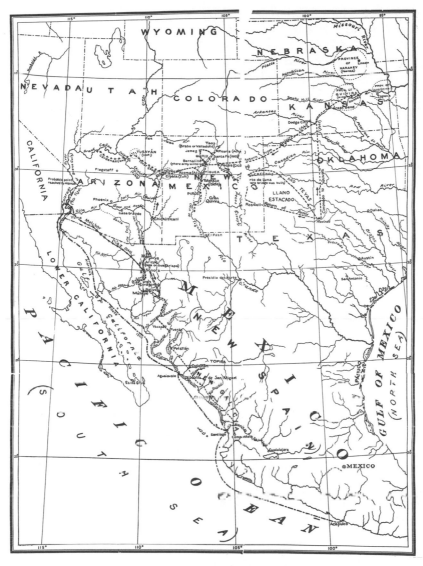

SPANISH THRUSTS FROM MEXICO, 1540–1542
-------- Coronado: from Compostela to Kansas.
— · — · — Melchior Diaz: from Sonora to the Lower Colorado.
+ + + + + + Cardenas: from Cibola to the Grand Canyon.
—— · —— Alarcon: from Acapulca through the Gulf of California.
Courtesy of the Map Division, The New York Public
Library, Astor, Lenox and Tilden Foundations.

an Indian who told Marcos what no doubt Marcos wished to hear: that a month's journey from Estévan's resting place was one of the cities of a province called Shiuona. There were seven such cities, the Indian related, and described the storied houses that were there, all of which were adorned with turquoises.

Shi-uo-na is a Zuñi Indian word meaning either tribal territories, or range, or as some have suggested, buffalo; perhaps it applied to both. To Estévan, first, and now to Friar Marcos, however, Shiuona sounded very much like Cibola which, taken together with the report of seven cities, made it all but conclusive.

The route taken by Estévan is not known, since he left no written memorials; but it must have been nearly the same as that followed by Friar Marcos, since he went with Estévan's messengers—north from Vacapa to the Yaqui River and through the valley of the Rio Sonora, where he raised two crosses "and took possession; for it appeared to me suitable from here on to perform acts of possession." By the time he reached the confines of the present United States, he found caches of food which Estévan had left for him.

How lovely was the land—in the valley of the San Pedro it was "like a garden" with villages a mile or so apart; it was a region, Marcos wrote, where turquoise was plentiful and adorned both men and women. When he reached the Gila River he learned that Estévan, with hundreds of Indians, was to the northeast.

Friar Marcos himself was now accompanied by many Indians, who volunteered their services, quite possibly because Estévan had prepared the way. Following him through a pass between the Sierra Mogoyan and Sierra Blanca, he emerged on a high plateau— the plateau of the Zuñis—where dread news greeted him.

"Here met us an Indian," he wrote afterward, "the son of one of the chief men that accompanied me, who had gone before with Estévan, who came in great fright, having his face and body all covered with sweat, and showing exceeding sadness in his countenance."

Estévan had been taken captive by the Zuñis, and some of his Indian followers had been killed, the rest fleeing in disorder, many with wounds.

Estévan had played the role of viceroy's emissary with special distinction. His dress, far from the viceregal court, was one of savage splendor. Bright feathers and tinkling bells adorned his arms and legs. He bore a gourd likewise hung with bells and decorated by a red and a white feather, which he sent before him by eager messengers as a symbol of authority, having seen this done in his wanderings in western Texas. Beside him paced two Spanish greyhounds; behind him followed a bevy of young Indian women, who had been given to him, or whom he had demanded, along the way. Eager Indians carried his provisions and supplied food. They also carried great stores of turquoises which he had collected.

"These had followed him from all the settlements he had passed," wrote Pedro de Castañeda, "believing that under his protection they could traverse the whole world without any danger."

Unfortunately for him and them, this did not apply to the Indians of the Zuñi pueblos. The magic gourd, in fact, proved his undoing, for to the Zuñis it was the rattle of an enemy, and they had dashed it to the ground. It may have been Apache. Estévan's messengers returned from Hawaiku bringing a warning not to proceed further. But to this he paid no attention, with what results we have seen.

The end of Estévan is related by Castañeda as follows:

"As the people in this country were more intelligent than those who followed Estévan, they lodged him in a little hut they had outside their village, and the older men and the governors heard his story and took steps to find out the reason he had come to that country.

"For three days they made inquiries about him and held a council. The account which the Negro gave them of two white men who were following him [Friar Marcos and another Franciscan], sent by a great lord, who knew about things in the sky, and how these were coming to instruct them in divine matters, made them think that he must be a spy or a guide from some nations who wished to come and conquer them, because it seemed to them unreasonable to say that the people were white in the country from which he came and that he was sent by them, he being black. Besides these other reasons, they thought it was hard of him to ask them for turquoises and women, and so they decided to kill him."

At dawn, "when the sun was about a lance high," Estévan was permitted to leave his hut. There was an outpouring of Indians. Perhaps, when he started to run, he heard for an instant the horizontal rain of their arrows.

The tradition of his death is retained in a Zuñi legend which places the event at the pueblo of Kiakima. Those who were next on the scene place it at Hawaiku. They brought the "short canes that spit fire and made thunder." And they marched and looted all the way to the Grand Canyon of the Colorado and the plains of Texas, Kansas and Nebraska, where the great buffalo herds were first seen and described by Europeans.

Estévan deserves his own memorial. He was the first man from a European expedition to travel across the entire United States, reach New Spain, and return, passing through southern Arizona to the Zuñi pueblos of western New Mexico. It was his urgent message to Friar Marcos about Cibola that started the chain of events that led to the expedition of Coronado, alluded to above.

Marcos was a seasoned campaigner, no longer young, and perhaps even eager for martyrdom. Learning that his life was threatened by some of the very Indians who had accompanied him and who had lost friends and kin by following Estévan, he divided his possessions among them, except for some religious articles, saying he did not fear death, since he would die a Christian. But, as he was so close to fabled Cibola, he said he was determined to have a view of it. Looking out over the plateau of the Zuñis he saw, in the clear, dry and magnifying light the pueblo of Hawaiku set against the Zuñi mountain range.

"It was situated on a plain at the foot of a round hill," he afterward wrote, "and maketh show to be a fair city. The houses are builded in order, according as the Indians told me, all made of stone with divers stories, and flat roofs, as far as I could discern from a mountain, whither I ascended to view the cities."

Exalted by the sight, he made a mound of stones, on which he placed a small cross, and took possession for the viceroy and the king-emperor, bestowing on the plain and the regions roundabout the name New Kingdom of St. Francis, for the founder of his order. This done, he turned south, and hurried back "with much more fear than victuals," as he afterward reported. The fear was not imaginary; he was no longer being received in friendly fashion by Indians along his route. On the journey to the north they had supplied him with deer, rabbits and partridges; perhaps on the return journey he was thankful to have dry corn to munch.

He made it back to Culiacán and, accompanied by Coronado, reached the City of Mexico in the summer of 1539. Rumors quickly spread that the Seven Cities, once sought by Nuño de Guzmán, had been found. The doubters heard from the pulpits of the Order of St. Francis that it was true; Friar Marcos himself had been elected Father Provincial, at Mendoza's insistence.

One of those who heard the rumors early was Hernando Cortez, who sent a fleet from Acapulco in July of 1539 to forestall exploration of the new lands by Mendoza. Commanded by Francisco de Ulloa, the ships sailed up the Gulf of California, then doubled the peninsula, and returned without additional news about the discoveries claimed by Father Marcos. One of the last acts of the conqueror of Mexico was to seek a royal order to continue his own explorations and prevent those of the viceroy, but he was recalled to Spain and never saw his empire again.

The stage was set for another invasion of American Indian lands, this time by an army of cavaliers, young men of good family and high station who thronged the City of Mexico with little to do but practice courtesies and await the call that would bring adventure, riches and fame. There was to be only a sprinkling of common soldiers in the Coronado expedition, but the result was the same for the Indians of the pueblos and the Plains.

"There were so many men of such high quality among the Spaniards," wrote Pedro de Castañeda, "that such a noble body was never collected in the Indies, nor so many men of quality in such a small body, there being 300 men. Francisco Vásquez de Coronado, governor of New Galicia, was captain general, because he had been the author of it all. The good viceroy Don Antonio [de Mendoza] did this because at this time Francisco Vásquez was his closest and most intimate friend, and because he considered him to be wise, skillful, and intelligent, besides being a gentleman. Had he paid more attention and regard to the position in which he was placed and the charge over which he was placed, and less to the estates he left behind in New Spain, or, at least, more to the honor he had and might secure from having such gentlemen under his command, things would not have turned out as they did. When this narrative is ended, it will be seen that he did not know how to keep his position nor the government that he held."

The author of the narrative, a native of the Ebro valley in Old Castile, was one of the original colonists in San Miguel Culiacán, founded by Nuño de Guzmán. He joined the expedition when it arrived there after its departure from Compostela. Little more is known of him; a quarter of a century later his widow and children —four sons and four daughters—filed a claim against the crown for his services in the field.

Compostela was the chief city of New Galicia, and the army assembled there because Mendoza wisely foresaw that mischief might be created among friendly Indians if an expedition passed through Mexico proper. The viceroy was present at the muster. Castañeda wrote:

"He made Don Pedro de Tovar ensign general, a young gentleman who was the son of Don Fernando de Tovar, the guardian and lord high steward of the Queen Doña Juana [daughter of Ferdinand and Isabella, wife of Philip I, mother of Charles V], our demented mistress—may she be in glory— and Lope de Samaniego, the governor of the arsenal at Mexico, a gentleman fully equal to the charge, army-master. The captains were Don Tristan de Arellano; Don Pedro de Guevara, the son of Don Juan de Guevara and nephew of the Count of Oñate; Don Garcia Lopez de Cardenas; Don Rodrigo Maldonado, brother-in-law of the Duke of the Infantado; Diego Lopez, alderman of Seville, and Diego Gutierres, for the cavalry.

"All the other gentlemen were placed under the flag of the general, as being distinguished persons, and some of them became captains later, and their appointments were confirmed by order of the viceroy and by the general, Francisco Vásquez. To name some of them whom I happen to remember, there were Francisco de Barrionuevo, a gentleman from Granada; Juan de Saldivar, Francisco de Ovando, Juan Gallego, and Melchior Diaz—a captain who had been mayor of Culiacán who, although he was not a gentleman, merited the position he held."

Diaz it will be recalled, had welcomed Cabeza de Vaca and his companions at Culiacán.

Father Marcos, together with some Franciscans, lay and clerical, accompanied the expedition, as did several hundred Indian auxiliaries and some Negroes. After hearing mass, cavaliers and soldiers were addressed by the viceroy; it was, says Castañeda, "a very eloquent short speech." Mendoza laid stress on the loyalty all owed to Coronado, their general, and then outlined "the benefits which this expedition might afford, from the conversion of those peoples as well as in the profit of those who should conquer the territory, and the advantage to His Majesty and the claim which they would thus have on his favor and aid at all times." This said, all present swore upon a missal "that they would follow their general on this expedition and would obey him in everything he commanded them, which they faithfully performed."

A day later, with colors flying, the army started north along the coast. The viceroy accompanied Coronado for two days, then turned back with his retinue. Off the coast, in support of the expedition, went two ships under Hernando de Alarcón having on board equipment and baggage which the soldiers could not transport overland. As in previous expeditions, ships and soldiers never met, although news of each other's presence came to both leaders in the wilderness. Alarcón sailed up the Gulf of California and explored the mouth of the Colorado River, by ship's boats and on foot.

For Coronado, the forms of the troubles to come appeared early. Logistics plagued his expedition, as it had earlier ones. At Chiametla, a foraging party attempted to requisition Indian provisions and was forced to fight; the quartermaster, Samaniego, fell dead with an arrow through his eye. Several soldiers were wounded. Reinforcements were brought up, and revenge took a macabre form. "They hanged those who seemed to belong to the district where the army-master was killed." Don García López de Cárdenas replaced Samaniego as quartermaster.

There was plenty of food at Culiacán, the inhabitants having stocked up in anticipation of the army's arrival, which took place on Easter Eve, 1540. The expedition was welcomed on the outskirts by citizens who requested Coronado not to enter until Easter Monday. On that day, a mock battle for the town was staged, the inhabitants coming out mounted and on foot in orderly ranks to face the "invaders." Cannon were shot off, the townspeople retired as though defeated, then ceased from play-acting to show their hospitality. It was all very gay, except for one artilleryman, "who lost a hand by a shot, from having ordered them to fire before he had finished drawing out the ramrod."

"Some of the townspeople were not ill repaid for this hospitality, because all had started with fine clothes and accoutrements, and as they had to carry provisions on their animals after this, they were obliged to leave their fine stuff."

The Franciscans appear to have forfeited their popularity as soon as the first difficult terrain was reached. Father Marcos, becoming aware of doubts and mutterings on the march to Culiacán, promised in a sermon "that he would place the army in a country where their hands would be filled." This satisfied the men temporarily; it is significant, however, that when Coronado pressed ahead with fifty horsemen, some foot soldiers and his Indian allies, the friars preferred to go along with him instead of staying with the main body of troops.

Castañeda was one of those left behind. What happened on the vanguard's march to Cibola is related by Coronado in a letter to the viceroy dated August 3, 1540. It is the first letter from an identifiable settlement in the United States. It gives the route of the march through New Galicia, Sonora, Arizona and New Mexico, and describes the battle for Cibola by the commander, who participated with courage and fortitude.

"I reached the Valley of Hearts [Corazones] at last, on the 26th day of the month of May, and rested there a number of days," Coronado wrote. "Between Culiacán and this place I could sustain myself only by means of a large supply of corn bread, because I had to leave all the corn, as it was not yet ripe. In this Valley of Hearts we found more people than in any part of the country which we had left behind, and a large extent of tilled ground. There was no corn for food among them, but as I heard that there was some in another valley called Señora, [whence Soñora], which I did not wish to disturb by force, I sent Melchior Diaz with goods to exchange for it, so as to give this to the friendly Indians whom we brought with us, and to some who had lost their animals along the way and had not been able to carry the food which they had taken from Culiacán.

"By the favor of Our Lord, some little corn was obtained by this trading, which relieved the friendly Indians and some Spaniards. Ten or twelve of the horses had died of overwork by the time that we reached this Valley of Hearts, because they were unable to stand the strain of carrying heavy burdens and eating little. Some of our Negroes and some of the Indians also died here, which was not a slight loss for the rest of the expedition. They told me that the Valley of Hearts is a long five days' journey from the western sea. I sent to summon Indians from the coast in order to learn about their condition, and while I was waiting for these the horses rested.

"I stayed there four days, during which the Indians came from the sea, who told me that there were seven or eight islands two days' journey from the seacoast, directly opposite, well populated with people, but poorly supplied with food, and the people were savages. They told me they had seen a ship pass not very far from the land. I do not know whether to think that it was the one which was sent to discover the country [by Cortez], or perhaps some Portuguese.

"I set out from the Hearts and kept near the seacoast as well as I could judge, but in fact I found myself continually farther off, so that when I reached Chichilticalli I found that I was fifteen days' journey distant from the sea, although the Father Provincial had said that it was only five leagues distant and that he had seen it. We all became very distrustful, and felt great anxiety and dismay to see that everything was the reverse of what he had told your Lordship. The Indians of Chichilticalli say that when they go to the sea for fish, or for anything else that they need, they go across the country, and that it takes them ten days; and this information which I have received from the Indians appears to me to be true. The sea turns toward the west directly opposite the Hearts for ten or twelve leagues, where I learned that the ships of your Lordship had been seen, which had gone in search of the port of Chichilticalli, which the father said was on the thirty-fifth degree."

Not only was Chichilticalli far in the interior, in southern Arizona, but the sea here mentioned was the Gulf of California. Chichilticalli is an Aztec name meaning "Red House." When Castañeda saw it a few weeks later "it appeared to have been a strong place at some former time when it was inhabited, and it was very plain that it had been built by a civilized and warlike race of strangers who had come from a distance."

Coronado's letter continues:

"I entered the borders of the wilderness region on St. John's Eve [June 23], and, for a change from our past labors, we found no grass during the first days, but a worse way through mountains and more dangerous passages than we had experienced previously. The horses were so tired that they were not equal to it, so that in this last desert we lost more horses than before; and some Indian allies and a Spaniard named Spinoza, besides two Negroes, died from eating some herbs because the food had given out.

"I sent the army-master, Don García López de Cárdenas, with fifteen horsemen, a day's march ahead of me, in order to explore the country and prepare the way, which he accomplished like the man that he is, and agreeably to the confidence

which your Lordship has had in him. I am the more certain
that he did so, because as I have said, the way is very bad for
at least thirty leagues and more, through impassable mountains.
But when he had passed these thirty leagues, we found fresh
rivers and grass like that of Castile, and especially one sort like
what we call *Scaramoio;* many nut and mulberry trees, but the
leaves of the nut trees are different from those of Spain. There
was a considerable amount of flax near the banks of one river,
which was called on this account El Rio del Lino [perhaps the
Little Colorado].

"No Indians were seen during the first day's march, after
which four Indians came out with signs of peace, saying that
they had been sent to that desert place to say that we were
welcome, and that on the next day the tribe would provide the
whole force with food. The army-master gave them a cross,
telling them to say to the people in their city that they need
not fear, and that they should have their people stay in their
own houses, because I was coming in the name of his Majesty
to defend and help them.

"After this was done, Hernando Alvarado came back to tell
me that some Indians had met him peaceably, and that two of
them were with the army-master waiting for me. I went to
them forthwith and gave them some paternosters and some
little cloaks, telling them to return to their city and say to the
people there that they could stay quietly in their houses and
that they need not fear. After this I ordered the army-master to
go and see if there were any bad passages which the Indians
might be able to defend, and to seize and hold any such until
the next day, when I would come up.

"He went, and found a very bad place in our way where we
might have received much harm. He immediately established
himself there with the force which he was conducting. The
Indians came that very night to occupy that place so as to defend it, and finding it taken, they assaulted our men. According to what I have been told, they attacked like valiant men,
although in the end they had to retreat in flight, because the
army-master was on the watch and kept his men in good order.
The Indians sounded a little trumpet as a sign of retreat, and
did not do any injury to the Spaniards.

"The army-master sent me notice of this the same night, so
that on the next day I started with as good order as I could, for
we were in such great need of food that I thought we should
all die of hunger if we continued to be without provisions for

another day, especially the Indians [allies], since altogether we did not have two bushels of corn, and so I was obliged to hasten forward without delay. The Indians [Zuñis] lighted their fires from point to point, and these were answered from a distance with as good understanding as we could have shown. Thus notice was given concerning how we went and where we had arrived."

FROM CORONADO'S CIBOLA
Pre-Columbian globular jar with black-on-white painted decoration. Height: 12 inches. Found in Apache County, Arizona. Photograph courtesy of the Museum of the American Indian, Heye Foundation.

It was from a spot overlooking the plateau of the Zuñis that Coronado and the vanguard had their first glimpse of Cibola. It must have been a bitter disappointment. Cavalier and commoner alike knew at once that someone had exaggerated. And yet, disappointing as it was, they knew that they would have to enter it, even if it meant fighting, for it contained food. Coronado wrote:

"As soon as I came within sight of this city, I sent the army-master, Don García López, Friar Daniel and Friar Luis, and Fernando Vermizzo, with some horsemen, a little way ahead, so that they might find the Indians and tell them that we were not coming to do them any harm, but to defend them in the name of our lord the Emperor. The summons, in the form which his Majesty commanded in his instructions, was made intelligible to the people of the country by an interpreter. But they, being a proud people, were little affected, because it seemed to them that we were few in number, and that they would not have any difficulty in conquering us. They pierced the gown of Friar Luis with an arrow which, blessed be God, did him no harm.

"Meanwhile I arrived with all the rest of the horse and the footmen, and found a large body of the Indians on the plain, who began to shoot with their arrows. In obedience to the orders of your Lordship and of [his Majesty], I did not wish my company, who were begging me for permission, to attack them, telling them they ought not to offend them, and that what the enemy was doing was nothing, and that so few people ought not to be insulted. On the other hand, when the Indians saw that we did not move, they took greater courage, and grew so bold that they came up almost to the heels of our horses to shoot their arrows.

"On this account I saw that it was no longer time to hesitate, and as the priests approved the action, I charged them. There was little to do, because they suddenly took to flight, part running toward the city, which was near and well fortified, and others toward the plain, wherever chance led them. Some Indians were killed, and others might have been slain if I could have allowed them to be pursued. But I saw that there would be little advantage in this, because the Indians who were outside were few, and those who had retired to the city were numerous, besides many who had remained there in the first place. As that was where the food was, of which we stood in such great need, I assembled my whole force and divided them as seemed to me best for the attack on the city, and surrounded it. The hunger which we suffered would not permit of any delay, and so I dismounted with some of these gentlemen and soldiers.

"I ordered the musketeers and crossbowmen to begin the attack and drive back the enemy from the defenses, so that they could not do us any injury. I assaulted the wall on one side, where I was told that there was a scaling ladder and that there was also a gate. But the crossbowmen broke all the strings of their crossbows and the musketeers could do nothing, because they had arrived so weak and feeble that they could scarcely stand on their feet.

"On this account the people who were on top were not prevented at all from defending themselves and doing us whatever injury they were able. Thus, for myself, they knocked me down to the ground twice with countless great stones which they threw down from above, and if I had not been protected by the very good headpiece which I wore, I think that the outcome would have been bad for me. They picked me up from the ground, however, with two small wounds in my face and an arrow in my foot, and with many bruises on my arms and legs, and in this condition I retired from the battle, very weak. I think that if Don García López de Cárdenas had not come to my help, like a good cavalier, the second time that they knocked me to the ground, by placing his own body above mine, I should have been in much greater danger than I was. But, by the pleasure of God, these Indians surrendered, and their city was taken with the help of Our Lord, and a sufficient supply of corn was found there to relieve our necessities."

Coronado says that he was singled out "because my armor was gilded and glittered, and on this account I was hurt more than the rest, and not because I had done more or was farther in advance than the others." He praised God that he was now well, "although somewhat sore from the stones." A number of his men were wounded, some by arrows, others by stones; three horses were killed, seven or eight wounded. As for Cibola, he wrote:

"It now remains for me to tell about this city and kingdom and province, of which the Father Provincial gave your Lordship an account. In brief, I can assure you that in reality he has not told the truth in a single thing that he said, but everything is the reverse of what he said, except the name of the city and the large stone houses. For, although they are not decorated with turquoises, nor made of lime nor of good bricks, nevertheless they are very good houses, with three and four and five stories, where there are very good apartments and good rooms with corridors, and some very good rooms under ground and paved, which are made for winter, and are something like a sort of hot baths [in reality, ceremonial chambers]."

He thought the Zuñis "well bred," with fine figures. Their corn cakes (tortillas) were the best he had ever seen. "They have the very best arrangement and machinery for grinding that was ever seen. One of these Indian women here will grind as much as four of the Mexicans. They have very good salt in crystals, which they bring from a lake a day's journey distant from here." The country was "all level," except for mesas. The climate was like Mexico's.

Mountain lions, wildcats, and deer are mentioned; "and some sheep as big as a horse, with very large horns and little tails. I have seen some of their horns, the size of which was something to marvel at." Castañeda also marveled. Beyond Chichilticalli

"the man in the advance guard [of the main force] saw a flock of sheep one day. I myself saw and followed them. They had extremely large bodies and long wool; their horns were very thick and large, and when they run they throw back their heads and put their horns on the ridge of their back. They are used to the rough country, so that we could not catch them and had to leave them. Three days after we entered the wilderness we found a horn on the bank of a river that flows in the bottom of a very steep, deep gully, which the general had noticed and left there for his army to see, for it was six feet long and as thick at the base as a man's thigh. It seemed to be more like the horn of a goat than of any other animal."

It was, in fact, the horn of a Rocky Mountain sheep, of which the Catalina Mountains in southern Arizona were once full.

Conquering armies are not noted for tenderness toward the conquered, but the Spaniards in America, bringing the cross and the crossbow, seem to have shown genius in sowing disaffection.

"Three days after I captured this city," Coronado told the viceroy, "some of the Indians who lived here came to offer to make peace. They brought me some turquoises and poor mantles, and I received them in his Majesty's name with as good a speech as I could, making them understand the purpose of my coming to this country, which is, in the name of his Majesty and by the commands of your Lordship, that they and all others in this province should become Christians and should know the true God for their Lord, and his Majesty for their king and earthly lord. After this they returned to their houses and suddenly, the next day, they packed up their goods and property, their women and children, and fled to the hills, leaving the towns deserted."

There was no gold in Cibola; worse—"The Seven Cities are seven little villages, all having the kind of houses I have described." When the main force under Tristan de Arellano came up—it had marched on foot, weapons on shoulders, even lances, all the horses being loaded with provisions—there was an outburst of **anger.**

"Such were the curses that some hurled at Friar Marcos," Castañeda wrote, "that I pray God may protect him from them."

His description of Cibola is contemptuous.

"There are haciendas in New Spain which make a better appearance at a distance."

The death of Estévan was made known to the army. "Many of
the things which he wore have been found," Coronado wrote Mendoza. He had been killed there "because he assaulted their women,
whom the Indians love better than themselves."

In honor of the viceroy's birthplace, he renamed the pueblo
"Granada," subscribing his letter: "From the province of Cibola,
and this city of Granada, the 3rd of August, 1540. Francisco
Vásquez de Coronado kisses the hand of your most illustrious
Lordship."

Juan Gallego carried the letter to the viceroy. He was accompanied by Father Marcos, who found Cibola uncomfortable. Melchior Díaz rode with them as far as Corazones, then headed for the
coast with twenty-five picked men to search for Alarcón's ships.
Somewhere on the lower Colorado Díaz learned from Indians that
the ships had been there and sailed away. At the foot of a tree bearing the legend, "Alarcón reached this place," the Spaniards dug
and found a letter from him stating that he was unable to proceed
further because the Isle of the Marquis (so named for Cortez) was
not an island but a peninsula and that he was returning to New
Spain.

Once more the Spanish pattern of exploration was being repeated
—the search for the sea, and the search for new provinces.

Twenty-five leagues west of Cibola was the Hopi pueblo of Awatobi, in northeastern Arizona. Thither went Captain Pedro de Tovar
with horsemen and foot soldiers. A Franciscan friar, Juan de Padilla, "who had been a fighting man in his youth,"—"hombre beli-
cose," perhaps not a soldier, but a brawler—accompanied them; he
was still a fighting man, as it turned out.

The expedition arrived at the very edge of the village at nightfall, so close that the Spaniards could hear voices in the pueblo.
Their presence was known, however; in the morning Indians poured
out with bows and war clubs, some of them bearing shields. The
Spaniards faced them in battle array.

"The interpreter was given a chance to speak to them and give them due warning, for they were very intelligent people," says Castañeda; "but nevertheless they drew lines and insisted that our men should not go across these lines toward their village."

The lines were drawn with ritual corn meal, almost under the noses of the horses.

"While they were talking, some men acted as if they would cross the lines, and one of the natives lost control of himself and struck a horse a blow on the cheek of the bridle with his club."

Friar Juan became impatient. Turning to Captain de Tovar, he said: "To tell the truth, I do not know why we came here."

"When the men heard this," Castañeda says, "they gave the Santiago [i.e., St. James, war cry; as in "St. George for England."] so suddenly that they ran down many Indians and the others fled to the town in confusion. Some indeed did not have a chance to do this, so quickly did the people in the village come out with presents, asking for peace."

There was no gold in Awatobi. The departing soldiers swapped beads and bells for corn, corn meal, piñon nuts and skins; a few lucky ones got turquoises.

Captain García López de Cardenas led an expedition to the northwest. With guides, porters and provisions obtained at the Hopi pueblo he pushed into territory already explored in part by Melchior Diaz; but venturing farther north, he inscribed a monumental moment in the annals of the discoverers:

"After they had gone twenty days they came to the banks of a river, which seemed to be more than three or four leagues in an air line across to the other bank of the stream which flowed between them. This country was elevated and full of low twisted pines, very cold, and lying open toward the north, so that, this being the warm season, no one could live there on account of the cold. They spent three days on this bank looking for a passage down to the river, which looked from above as if the water was six feet across, although the Indians said it was half a league wide. It was impossible to descend, for after these three days Captain Melgosa and one Juan Galeras and another companion, who were the lightest and most agile men, made an attempt to go down at the least difficult place, and went down until those who were above were unable to keep sight of them.

"They returned about four o'clock in the afternoon, not having succeeded in reaching the bottom on account of the great difficulties which they found, because what seemed to be easy from above was not so, but instead very hard and difficult. They said that they had been down about a third of the way and that the river seemed very large from the place which they reached, and that from what they saw they thought the Indians had given the width correctly. Those who stayed above had estimated that some huge rocks on the sides of the cliffs seemed to be about as tall as a man, but those who went down swore that when they reached these rocks they were bigger than the great tower of Seville [the bell tower of the cathedral]."

This is the first description of the Grand Canyon of the Colorado by a white man. Nothing else came of Cardenas' expedition.

Striking to the east went Captain Hernando de Alvarado with twenty men and some Indian allies, among them a chief with a long mustache instantly dubbed "Whiskers" (Bigotes) by the soldiers. He had come voluntarily to Hawaiku to tell Coronado "that if he wanted to go through their country they would consider us as their friends," Castañeda wrote; this turned out to be premature. "Whiskers" brought presents of tanned hides, shields and headpieces, "which were very gladly received." The Indians with him "described some cows which, from a picture that one of them had painted on his skin, seemed to be cows, although from the hides this did not seem possible, because the hair was woolly and snarled so that we could not tell what sort of skins they had."

The expedition set out on Sunday, August 29, 1540. Accompanying Alvarado was the fighting friar, Juan de Padilla. Five or six miles from Hawaiku the Spaniards came upon vestiges of a vanished people and culture. In his report to Coronado, Alvarado wrote:

> "After we had gone two leagues, we came to an ancient building like a fortress, and a league beyond this we found another, and yet another a little farther on, and beyond these we found an ancient city, very large, entirely destroyed, although a large part of the wall was standing, which was six times as tall as a man, the wall well made of good worked stone, with gates and gutters like a city in Castile. Half a league or more beyond this, we found another ruined city, the walls of which must have been very fine, built of very large granite blocks, as high as a man and from there up of very good quarried stone."

Five days later, going at the rate of about ten miles a day over an ancient lava bed, Alvarado's expedition reached the pueblo of Acoma, said to be the oldest continuously occupied settlement in the United States. The pueblo stood on its 357-foot mesa like a fortress, which it was; the only way to get to it was by ever-narrowing steps, the last being mere toeholds. On the top was a wall, or mound, of large and small stones, which could be rolled down on an assaulting force.

Seeing the Spaniards approach, the Indians of the pueblo ranged themselves on the plain, after drawing the sacred lines in corn meal, then changed their minds and offered friendship. Castañeda describes the ceremony thus: "They went through their forms of making peace, which is to touch the horses and take their sweat and rub themselves with it, and to make crosses with the fingers of the hands. But to make the most secure peace they put their hands across each other, and they keep this peace inviolably." Following this, presents poured from the pueblo—turkeys, corn, corn bread, corn meal, piñon nuts, and deerskins. The turkeys had "very big wattles."

From Acoma, the expedition pressed on to Tiguex (the modern Bernalillo, New Mexico) on the Rio Grande, and thence to Cicuye (Pecos). As "Whiskers" was a Cicuye chief, the Spaniards were greeted joyously, with drums as well as flutes, and presents of cloth, turquoises and food. There were ten other villages situated, like the two named, on either side of the river.

> "The country is so fertile," Castañeda wrote, "that they do not have to break up the ground the year round, but only have to sow the seed, which is presently covered by the fall of snow, and the ears come up under the snow. In one year they gather enough for seven. A very large number of cranes and wild geese and crows and starlings live on what is sown, and for all this, when they come to sow for another year, the fields are covered with corn which they have not been able to finish gathering."

"In general," Castañeda noted, "these villages all have the same habits and customs." The men spin and weave; the women bring up the children and prepare the food, he wrote.

> "They keep the separate houses where they prepare the food for eating, and where they grind the meal, very clean. This is a separate room or closet, where they have a trough with three stones fixed in stiff clay. Three women go in here, each one having a stone, with which one of them breaks the corn, the next grinds it, and the third grinds it again. They take off their shoes, do up their hair, shake their clothes, and cover their heads be-

fore they enter the door. A man sits at the door playing on a fife while they grind, moving the stones to the music and singing together. They grind a large quantity at one time, because they make all their bread of meal soaked in warm water, like wafers."

Young men lived in separate quarters—*estufas*. Unmarried women went around nude until they took husbands. Marriages were arranged by the village elders; when this was done, "the man had to spin and weave a blanket and place it before the woman, who covers herself with it and becomes his wife."

To this idyllic and fruitful province of pueblos, the army of Coronado came to set up winter quarters, on the advice of Alvarado. "As it was necessary that the natives should give the Spaniards lodging places, the people in one village had to abandon it and go to others belonging to their friends, and they took with them nothing but themselves and the clothes they had on." In charge of this operation was Captain López de Cárdenas.

The fatal moment was now approaching when the Spaniards were to hear what they had left home to learn; but this time it came from an unusual source—not from a chief anxious to speed their departure from his lands, not from a captive of their own, run down by a horseman with a lance, but from an Indian slave in Cicuye, whom the soldiers had dubbed "El Turco." Castañeda says he resembled one; but if he was a Pawnee, as some think, he may have looked like a Turk only because of the way he wore his hair.

This Indian told Alvarado that in Quivira where he came from

"there was a river in the level country which was two leagues wide, in which there were fishes as big as horses, and large numbers of very big canoes, with more than twenty rowers on a side, and that they carried sails, and that their lords sat on the poop under awnings, and on the prow they had a great golden eagle. He said also that the lord of that country took his afternoon nap under a great tree on which were hung a great number of little gold bells, which put him to sleep as they swung in the air. He said also that everyone had their ordinary dishes made of wrought plate, and the jugs and bowls were of gold."

Much of what he said was in sign language and pantomime. His word for gold was "acochis," Spanish for *hakwichis*, meaning metal. It would appear from this that "El Turco" had encountered other Spaniards and knew what they were searching for. He may have known the Mississippi, or heard about it; the rest, of course, was

fiction. One of his motives in concocting the tale he told the gul-
lible Spaniards was to escape from his slavery; another, if believed,
was more sinister and was the cause of his death. When Alvarado
started back to Tiguex, "El Turco" was taken along. On meeting
Coronado, he embroidered some more. If the Spaniards did not
believe he knew about gold, let them demand the bracelets which
had been taken from him. This appeared plausible enough, and
Alvarado, with a guard, returned to Cicuye, where he was told "El
Turco" was a liar. Alvarado preferred the word of a stranger to the

word of friends. He invited "Whiskers" and the chief elder of the
village to his tent, where both were seized, put in chains, and taken
to Tiguex.

"This," wrote Castañeda, "began the want of confidence in the
word of the Spaniards whenever there was talk of peace from this
time on."

It was the winter of 1540. The setting is now the classical one
for the events that followed: an aroused province, and distrust met
by arrogance and force. Castañeda's account is vivid.

> "The general wished to obtain some clothing to divide among
> his soldiers, and for this purpose he summoned one of the chief
> Indians of Tiguex, with whom he had already had much inter-
> course and with whom he was on good terms, who was called
> Juan Aleman by our men, after a Juan Aleman who lived in
> Mexico, whom he was said to resemble. The general told him
> that he must furnish about three hundred or more pieces of
> cloth, which he needed to give his people. He said that he was
> not able to do this, but that it pertained to the governors
> [elders]; and that besides this, they would have to consult

together and divide it among the villages, and that it was necessary to make the demand of each town separately.

"The general did this, and ordered certain of the gentlemen who were with him to go and make the demand; and as there were twelve villages, some of them went on one side of the river and some on the other. As they were in very great need they did not give the natives a chance to consult about it, but when they came to a village they demanded what they had to give, so that they could proceed at once. Thus these people could do nothing except take off their own cloaks and give them to make up the number demanded of them. And some of the soldiers who were in these parties, when the collectors gave them some blankets or cloaks which were not such as they wanted, if they saw any Indian with a better one on, they exchanged with him without more ado, not stopping to find out the rank of the man they were stripping, which caused not a little hard feeling.

"Besides what I have just said, one whom I will not name, out of regard for him, left the village where the camp was and went to another village about a league distant, and seeing a pretty woman there he called her husband down to hold his horse by the bridle while he went up; and as the village was entered by the upper story, the Indian supposed he was going to some other part of it. While he was there the Indian heard some slight noise, and then the Spaniard came down, took his horse, and went away. The Indian went up and learned that he had violated, or tried to violate, his wife, and so he came with the important men of the town to complain that a man had violated his wife, and he told how it happened.

"When the general made all the soldiers and the persons who were with him come together, the Indian did not recognize the man, either because he had changed his clothes or for whatever other reason there may have been, but he said that he could tell the horse, because he had held his bridle, and so he was taken to the stables, and found the horse, and said that the master of the horse must be the man. He denied doing it, seeing that he had not been recognized, and it may be that the Indian was mistaken in the horse; anyway, he went off without getting any satisfaction. The next day one of the Indians who was guarding the horses of the army came running in, saying that a companion of his had been killed, and that the Indians of the country were driving off the horses toward their villages.

The Spaniards tried to collect the horses again, but they were lost, besides seven of the general's mules."

The province was in revolt; riding up to the closed palisade of a village Captain de Cárdenas heard the hoofs and terrified neighs of horses "being chased as in a bullfight and shot with arrows." He also saw Indians arming for battle.

It was decided to attack one of the villages, to make an example; the one chosen was the one "where the greatest injury had been done and where the affair with the Indian woman occurred." While horsemen under Captain de Cárdenas surrounded the village, Coronado led the assault.

"Several captains who had gone on in advance with the general, Juan de Saldivar, and [Francisco de] Barrionuevo and Diego López and [Pablo de] Melgosa, took the Indians so much by surprise that they gained the upper story, with great danger, for they wounded many of our men from within the houses. Our men were on top of the houses in great danger for a day and a night and part of the next day, and they made some good shots with their crossbows and muskets.

"The horsemen on the plain with many of the Indian allies from New Spain smoked them out from the cellars [underground ceremonial chambers] into which they had broken, so that they begged for peace. Pablo de Melgosa and Diego López, the alderman from Seville, were left on the roof and answered the Indians with the same signs they were making for peace, which was to make a cross. They then put down their arms and received pardon."

Those who submitted numbered two hundred. They were led from the pueblo to the tent of Cárdenas on the plain.

"As he had been ordered by the general not to take them alive, but to make an example of them so that the other natives would fear the Spaniards, he ordered two hundred stakes to be prepared at once to burn them alive. Nobody told him about the peace that had been granted them, for the soldiers knew as little as he, and those who should have told him about it remained silent, not thinking that it was any of their business. Then when the enemies saw that the Spaniards were binding them and beginning to roast them, about a hundred men who were in the tent began to struggle and defend themselves with what there was there and with the stakes they could seize. Our men who were on foot attacked the tent on all sides, so that there was great confusion around it, and then the horsemen chased those who escaped. As the country was level, not a man of them remained alive, unless it was some who remained hidden in the village and escaped that night to spread throughout the country the news that the strangers did not respect the peace they had made, which afterward proved a great misfortune."

Snow fell on pueblo and plain.

"It snowed so much that for the next two months it was impossible to do anything except to go along the roads to advise them to make peace and tell them that they would be pardoned and might consider themselves safe, to which they replied that they did not trust those who did not know how to keep good faith after they had once given it."

Cárdenas himself went with thirty men to Tiguex to talk to the Indian chief dubbed "Juan Aleman" by the Spaniards. He was told to dismount and send his men away. This done, the chief and two other Indians approached him, pausing only to say they had no weapons and he must take his off. Cárdenas complied. "Juan Aleman" thereupon embraced him; the other Indians, taking war clubs from under their cloaks, almost knocked him off his feet with two resounding blows on his helmet. The horsemen dashed toward the village and carried him off despite a shower of arrows, which wounded some. Tiguex was surrounded and besieged for fifty days.

"One day, before the capture was completed, they asked to speak to us, and said that, since they knew we would not harm the women and children, they wished to surrender their women and sons, because they were using up their water. It was impossible to persuade them to make peace, as they said that the Spaniards would not keep an agreement made with them. So they gave up about a hundred persons, women and boys, who did not want to leave them.

"Don Lope de Urrea rode up in front of the town without his helmet and received the boys and girls in his arms, and when all of these had been surrendered, Don Lope begged them to make peace, giving them the strongest promises for their safety. They told him to go away, as they did not wish to trust themselves to people who had no regard for friendship or their own word which they had pledged. As he seemed unwilling to go away, one of them put an arrow in his bow ready to shoot, and threatened to shoot him with it unless he went off, and they warned him to put on his helmet, but he was unwilling to do so, saying that they would not hurt him as long as he stayed there. When the Indian saw that he did not want to go away, he shot and planted his arrow between the forefeet of the horse, and then put another arrow in his bow and repeated that if he did not go away he would really shoot him. Don Lope put on his helmet and slowly rode back."

Early one morning the Indians were seen leaving their pueblo.

"The alarm was given by those in the camp of Don Rodrigo Maldonado. The enemy attacked them and killed one Spaniard and a horse and wounded others, but they were driven back with great slaughter until they came to the river, where the water flowed swiftly and very cold. They threw themselves into this, and as the men had come quickly from the whole camp to assist the cavalry, there were few who escaped being killed or wounded."

Another village was besieged; when the people fled "they pursued and killed large numbers of them. At the same time those in the camp were ordered to go over the town, and they plundered it, making prisoners of all the people who were found in it, amounting to about a hundred women and children."

The province was pacified as far as the pueblo of Sia. The elder abducted from Cicuye was returned to his people by Coronado himself, who promised that "Whiskers" would be freed on the departure of his army. He thus left Cicuye "at peace." His persuasive powers had no effect in his region. "The twelve villages of Tiguex were not repopulated at all during the time the army was there, in spite of every promise of security that could possibly be given to them."

On April 23, 1541, the army left Tiguex for Cicuye, a march of sixty-five miles. "Whiskers" was freed; his people, rejoicing, gave Coronado food and guides. "El Turco" advised against loading all the pack animals with provisions, saying they would be needed to transport the gold in the province of Quivira beyond the country of cows. If his last statement, as given by Castañeda, is believed, it was during this period that he and "Whiskers" plotted the destruction of the army.

Descending from the mountains, the expedition came to the Pecos River, which was bridged and crossed, "by much diligence and rapid work," in four days. Before the Spaniards stretched the plains where the buffalo roamed.

"Who could believe," Castañeda wrote with astonishment recollected in tranquillity, "that 1,000 horses and 500 of our cows and more than 5,000 rams and ewes and more than 1,500 friendly Indians and servants, in traveling over those plains, would leave no more trace where they had passed than if nothing had been there—nothing—so that it was necessary to make piles of bones and cow dung now and then, so that the rear guard could follow the army. The grass never failed to become erect after it had been trodden down."

Although Cabeza de Vaca had seen and was the first white man to describe the American bison—"They have small horns like the cows of Morocco; the hair is very long and flocky like the merino's" —it remained for Castañeda to fill in the details:

"They have a narrow, short face, the brow two palms across from eye to eye, the eyes sticking out at the side, so that, when they are running, they can see who is following them. They have very long beards, like goats, and when they are running they throw their heads back with the beard dragging on the ground. There is a sort of girdle round the middle of the body. The hair is very woolly, like a sheep's, very fine, and in front of the girdle the hair is very long and rough like a lion's. They have a great hump, larger than a camel's. The horns are short and thick, so that they are not seen much above the hair. In May they change the hair in the middle of the body for a down, which makes perfect lions of them. They rub against the small trees in the little ravines to shed their hair, and they continue this until only the down is left, as a snake changes his skin. They have a short tail, with a bunch of hair at the end. When they run, they carry it erect like a scorpion."

The buffalo followed the grass, and Indians followed the buffalo, living off them, the first encountered being the Querechos of the Plains:
"They travel like the Arabs, with their tents and troops of dogs loaded with poles and having Moorish packsaddles with girths. When the load gets disarranged, the dogs howl, calling someone to fix them right."
Other fauna:

"There are very great numbers of wolves on the plains, which go around with the cows. They have white skins. The deer are pied with white. Their skin is loose, so that when they are killed it can be pulled off with the hand while warm, coming off like pigskin. The rabbits, which are very numerous, are so foolish that those on horseback killed them with their lances. This is when they are mounted among the cows. They fly from a person on foot."

The first Querechos were encountered nine or ten days after the crossing of the Pecos, in the Staked Plains of western Texas.

"They did nothing unusual when they saw our army, except to come out of their tents to look at us, after which they came to talk with the advance guard, and asked who we were. The general talked with them, but as they had already talked with the Turk, who was with the advance guard, they agreed with what he had said."

This may account for what they told Coronado.

"They said that there was a very large river over toward where the sun came from, and that one could go along this river through an inhabited region for ninety days without a break from settlement to settlement. They said that the first of these settlements was called Haxa."

"El Turco" embellished—it was only one or two days away. The next day the Querechos folded their tents and with their dogs dragging tent poles and other gear faded into the buffalo grass.

"The general sent Captain Diego López with ten companions lightly equipped and a guide to go at full speed toward the sunrise for two days and discover Haxa, and then return to meet the army, which set out in the same direction next day."

Haxa—which remains unidentified—was not found; López and his men reported "that in the twenty leagues they had been over they had seen nothing but cows and the sky."

It is curious to reflect that the two Spanish expeditions—de Soto's from the east, Coronado's from the southwest—were now approaching each other and were at length separated by only a few hundred miles. It is even thought by some that Coronado's persistence in moving toward the province of Quivira was due to the rumors of a king who might have been, not an Indian, but de Soto himself. The strands are inextricably woven; Coronado's army came to a village in a ravine where Cabeza de Vaca and his companions had rested on their memorable trek, and an Indian woman told some of the soldiers that "she had run away from other men like them nine days," and named several of de Soto's officers. (This does not appear to have reached the ears of Coronado, and Casteñeda himself did not learn of it until he was back in Mexico.)

The army was now among the Teyas (whence Texas) who, like the Querechos, traveled with their gear drawn by dogs and pitched their tepees where the buffalo roamed.

"These people are very intelligent; the women are well made and modest. They cover their whole body. They wear shoes and buskins made of tanned skin. The women wear cloaks over their small under-petticoats, with sleeves gathered up at the shoulders, all of skin, and some wore something like little *sanbenitos* with a fringe, which reached halfway down the thigh over the petticoat" (the *sanbenito,* a fashion creation of the Inquisitors, was made of yellow cloth with a hole for the head, a flap hanging down before and behind. With a St. Andrew's cross on each flap, it represented a confessed and penitent heretic; but made of black cloth decorated with flames and devils, it denoted impenitence, and was worn at the stake).

The Teyas told Coronado that Quivira was to the north, and that there were no good roads. They said they knew nothing of large settlements with stone houses, where there was gold and silver, only huts of straw and skin. "El Turco" was not permitted to talk to them.

It was the end of May. The army had been on the move for thirty-seven days, traveling, says Castañeda, six or seven leagues a day (with a foot soldier counting off the steps). Coronado had come 250 leagues, or approximately 657 miles, from Tiguex. His provisions, chiefly corn, had given out. He concluded that it would be risky to take a large body of men and pack animals through the trackless waste; nevertheless, he did not wish to give up the quest.

His decision was to press forward himself, accompanied by Juan de Padilla, thirty horsemen and half a dozen foot soldiers, with Teyas for guides, while the main force, under Tristan de Arellano, returned to Tiguex. As the men did not wish their commander to leave, he promised to send messengers to them in eight days—it turned out to be two weeks—with new orders to follow him, or return. So certain were the soldiers that they would be asked to follow that they spent their time killing buffalo and drying the meat to take with them. Castañeda's account of their activities during the waiting period is lively:

"It was estimated that during this fortnight they killed five hundred bulls. The number of these that were there without cows was something incredible. Many fellows were lost at this time who went out hunting and did not get back to the army for two or three days, wandering about the country as if they were crazy, in one direction or another, not knowing how to get back where they started from, although this ravine extended in either direction so that they could find it.

"Every night they took account of who was missing, fired guns and blew trumpets and beat drums and built great fires, but yet some of them went off so far and wandered about so much that all this did not give them any help, although it helped others. The only way was to go back where they had killed an animal and start from there in one direction and another until they struck the ravine or fell in with somebody who could put them on the right road."

The orders came to return to Tiguex. Teyas guided the army: "In the morning they notice where the sun rises and observe the direction they are going to take, and then shoot an arrow in this direction. Before reaching this they shoot another over it, and in this way they go all day." It took only twenty-five days to get back, even though the Teyas paused from time to time to hunt buffalo. Arellano found the whole province in revolt, and the usual measures followed. To get food, patrols went as far as Taos.

It took Coronado forty-eight days to reach Quivira, which was a habitation of the Wichita Indians who alone of the northern plains tribes lived in grass or straw lodges. The little expedition was now in Kansas, having crossed the Arkansas River east of the present Dodge City. With the Spaniards was "El Turco," in chains. The fatal confrontation took place.

"They asked the Turk why he had lied and had guided them so far out of their way. He said that his country was in that direction and that, besides this, the people at Cicuye had asked him to lead them off on to the plains and lose them, so that the horses would die when their provisions gave out, and they would be so weak if they ever returned that they could be killed without any trouble, and thus they could take revenge for what had been done to them. This was the reason why he had led them astray, supposing that they did not know how to hunt or to live without corn, while as for gold, he did not know where there was any of it. He said this like one who had given up hope."

DE SOTO–MOSCOSO ROUTE MAP

A quill-and-ink map made by a member of de Soto's expeditionary force. The territory depicted extends from South Carolina to the Panuco River north of Veracruz. The Indian place names are those given by the Gentleman of Elvas and other narrators, although the spelling varies; see, for example, "Tascalussa" (center of map). The *"Rio del espiritu santo,"* flowing from the mountains (upper left), is the Mississippi. The large bodies of water (upper right) may represent the Florida or Carolina Indians' tales of the Great Lakes. At extreme left is the following inscription: *desde quevira hasta acqui hay grandisimas manadas de vacas*— "from quevira to here there are very great herds of cattle" (meaning buffaloes). It was probably inserted after Moscoso had talked with Coronado in Mexico about the latter's expedition to Quivira. The map is in the Archives of the Indies, Seville. Reproduction from Harrisse, *The Discovery of North America*, the Rare Book Division, The New York Public Library.

He was right.

They garroted him.

Coronado later wrote to the emperor: "What I am sure of is that there is not any gold nor any other metal in all that country." He was there twenty-five days. He erected a huge cross inscribed, "Francisco Vásquez de Coronado, general of an expedition, reached this place," and took possession for Spain.

In the letter already referred to he told Charles V:

"The country itself is the best I have ever seen for producing all the products of Spain, for besides the land itself being very fat and black and being very well watered by the rivulets and springs and rivers, I found prunes like those of Spain and nuts and very good sweet grapes and mulberries."

The letter was written in October at Tiguex, where the army spent the winter of 1541–1542.

It was generally believed that Coronado would return to the province of Quivira in the spring. To this end, preparations were being made when, on an unspecified feast day, the general and Captain Rodrigo Maldonado had a race on horseback. The general was mounted on a powerful horse with a new girth, which broke, and he fell to the ground in Maldonado's path. A hoof struck him in the head.

Coronado's recovery was long and painful. His desire in these circumstances was a natural one, although he was much criticized for it: he wished to see his wife and children. He persuaded some of his captains and other gentlemen serving with him to start the men talking about returning to New Spain. There were many who were eager to do so. In April the army set out for Cibola on the return journey.

Friar Juan de Padilla went back to Quivira. His death was priestly and heroic. He was attended on foot by two oblates dressed as friars, two Indians who had served as sacristans with the army, and a Portuguese soldier on horseback. The cross at Quivira was still standing when the little group arrived and was welcomed. One day, setting out to save more souls, he and his companions were met by Indians on the warpath—some think that among them were Coronado's guides from Tiguex. Juan de Padilla told the horseman to flee with the others, since they were young and could run; he himself knelt in prayer and received the arrows of martyrdom.

Thus ended, for the time being, the hopes, sacred and profane, which were so high when Coronado, escorted by the viceroy, led his army from Compostela two years before. "It was God's pleasure that these discoveries should remain for other peoples and that we who had been there should content ourselves with saying that we were the first who discovered it," wrote Castañeda in dejection.

Had Coronado tarried in New Mexico he might have received a letter from Port of the Possession (Port San Quentín) on the Pacific Coast, claimed for Spain "in the name of his Majesty and of the most Illustrious Señor Don Antonio de Mendoza" on August 22, 1542. The letter writer was a Portuguese navigator sent by the viceroy to explore Alta California and the coast beyond whither it led—hopefully, to a "Passage from the South Sea at the North" to the Orient.

August 22 was a Tuesday. The following is from the *Relation, or Diary, of the Voyage Made by Juan Rodríguez Cabrillo with Two Ships* (the ships were the *San Salvador* and *Victoria*, from Alvarado's fleet).

"On the Friday following, on going to get water, they found· in the watering place some Indians who remained quiet and showed them a pool of water, and a saline which contained a large quantity of salt. They said by signs that they did not live there, but inland, and that there were many people.

"This same day, in the afternoon, five Indians came to the beach; they [the Spaniards] brought them to the ships and they appeared to be intelligent Indians. Entering the ship they pointed at and counted the Spaniards who were there, and said by signs that they had seen other men like them, who wore beards, and who brought dogs, and crossbows, and swords.

"The Indians came smeared over with a white paste on the thighs, body, and arms, and wore the paste like slashes, so that they appeared like men in hose and slashed doublets. They made signs that Spaniards were five days from there. They made signs that there were many Indians, and that they had much maize and many parrots.

"They came covered with deerskins; some wore the deerskins dressed in the way the Mexicans dress the skins which they use for their *cutaras*. They are a large and well-featured people. They carry their bows and arrows like those of New Spain, the arrows being tipped with flints.

"The captain gave them a letter to carry to the Spaniards who they said were in the interior."

San Diego Bay, September 28:

"They went about six leagues along a coast running north-northwest, and discovered a port, closed and very good, which they named San Miguel. It is thirty-four and one-third degrees. Having cast anchor in it, they went ashore where there were people. Three of them waited, but all the rest fled. To these three they gave some presents and they said by signs that in the interior men like the Spaniards had passed. They gave signs of great fear.

"On the night of this day they went ashore from the ships to fish with a net, and it appears that here there were some

Indians, and that they began to shoot at them with arrows and wounded three men [so phrased, as having been expanded from the log or diary]. Next day in the morning they went with the boat farther into the port, which is large, and brought two boys, who understood nothing by signs. They gave them both shirts and sent them away immediately.

"Next day in the morning three adult Indians came to the ships and said by signs that in the interior men like us were traveling about, bearded, clothed, and armed like those of the ships. They made signs that they carried crossbows and swords; and they made gestures with the right arm as if they were throwing lances, and ran around as if they were on horseback. They made signs that they were killing many native Indians, and that for this reason they were afraid."

Cabrillo heard of Spaniards in the interior at several other places; at one of them (San Buenaventura) which he named Pueblo of the Canoes, from their number, the Indians "indicated by signs that in seven days they could go to where the Spaniards were, and Juan Rodríguez decided to send two Spaniards into the interior. They also indicated that there was a great river. With these Indians they sent a letter at a venture to the Christians."

Cabrillo's ships reached the latitude of Rogue River, Oregon, and brought back a "Description of the Coast, Ports, Bays, and Islands which he Examined, and their Distances, on the Whole Extent of that Coast." Cape Mendocine was named in honor of the viceroy. When Coronado appeared before Mendoza to make his report, he was received coldly. A short time later he was asked to relinquish his post as governor of New Galiacia.

That summer of 1542, as Coronado's army marched forlornly back from Cibola, the army of de Soto, under Moscoso, likewise set out for New Spain from the banks of the Mississippi.

"Some were glad of the death of Don Hernando de Soto," wrote the gentleman of Elvas, "holding it certain that Luis de Moscoso, who was given to leading a gay life, preferred to see himself at ease in a land of Christians, rather than continue the toils of war, discovering and subduing, which the people [of the army] had come to hate, finding the little recompense that followed."

Moscoso shared their view—"it was his desire to get out of the land of Florida in the shortest time." The question was how—by marching overland, or going down the river to the sea?

"To everyone it appeared well to march westwardly, because in that direction was New Spain, the voyage by sea being held more hazardous and of doubtful accomplishment, as a vessel of sufficient strength to weather a storm could not be built, nor was there captain nor pilot, needle nor chart, nor was it known how distant might be the sea; neither had they any tidings of it, or if the river did not take some great turn through the land, or might not have some fall over rocks where they might be lost."

Such is the catalogue of perils by water which determined the Spaniards to go by land. It is quoted here because, formidable though the perils were, in the end they had to be faced. They were also surmounted.

The army proceeded through Arkansas in the usual manner—portered by captives, demanding and receiving provisions and guides, and meting out the punishments that were necessary to strike terror in the hearts of those ahead who might presume to bar the way; some nevertheless did.

Leaving Guachoya on June 5, the army passed through desert country, reaching Chaguate (in Saline County) on the 20th. Here, one of the gentleman adventurers, Francisco de Guzmán, "a bastard son of a gentleman of Seville," having found his heart's desire in the New World, and being loath to part from her, decided to remain behind. It was not that he could not have taken her along—there were now many Indian concubines with the officers and men; it was "in fear of being made to pay for gaming debts in the person of [this] Indian girl." When his absence was noticed, Chaguate was far behind.

Guacay was reached on July 4; it was "unoccupied," which made it convenient for temporary lodgers. The usual patrols went out: "many Indians of both sexes were captured." The next bivouac was by a salt lake on the west side of the Ouachita River (in Clark County); "some salt was made." Stopping at times only overnight the army continued on its way, its advance heralded by fugitives and scouts. On July 22, a Saturday, "along a clump of luxuriant woods" (perhaps on Prairie de Roane), Indians attacked in numbers, and were repulsed with heavy losses, inflicted by the pursuing cavalry.

"One Indian, brought back alive, being asked by the Governor who they were that had come to give him battle, said the cacique of Naguatex, the one of Maya, and another of a province called Hacanac, lord of great territories and numerous vassals, he of Naguatex being in command. The Governor, having ordered his right arm to be cut off, and his nose, sent him to the cacique, with word that he would march the next day into his territory to destroy it, and that if he wished to dispute his entrance to await him."

PHILIP II

Son of Charles V, oppressor of the Netherlands and foe of Elizabeth. He is wearing the basket hat typical of the period for both men and women. Pendant is the Order of the Golden Fleece. His vaunted sea power is part of the artist's flattery. Portrait, after Antonio Moro, from Emanuel van Meteren's *Historien der Nederlander*. Courtesy of the Prints Division, The New York Public Library, Astor, Lenox and Tilden Foundations.

The territory of the cacique of Naguatex spanned both sides of the Red River. He submitted when the army passed over and approached his own village. The guides given Moscoso appeared to him to be leading him to the east, and were hanged from a tree;

another guide obtained in Texas confessed under torture that he had been ordered to lead the Spaniards astray. "He was commanded to be cast to the dogs."

There were now rumors of men like themselves on the move not far to the west. At a place called Guasco (which some writers relate to Waco) Indians told the governor "that ten days' journey from there, toward the sunset, was a river called Daycao, whither they sometimes went to drive and kill deer, and whence they had seen persons on the other bank, but without knowing what people they were."

The thought that Spaniards from New Spain were not far away sent a surge of hope through the army. Loading their horses and tamemes with all the provisions that could be seized, they marched ten days through wilderness, only to find a few huts in a land devoid of maize. Two wretched natives were caught and questioned, without result, as no one knew their language.

At this barren spot in Texas, and at the lowest ebb of their fortunes, the Spaniards again debated the question—whether to proceed by land, or return and go down the great river to the sea. "The Governor, who longed to be again where he could get his full measure of sleep, rather than govern and go conquering a country so beset for him with hardships, directly returned." Retracing their steps, perhaps for once the invaders regretted the burned villages, and the destroyed cornfields.

Reaching Chaguate again, Moscoso sent a letter to Francisco de Guzmán by an Indian, together with paper, pen and ink; the letter reminded the lover that he was a Christian and offered pardon if he returned, the writing material was to enable him to tell his commander whether he was being detained against his will. The reply came: de Guzmán's name, written on the back of Moscoso's letter, signifying that he was alive, and nothing more. A cavalry detachment was sent to find him, without success.

"For want of maize the Governor could not tarry longer to look for him." But when Nilco was reached, it was learned that the Indians of this fertile region had not dared to plant corn while the Spaniards were at Guachoya. "Everybody was confounded," says the gentleman of Elvas, forgetful of the slaughter of the inhabitants by de Soto's orders.

The Indians of Nilco were also alarmed. Not only was there a shortage of maize for themselves—the Spaniards were back in their midst, and there was no knowing what they would do. They now revealed that, above Guachoya, on the Mississippi, there were two towns "in a fertile country named Aminoya." Thither dashed horsemen and infantry, and seized one of the towns, together with many prisoners and a large quantity of corn. A message to Moscoso told the result, and the army marched to Aminoya through December weather, undergoing great exposure; "for they passed through much water, and rain fell many times, bringing a north wind, with severe cold, so that when in the field they had the water both above and below them; and if at the end of a day's journey they found dry ground to lie upon, they had occasion to be thankful." Many arrived "sick of severe and dangerous diseases, marked with inclination to lethargy." André de Vasconcelos died, as did several other Portuguese. "Nearly all the Indians in service died" (meaning the tamemes).

Thus ended the year 1542 in "Florida of the Indies," in the New World.

Moscoso chose for his base of operations what appeared to be the better town, it being palisaded and only a quarter of a league from the river. The corn from the other was seized and brought there; "together, the quantity was estimated to be 6,000 fanegas," a Lisbon fanega being somewhat more than a pint. Also heartening: "For the building of ships better timber was found than had been seen elsewhere in all Florida." It was only now that those skilled in the arts of peace stood out and were admired:

"A Portuguese, of Ceuta, had learned to saw lumber while a captive in Fez; and saws had been brought for that purpose, with which he taught others, who assisted him. A Genoese, whom God had been pleased to spare, as without him we could not have gone away, there being not another person who knew how to construct vessels, built the brigantines with the help of four or five Biscayan carpenters, who hewed the planks and ribs for him; and two calkers, one a Genoese, the other a Sardinian, closed them up with the oakum, got from a plant like hemp, called enequen; but from its scarcity the flax of the country was likewise used, as well as the ravelings of shawls. The cooper sickened to the point of death, and there was not another workman; but God was pleased to give him health, and notwithstanding he was very thin, and unfit for labor, fifteen days before the vessels sailed, he had made for each of them two of the half-hogsheads sailors call quartos, four of them holding a pipe of water [equivalent to 126 American gallons]."

Seven brigantines were built. To make the spikes to hold the planks all the iron was collected—the chains used for captive Indians, the iron in shot, even the ornamental work on crossbows. Stirrups were melted down to make anchors, and were replaced by wooden ones. Deerskins were stitched together for sails. Some ropes were obtained from Indians; the bark of mulberry trees was twisted into cables.

Contrasting strongly with the energy displayed by the Spaniards was the state of the Indians of Aminoya, who came to offer their services, "being compelled by hunger to beg some ears of that corn which had been taken from them." So weak and lean were some that they died nearby. Despite Moscoso's orders not to feed them, the men shared what they could, "when it was seen that they were willing to work, and that the hogs had aplenty."

Work was suspended in March when the Mississippi rose, flooding Aminoya. "The river became so enlarged that it reached Nilco, nine leagues off, and the Indians said that on the opposite side it also extended an equal distance over the country." Not until May was the work resumed, the Spaniards having passed the time in extreme discomfort, but on the alert for plots against themselves and the unfinished brigantines, which drew many visitors in canoes. The dangers were real; an Indian put to the torture confessed that the chiefs of Nilco, Guachoya, Taguanate and some others were planning a concerted attack. More atrocities followed—on one day, thirty men from Guachoya, having brought presents of fish, were sent back mutilated.

The vessels were finished in June. The gentleman of Elvas says they were "small, drawing but little water," but of "good build, except that the planks were thin, on account of the shortness of the spikes" (made short to conserve iron). Instead of decks they had planks which gave some shelter, and enabled the men to handle the sails as well as to row. To command them, Moscoso appointed six captains who swore allegiance to him until they should reach New Spain; he himself took the brigantine "he liked best." As the Mississippi had long since passed flood stage, it seemed a miracle to all that the river rose once more and floated the vessels into deep water.

On July 1, a number of captive Indians were put on board the brigantines by Moscoso "and by those he favored," as prizes of the campaign, perhaps to be sold later as slaves; the rest of the captives, numbering about five hundred men, women and children—some of whom had learned Spanish—were given their freedom. Many wept, as did some Spaniards. Their doom was certain, for they were left in the midst of enemies.

On July 2, the brigantines began the descent of the river, with

"canoes," or longboats, in tow. Aboard were 322 men, the survivors
of the army that landed at Tampa Bay. Twenty-two horses were
also taken along; all the rest had been slaughtered to provide meat
for the voyage, as were the remaining hogs. In addition to jerked
horsemeat and pork, there was corn and water. Sails were as yet
stowed, the vessels being propelled by oars.

It is not clear whether some or all or any of the horses were
actually on board the brigantines. They appear shortly in plain
view, being rowed along, perhaps on the rafts "made of trees, upon
which were placed many boughs," that were used to save them
when the river flooded Aminoya in March. Perhaps canoes were
attached to the rafts; the gentleman of Elvas speaks of "the men
with the horses in the canoes" which, admittedly, is ambiguous.
Some longboats or canoes were used to transport infantry to protect the brigantines.

It is thought that Aminoya was in upper Louisiana, and white
men now saw, for the first time, those places whose present names
are memorable to Americans—Vicksburg, Natchez, Baton Rouge
and New Orleans. Passing Guachoya, where de Soto died, and the
spot where his body was committed to the river, the Spaniards
came to a clump of trees on the Mississippi side where the vessels
paused and men went ashore, returning at nightfall. On July 3
horsemen found a deserted town stored with ripe corn; men from
the brigantines followed, and the whole day was spent shucking
the corn and carrying it on board. War canoes that menaced the
brigantines were driven off by crossbowmen.

At a town near Vicksburg Bluffs, whither the canoes had fled,
other Indians had already massed, and Moscoso decided on a show
of force. It is not easy to conjecture from the materials that have
come down to us why he should have found this necessary; probably it was done to demonstrate that the Spaniards were still to
be feared, and so gain an unobstructed passage. Horse and foot
soldiers went ashore, the Indians were put to flight, and the town
burned.

To no avail—the next day, a hundred canoes barred the way, each
carrying sixty or seventy armed and painted warriors; some of the
canoes had awnings, under which sat plumed and painted chiefs.
A captain of infantry with twenty-five men in armor set out to meet
them in longboats. The canoes parted until the Spaniards came up
to them, then closed to give them battle hand to hand. The brigantines drifted past unable to render aid, the men on board seeing the
men in the longboats sink beneath the water from the weight of
their armor. Eleven died there; those who were able to get away

reported that they had seen their commander carried off in an Indian canoe.

Now the brigantines came under attack. Short of crossbows, crowded together on the planks that served as decks, the Spaniards "had little else to do than to stand as objects to be shot at, watching for the shafts." Sometimes the steersman and oarsman dived beneath the planking, letting the vessels swing helplessly in the current. Many were wounded—on one brigantine alone more than a score at the first volley. The Indians ranged at will from one vessel to another, discharging their arrows, and darting swiftly away. "Not satisfied with this, they strove to get at the men with the horses; but the brigantines were brought about the canoes in which they were, to give them protection, and in this position conducted them along." It was found, however, that they could not keep up, and Moscoso decided to eliminate this hazard. At the first landing place deemed suitable the horses were led ashore and slaughtered, and the meat cut up, dried and taken on board.

Thus the flotilla continued, the men aboard embattled by day, and startled by wild yells at night. On July 16 they reached the Gulf, having consumed their meat supply and subsisting for several days on boiled corn in a daily ration of a helmetful for three; here, their leaders discussed how to proceed to New Spain without chart or compass.

Juan de Añasco thought it best to put out to sea and cross the Gulf diagonally to shorten the voyage; other captains, and most of the men, believed that safety lay in hugging the shore. Both procedures, as it turned out, were followed, at the whim of wind and wave.

On July 18, the sails made of deerskin were hoisted, and the brigantines left the river, those commanded by Moscoso and de Añasco standing farther out, and sailing all day, that night, and the next day "until vespers," in fresh water; like de Vaca before them, "they were greatly amazed, for they were very distant from the shore, and so great was the strength of the current of the river, the coast so shallow and gentle, that the fresh water entered far into the sea."

Getting closer to land, many places were sighted where the brigantines hove to. "Fish abounded there." The men fished with nets and lines. "A man having thrown out a cord made fast to his arm, a fish caught at the hook and drew him into the water up to the neck, when, remembering a knife that he had providentially kept, he cut himself loose." Not only were many fish caught— "wherever the people dug along the shore they found fresh water."

On September 10, fifty-four days after leaving the mouth of the

Mississippi, the brigantines reached a river 150 miles north of Veracruz. Going ashore, they saw Indians wearing Spanish clothes; curiously enough, they themselves were wearing cloaks, jackets, trousers and shoes made of deerskin dyed black. Asked in what country they were, the Indians answered in Spanish that they were in the province of Panuco. Asked where the Christians were, the Indians said fifteen leagues inland. The Spaniards knelt, prayed and kissed the ground.

For the third time since taking office, the viceroy Mendoza welcomed countrymen who had been in the service of his king and were thought lost. Francisco Maldonado, still seeking de Soto, arrived in Veracruz in October, and returned with the dire tidings to Doña Isabel, who died of grief in a few days.

There were those who thought that not the sword, but the cross, was the way to win this newer world. The master expositor of this doctrine was the Dominican, Bartolomé de Las Casas, who had for disciple a monk named Louis Cancer de Barbastro, a native of Saragossa. Friar Luis had gone to Hispaniola (Santo Domingo) to work among the natives, but found little to do, so greatly had the population been reduced by the avarice and ferocity of the original Spanish settlers. He had then gone to Puerto Rico, where he founded a convent of his order; but here, too, slaughter and slavery had all but wiped out the natives of that island. For a time he worked in an unconquered province in Guatemala, where Las Casas obtained from the governor an order excluding other Spaniards for a period of five years. As a result, the province, once called Tierra de Guerra, was renamed Provincia de la Vera Paz, and Friar Luis found himself acclaimed as Alférez de la Fé—"Standard-Bearer of the Faith."

Still full of zeal, he set himself a greater task—to carry that standard to unconquered Florida. In 1549, Mendoza gave him a ship, a pilot and provisions. The ship, *Santa Maria de la Encina*, was unarmed. Aboard her were three other friars, an oblate named Fuentes, and an Indian woman captured in Florida, now a convert with the name Magdalena. She was to serve as interpreter. The pilot's orders were to stay away from any place where the fleets of Ayllón, Narváez, or de Soto had been, and to seek instead a landing place where fear of the Spaniard was yet unknown. Although this would have been difficult to achieve in any case, by an extraordinary twist of fate the *Santa Maria de la Encina,* after an uneventful voyage from Veracruz, dropped anchor near Tampa Bay.

The friars, the Indian woman and the oblate were rowed close to the beach. Friar Diego de Tolosa waded ashore and climbed a tree to spy out the land. As he did so, Indians, by ones and twos, came out of the woods, until about twenty stood there in plain view of those in the boat.

The next to land were Magdalena and the oblate. They were followed by Friar Luis, despite the pleas of sailors that he remain in the boat. Reaching the beach, he fell on his knees and prayed. Then he approached the Indians, falling on his knees a second time before offering them gifts—"some articles of Flanders, which though of small account and of little value to Christians were much prized by them and highly appreciated" (from the account by Friar Luis written on board the *Santa Maria de la Encina* before his death).

The two friars embraced and knelt together, and were joined by Magdalena and the oblate Fuentes. Friar Luis drew out his missal, and they recited litanies in unison. The Indians appeared to be in a friendly mood, and having learned from them that there was a good harbor distant, they said, about a day and a half, Friar Diego, Fuentes and Magdalena decided to go by land. Friar Luis returned to the ship to get more gifts.

When he approached the shore a second time, Friar Diego, Fuentes and Magdalena were no longer there. A sailor, enticed ashore, was quickly carried off. Perhaps the intended victim was Friar Luis, who remained in the boat until sunset, his eyes on the deserted beach.

The next day the *Santa Maria de la Encina* sailed to find the harbor where, it was hoped, the missing men and the converted Indian woman would be waiting. The day and a half stretched to sixteen before the harbor was reached and entered.

Friar Luis and Friar Juan García went ashore and said mass. On the following day Friar Luis continued the vigil with Friar Gregorio de Beteta. When they were about to leave, two Indians approached. One of them was carrying a staff to which palm leaves were fastened, while the other cried out in broken Spanish: "Friends, friends —good, good."

It appeared that all would be well.

The next day, as the boat with the three friars was approaching land, a number of Indians waded out. One of them begged Friar Luis for a small wooden cross which he kissed and then carried ashore, where everyone kissed it, including a naked Indian woman who was not recognized at once, but turned out to be Magdalena.

She said that Friar Diego and Fuentes were in the house of the cacique, where many Indians had gathered. Perhaps she did not know that both were dead. But there was someone who did.

While the conversation with Magdalena was taking place, a canoe put out from shore for the *Santa Maria de la Encina*. In it was a sun-blackened Spaniard named Juan Muñoz, the soldier from de Soto's army who had been a captive for ten years. Not only were the two men dead—he had held in his own hands the scalp of Friar Diego. The sailor was still alive.

Such was the news that greeted Friar Luis when he returned to the ship. To judge from the account he wrote, he had determined to continue his work of winning over the Indians, not overlooking the possibility that if he persisted he, too, would die at their hands.

On Wednesday, June 26, he was rowed to the shore. There were Indians in the trees, who descended and ran to a hillock where stood others with bows and arrows, darts and war clubs.

Juan Muñoz stood up and shouted at them: "We know what you have done!"

Friar Luis said: "Be silent, brother; do not provoke them."

Friar Gregorio to Friar Luis: "No people in the world could be more enraged than they are. For the love of God wait a little—do not land."

But he leaped into the water. Reaching land, he called for someone to bring him a cross, but Friar Gregorio shouted back: "Father, for mercy's sake, will not your Reverence come for it, as there is no one here who will take it to you."

Nearing the hillock, Friar Luis knelt and prayed. As he rose, one of the Indians came forward and embraced him. Perhaps for a moment he felt he had been right; then the Indian took him by the arm and rushed him along. Another snatched his hat, and still another struck him with a club, knocking him down.

"We were very near, so that we saw and heard very distinctly what they said," Friar Gregorio afterward recalled. "Then he gave a scream, 'Hay vala,' but they did not let him finish, and so many rushed upon him that they made an end of him there."

The sailors rowed swiftly back to the *Santa Maria de la Encina*. Some arrows followed them.

Two more attempts were made to gain a foothold in Florida—the first, in 1559, at Ochuse (Pensacola Bay) where Maldonado waited for de Soto; the second, 1561, on the Atlantic coast in the region where Ayllón had met disaster and death.

These were colonizing expeditions, for there were now those who thought that colonists and clergy were the answer to Indian hostility

—"not to do what has been done in the discovery of the Indies, but to settle, and by good example, with good works and with presents, to bring them to a knowledge of our Holy Faith" (from the instructions of Don Luis de Velasco, viceroy, to Tristán de Luna y Arellano, captain general of the expedition to Ochuse).

Nothing came of either. De Luna proved an inept leader and good intentions gave way to necessity. His search for food extended to the province of Coça; by the spring of 1560 the wives and children of the settlers wandered about seeking fresh shoots, even leaves and twigs, to eat. He was supplanted by Angel de Villafañe, who was ordered to start a colony at Santa Elena (Port Royal Sound, South Carolina). Although he landed at several places on the coast and took possession, he saw no suitable harbor for his ships, which found a haven at length in Hispaniola, July 9, 1561. He had explored as far as Chesapeake Bay.

On September 23, Philip II forbade any new attempts at colonization of the eastern coast, certain that what Spaniards had failed to accomplish would be beyond the capacity of the French.

Perrenot de Chantone, Spanish ambassador in France, to Philip II, January 13, 1562: "The three ships which I wrote Your Majesty

GREETINGS ON THE RIVER OF MAY (THE ST. JOHNS)

Engraving by De Bry after Le Moyne. From De Bry's *Voyages*, Part II, Florida. Courtesy of the Rare Book Division, The New York Public Library.

F. May

were preparing to sail for Florida have come to be six, and a number of people will go in them, and they will leave after the close of this month with the first fair weather."

There were five ships: two Dutch three-masters, a large sloop, and two smaller ones carried aboard the larger vessels for coastal reconnoitering and landings. The crew numbered 150, half of them arquebusiers. The pilot was a Portuguese, "than whom there was none more competent to show them the way," according to Chantone. Although this was a Huguenot expedition, sponsored by Gaspard de Coligny, the Protestant Admiral of France, it also had the backing of Catherine de Medici, the Queen Mother, and Antoine de Bourbon and the Prince of Condé, united for once, despite religious differences, in order to weaken Philip abroad, who was a harsh and overbearing neighbor at home. There was also a chance for large returns on a modest investment. The fleet was bound for Santa Elena, off whose shores, in the so-called Bahama Channel, a golden galleon or two could be picked off periodically from the treasure fleets of Mexico and Peru sailing in convoy for the ports of Spain.

The leader of the expedition was Jean Ribaut, a full-bearded soldier, sailor and diplomat, and like most of the others, a Protestant. Among the gentlemen and officers under his command was one René de Laudonnière. In addition to stores of food, a forge, many cannon, small arms and ammunition, the ships carried several stone columns engraved with the crown and arms of France. Ribaut's aim was to take possession of Florida of the Indies.

On February 16, 1562, the ships left Dieppe bound, it was said, "for Canada"; instead, avoiding the Canaries and the Azores to escape ·surveillance, they reached a Florida headland not far from the future site of St. Augustine. Sailing up the coast, they arrived on May 1 at a river which Ribaut named Rivière de Mai (the St. Johns River near present-day Jacksonville). Here he was greeted by friendly Indians, and after tarrying a day, erected the first of the stone pillars.

He now sailed sixty leagues to the north, seeking a favorable harbor, and came at last to a place where the largest French ships could enter at flood tide. He named it Port Royal. Many Indians were hiding in the woods, but came out when Ribaut displayed "merchandise" and indicated by signs that he had come to trade, not fight. Again he made friends. Several leagues in the interior he erected a second stone column.

"We found the place as pleasant as was possible, for it was

A TIMUCUAN WARRIOR
Watercolor by John White, after a drawing by Jacques
Le Moyne. Courtesy of the Trustees of the British Museum.
Copyright 1964. White, artist and future governor of the
"lost colony" of Roanoke, knew Le Moyne in London.

all covered over with mighty high oaks and infinite store of
cedars, and with lentiskes [gum trees: mastics] growing underneath them, smelling so sweetly, that the very fragrant odor
only made the place to seem exceedingly pleasant. As we
passed through these woods we saw nothing but turkeycocks
flying in the forests, partridges, grey and red, little different
from ours, but chiefly in bigness. We heard also within the
woods the voices of stags, bears, lusernes [lynx], leopards, and
divers other sorts of beasts, unknown to us. Being delighted

with this place, we set ourselves to fishing with nets, and we caught such a number of fish, that it was wonderful." (From Ribaut's *Whole and True Discovery of Terra Florida,* translated by Richard Hakluyt.)

Many Spaniards had searched in vain for such a place: a deep-water port, a salubrious site, and friendly natives. Frenchmen had found it. Ribaut exhorted his men to prosper the enterprise for their young king, Charles IX, twelve years old. When he asked for volunteers to remain while he returned to France to get more ships and supplies, almost all stepped forward. Of these he selected twenty-six. For their greater safety a fort was begun, consisting of a log house behind earthworks defended by eight cannon. Ribaut named it Charlesfort. A map entitled "La Florida Françoise" shows that it was built upriver from Port Royal at the confluence of two streams.

Ribault sailed from Port Royal June 11, 1562, promising to be back in six months. He left one Captain Albert in command, who proved unequal to his task; but perhaps he was a little mad.

Had those behind the scheme of colonization sent farmers as well as soldiers, all might have been well; but improvidence and idleness brought doom to the colony. Stores dwindled; dissensions broke out. A drummer was hanged; another colonist, by name Lachère, was banished to a nearby island. One day, a soldier who had been beaten by Albert ran him through with a sword. A new leader was elected, one Nicholas Barre. The castaway was rescued.

The six months passed. A longing to return to France filled the men. A vessel was constructed, calked with moss and pine pitch, and with sails stitched from odds and ends of materials, including shirts. The Indians gave them ropes and other cordage, and a plentiful supply of food to speed the parting guests. When they were ready to cast off, a young sailor named Guillaume Rufin, eyeing the vessel, said he would remain where he was, on dry land.

The vessel, which is thought to have been about twenty tons, scudded before the wind for a considerable distance, then was becalmed. Rations were reduced to twelve grains of corn a day, and some of the men gnawed their leather jerkins and shoes. There was no water but sea water and urine. The men turned cannibal, the first victim being the castaway Lachère. The survivors were picked up by an English vessel.

"So quick bright things come to confusion."

Ignorant of the disaster that had befallen the colonists, a Spanish frigate was sent from Cuba to destroy Charlesfort and uproot the

A TIMUCUAN LADY
Watercolor by John White, after a drawing by Jacques
Le Moyne. Courtesy of the Trustees of the British Museum.
Copyright 1964.

stone columns set up by Ribaut. The Spaniards did not find the first
one, on the St. Johns, but when they reached Port Royal they
learned of a white man in the interior, to whom an Indian was sent
bearing a cross.

Guillaume Rufin, dressed in deerskin, came to the ship and led
them to the log house. The Spaniards burned it to the ground. He
then showed them where the second column claiming Florida for
France had been erected. This was pulled up and placed aboard
the frigate. So was Rufin.

IV

$\mathscr{F}$ORT
$\mathcal{C}$AROLINE

A few ships, a few hundred men, a few hundred thousand ducats' worth of supplies sent in time might have given France the Atlantic coast, perhaps America itself north of Mexico, had it not been torn asunder, when Ribaut arrived, in a religious civil war. It was only after the Peace of Amboise that Coligny was able to give any thought to Florida; Ribaut, meanwhile, had gone to England to seek the aid of the Protestant queen, and the command of the new expedition was given to his companion of the first voyage, the gentleman soldier René de Laudonnière.

The muster took place at Le Havre. There were three ships—the *Isabella,* the *Little Breton,* and the *Falcon,* the largest one being a man-of-war between two hundred and three hundred tons. These were manned by 110 sailors. On board went 120 soldiers, together with carpenters, craftsmen of various sorts, an apothecary, servants, pages and four women, one of whom was described as Laudonnière's "housekeeper." He had picked her up at an inn. There were also some gentlemen adventurers, and an artist named Jacques Le Moyne. The pilots were a Basque and a Portuguese.

The ships sailed April 22, 1564, and reached the Florida coast a month later at or near the future site of St. Augustine. To the river which the natives called Seloy, after their chief, Laudonnière gave

THE ARMS OF FRANCE IN FLORIDA

Chief Athore, son of Saturiova, shows Laudonnière the pillar set up by Ribaut, "crowned with crowns of bay, and at the foot thereof many little baskets full of mill." The object in the foreground is a quiver. Engraving by De Bry after Le Moyne's resplendent gouache, the original of which is in the Print Room of the New York Public Library.

the name River of Dolphins, but he did not tarry. On June 25 he came to the River of May (the St. Johns), where Ribaut had left the first of the stone columns.

"Being come to the place where it was set up, we found the same crowned with crowns of bay, and at the foot thereof many little baskets of mill [produce]." (Laudonnière, *A Notable History,* translated by Hakluyt.)

Here Laudonnière renewed his acquaintance with the friendly Indians he had met two years before with Ribaut. The chief, Saturiova, presented him with a wedge of silver, and when asked where it was from replied that it came from an enemy province called Thimogoa (Timuqua), a journey of several days up the river. Laudonnière now told his men that Port Royal, for all that it was an excellent harbor, "for our inhabiting, it was much more needful for us to plant in places plentiful of victual[s], than in goodly havens." He did not hesitate to appeal to their cupidity, which matched his own; they had seen ornaments of gold, and the silver gift. All agreed that the River of May was the place to plant their colony.

The site chosen for a fort was near a spring on the right bank of the river several miles from the coast where the St. Johns narrows, and probably not far from St. Johns Bluff if not on it.

"Our fort was built in form of a triangle. The side toward the west, which was toward the land, was enclosed with a little trench and raised with turf made in form of a battlement of nine feet high. The other side, which was toward the river, was enclosed with a palisade of planks of timber after the manner that cabins are made. On the south side there was a kind of

FORT CAROLINE

A view to the east. Engraved by De Bry after Le Moyne's drawing. Laudonnière's house was located inside the west wall, with an escape route to the river.

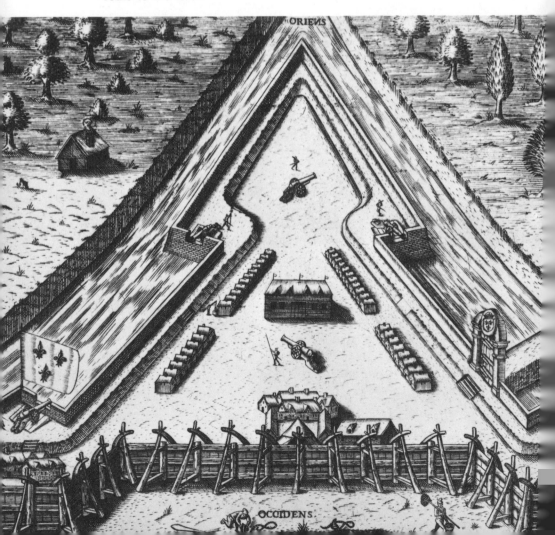

Outina.

.13.

GRAND ILLUSION

The French battle Potauou on the side of Outina, whose territory was
thought to be the gateway to the gold and silver of the Appalachian
Mountains. Engraving by De Bry after Le Moyne.

bastion within which I caused an house for the munition to be
built." (*A Notable History;* see, also, De Bry's engraving of Le
Moyne's drawing.)

There were other buildings—a storehouse, bakehouse and Laudonnière's lodging for himself and his housekeeper, which was
built near the palisade on the river side with a view of the parade
or muster ground and the tents of soldiers. Seven cannon commanded both sides of the river, and the fleur-de-lys flew from a
standard on the south bastion. The name given to the fort, once
more in honor of the boy king, was Fort Caroline.

On July 28 the *Isabella* sailed to France, bearing letters to the
lords of the council and gifts for the queen mother—some pearls,
bits of gold and silver, and the skin of an unusual beast, the alli-
gator. The gold and silver were taken by the Indians from streams
and rivers flowing from the Appalachian Mountains.

In a fruitful province, surrounded by friendly natives, and with the prospect of wealth if the colony flourished, everything depended on the qualities of leadership displayed by Laudonnière. He appears to have been lacking in most of them. Saturiova had not permitted him to build a fort in his domain for nothing; he expected, in return, French aid against his enemy of Thimogoa, which was not forthcoming. When he returned victorious with captives, Laudonnière attempted to free some of them to get the good will of the Indians of Thimogoa, whence came the silver and gold. He also permitted a detachment of his men to help one chief defeat another, again with the terrain in view, but with immediate benefits: a supply of corn. He confesses that he "travailed to purchase friends, and to practice [play upon] one while with one here, and another while with another there."

The distrust of his neighbors was matched by the discontent of his garrison. On September 20 thirteen well-armed men stole a bark which they had secretly provisioned and set out for Spanish waters in search of treasure. Off Cuba they captured a vessel laden with gold and silver, but were themselves captured in the harbor of Arcos. Some were sent to Spain, the rest held in Havana.

In November, sixty-six men conspired to seize two barks nearing completion, and taking Laudonnière prisoner, compelled him to furnish arquebuses, cannon, ammunition, supplies and a pilot. They sailed away on December 8. One of the barks ended up in Havana; the other captured a brigantine with a cargo of cassava, and as it was not only larger but better constructed than their own vessel, the Frenchmen transferred themselves to it, retaining the bark as an auxiliary. Off Jamaica they captured a caravel of fifty tons, off the Cape of Tiburon a vessel from Santo Domingo bound for Cuba; on board the latter were Negro slaves, sugar, wine (and, according to one account, the governor of Jamaica as well). The Frenchmen decided to return to Jamaica to trade captives and merchandise for food, but while in harbor were attacked by three Spanish vessels. The Frenchmen aboard the caravel were forced to surrender, and were afterward hanged as pirates. The bark with the remaining Frenchmen escaped during the sea fight, and returned to the St. Johns River. They were overpowered by men from Fort Caroline, and after a summary trial four of the leaders were sentenced to be hanged, but on the pleas of the garrison were executed by shooting. As a gibbet had already been erected, their bodies were strung up.

Such was the situation at the first French outpost in Florida in 1565, its garrison shrunk, its stores of food dwindling. Unlike the Indians, who had gone into the forests to hunt while their crops ripened, the colonists seemed unable to provide for themselves.

STAG HUNT, 1564
Indians creeping up on their prey. Engraving by De Bry after a drawing by Le Moyne.

Outina, a chief west of the St. Johns, was seized, Spanish fashion, and held for a ransom of corn, which was paid; but as the French force left his village it was ambushed. Two men were killed, twenty-two wounded, among them Le Moyne, with an arrow in his leg. The corn, so triumphantly borne off, strewed the forest floor.

There were other occurrences which, in effect, turned Fort Caroline into a beleaguered place. Laudonnière had begun to make preparations to leave when, on a July day, peering out to sea, he descried four sails and hastened back to announce the news to his men. "One would have thought them to be out of their wits to see them laugh and leap for joy," he was to write.

The ships turned out to be English, under the command of Master John Hawkins, afterward knight, captain of the *Jesus of Lubeck*—a galleon of 700 tons belonging to Queen Elizabeth—and "general of the *Salomon,* and two other barks going in his company," the *Tiger* and *Swallow.* He had left Plymouth October 18, 1564, "with a prosperous wind," sailed to Guinea on the African coast, loaded his ships with slaves, and having sold them in the West Indies under threat of bombardment if the Spaniards refused to buy, was now proceeding up the American coast on the return voyage to England, "with great profit to the venturers of the said voyage, as also to the whole realm, in bringing home both gold, silver, pearls and other jewels great store." The queen was one of the venturers—that is, a shareholder.

From the narrative of John Sparke the younger, "who went upon the same voyage, and wrote the same," after describing the plight of the French garrison:

> "In which perplexity our captain seeing them, spared them out of his ship twenty barrels of meal and four pipes of beans, with divers other victuals and necessaries which he might conveniently spare [oil, vinegar, olives, rice, biscuits, and fifty pairs of shoes]; and to help them the better homeward, whither they were bound before our coming, at their request we spared them one of our barks of fifty ton."

The bark was paid for in artillery and powder; for the rest, Laudonnière gave his personal note.

On July 28 Hawkins sailed away, leaving Laudonnière preparing to follow suit. Hawkins was the first English navigator to go up the American coast. Contrary winds kept him from reaching Newfoundland until August 23; his own provisions ran short, and his men fished merrily for cod, then ran into two French fishing vessels,

> "and had of them so much fish," wrote John Sparke the younger, "as would serve us plentifully for all the rest of the way, the captain paying for the same both gold and silver, to the just value thereof, unto the chief owners of the said ships; but they not looking for anything at all, were glad in themselves to meet with such good entertainment at sea as they had at our hands."

After this encounter, "a good large wind" sped the English to Padistow in Cornwall.

Sparke's account, published by Hakluyt, gave the English nation its first account of Florida as seen through English eyes. In the short time that Hawkins was ashore he observed the organization, housing, customs and weapons of the Florida Indians, which are all set down in the narrative of the voyage, together with remarks on the fruitfulness of the land and the necessity of keeping the peace with the native tribes: "Notwithstanding the great want that the Frenchmen had, the ground doth yield victuals sufficient, if they would have taken pains to get the same; but they being soldiers desired to live by the sweat of other men's brows."

Half a century had passed since Juan Ponce de León had named Florida—more since Spaniards had first seen it, if account be taken of slavers, and the mysterious voyagers whose knowledge of the

MIXED GRILL, FLORIDA, 1565
(De Bry, after Le Moyne)

peninsula went into the Cantino map of 1502. But there was still no haven for galleons from New Spain sailing to rendezvous in Havana with those from Tierra Firma (South America), none in the dangerous straits where the combined fleets, going twice a year to Spain, could find a refuge or put in for repairs.

To this old hazard the French had added a new danger. If permitted to remain in possession, they could sally out at will when the treasure fleets were on the move, pick off one or more galleons, and return with impunity to their fortified lair—just as the English were doing at the other end of the run, in the Azores.

The stage is now set for the first battle between two European powers on American soil.

V

ST. AUGUSTINE

While Laudonnière was refitting his two ships, a fleet from France arrived at the mouth of the St. Johns. Its commander was Jean Ribaut, serving once more under Coligny, and bringing Laudonnière orders to return and answer certain charges. One was the matter of his housekeeper, which offended the Protestant Admiral of France who once had a mistress of his own, none other than the most celebrated of French courtesans, Ninon de Lenclos, whom he shared with others; but she was refined, and they were noblemen. More serious was the second charge, which dealt with the manner in which Laudonnière had exercised his authority. A third was that he had communicated with the lords of the council directly, instead of through the admiral. His defense was forceful enough to induce Ribaut to offer to share his command, but Laudonnière declined; there could be but one lieutenant of the king, he said. The two men remained on good terms, and Laudonnière sat in on all deliberations.

Ribaut had arrived with seven ships, one of them commanded by his son Jacques. Aboard them were three hundred soldiers, colonists and their wives and children, and assorted artisans. Three of the smaller ships crossed the harbor bar, one of them going up the river to the fort. The four larger ships anchored about a mile offshore.

At four o'clock in the afternoon, Tuesday, September 4, 1565, sailors aboard the French ships sighted five vessels approaching from the south. Before they could make out what manner of ships they were a thunderstorm broke, followed by a calm, and the two fleets remained in sight of each other a mile or so apart. It was not until ten that night that the approaching vessels were able to move in an offshore breeze, and they came up bow to bow. Trumpets sounded from one of the newcomers. It was a salute to begin a parley.

"Gentlemen, from where does this fleet come?"

"From France."

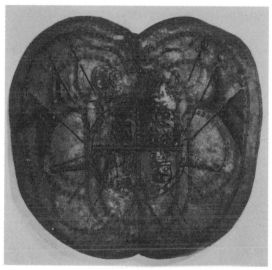

SPANISH SHIELD

The double-oval design was copied from the Moors. This one belonged to a guard of Philip II. It is made of three layers of leather and is ornamented with the arms of Castile and León. Height: 19¼ inches; width: 19½ inches. Courtesy of the Metropolitan Museum of Art, gift of William H. Riggs, 1913.

"What are you doing here?"

"Bringing infantry, artillery, and supplies for a fort which the King of France has in this country, and for others which he is going to make."

"Are you Catholic or Lutherans?"

"Lutherans, and our general is Jean Ribaut. Who are you, and who commands?"

"I am the general. My name is Pedro Menéndez de Avilés. This is the armada of the King of Spain, who has sent me to this coast and country to burn and hang the Lutheran French who should be found there, and in the morning I will board your ships; and if I find any Catholics they will be well treated."

(A priest aboard the *San Pelayo,* Avilés' flagship, afterward reported "a stillness such as I never heard since I came into the world.")

The response of the Protestant sailors was derisive. Avilés drew his sword and ordered his men to close and board the enemy vessels. The order was also heard by the French, who cut their cables and passed right through the Spanish fleet, three of them veering to sail north, the fourth going south, with the Spaniards following.

The dialogue given above is from a letter dispatched by Avilés to Philip II on September 11. He had arrived with the van of his fleet on the River of Dolphins on August 28, the festival day of St. Augustine, and to this place he returned after a vain pursuit of the French ships. There was a large communal Indian house near the water; this was taken over and converted into a fort, with a moat and breastworks of earth and fagots. Soldiers and supplies were put ashore, and were followed by settlers. On September 8 Avilés himself made a triumphal landing, amid flags, trumpet calls and the booming of cannon. He was met by a priest carrying a cross and chanting the *Te Deum Laudamus.* The assembled company fell on their knees. In that solemn moment, watched by Indians, Avilés took possession for Philip II and Spain. Among the onlookers, in chains, were three Frenchmen, mutineers from Fort Caroline sent from Cuba to Spain, and brought back to Florida by Avilés.

Such was the birth of the oldest city in the United States.

The three smaller Spanish ships were able to enter the harbor, leaving two galleons, the *San Pelayo* and the *San Salvador,* riding in the roads. These were rapidly unloaded, Avilés being certain that the French would attack him by sea. It is, in fact, what was attempted; Ribaut arrived with his fleet on the morning of the 11th, to find the *San Pelayo* and the *San Salvador* hull down on the horizon, en route to Hispaniola, and started in pursuit. On board his ships were two hundred sailors and four hundred soldiers.

From his Indian neighbors Avilés had learned that Fort Caroline could be reached without going to sea. Two days later, on the 13th, a "norther" struck the coast, and Avilés, foreseeing that Ribaut's ships could not return in time to be of assistance, decided to attack the fort by land.

On September 16 he assembled three hundred arquebusiers, and two hundred pikemen and targeteers. The rations issued consisted of a bottle of wine and six pounds of biscuits per man, including Avilés himself. After Mass, the expedition set out, guided by two Indian chiefs who had a score to settle with Laudonnière, and with one of the French prisoners in chains. Twenty sturdy Spaniards went ahead with axes to hack a path through palmetto thickets and cypress swamps. It was still pouring when the march began.

For three days, through wet woods, swamps, and swollen streams, sometimes knee-deep and waist-deep in water, the soldiers moved in sullen groups or single file. It is said that Avilés pretended not to hear their grumblings. For two of those days fires were permitted during halts; on the third they were forbidden.

At dawn on the 20th—the feast day of St. Matthew—the Spaniards reached a rise beyond which, said the French prisoner, lay the fort and the river; he was now on a leash held by Avilés himself, his hands bound behind him. Soaked match cords and wet powder made the arquebuses more useful as clubs; the slaughter was to be carried out by pikes (shafts with blades, the bayonet of that day), halberds, swords, knives, daggers, and the axes of the trail blazers.

Inside the fort were some two hundred men—soldiers, artisans, servants, including some newly arrived on Ribaut's ships; and women and children, perhaps as many as fifty. (The accounts vary as to the number of fighting men; Laudonnière, trying to explain the disaster, minimizes the number of soldiers and their fitness. Of those left behind by Ribaut, he says "I found nine or ten whereof not past two or three had ever drawn sword out of the scabbard," and "those that were left me of mine own company were about sixteen or seventeen that could bear arms, and all of them poor and lean; the rest were sick and maimed in the conflict which my lieutenant had against Outina." Nevertheless, a surprising number were agile enough to vault palisade and ditch and escape to the woods.)

Two Spaniards went forward, commando style, and were hailed. "Who goes there?"

"Frenchmen," they answered, creeping closer. The sentry was able to shout before the thrust came. Hearing him, Avilés cried out: "Santiago, at them! Victory!"

The attack on the fort was made from three sides—the north, west and south. The French, aroused from their slumbers by Laudonnière's trumpeter, rushed from their beds naked or in nightshirts, snatching up arms. Laudonnière himself was clad in nothing but a shirt, and fought with sword and shield. He was pointed out to Avilés by his bound prisoner, and a charge of pikemen swept Laudonnière and his men to the south end of the fort, where he escaped through his house. So did his housekeeper, with a stab wound in her breast. The court was now full of Spaniards hacking the defenders with halberds or thrusting them through with pikes; others were slaughtering the sick and the wounded in their beds. Urged by a priest, Avilés shouted orders to spare the women and children. By now, three Spanish ensigns had been planted on the ramparts and Spanish trumpets were sounding victory beside them.

The artist, Le Moyne, had just stretched himself out in his hammock after sentry duty when the attack began. One sight of the court sufficed for Le Moyne, and clambering over bodies, he leaped into the ditch outside the fort and headed for the woods. So did a carpenter, named Le Challeux, aged sixty, who with chisel in hand, had left his hut to begin his day's work when the Spaniards began to pour in; two armed with pikes ran toward him. Despite his age he leaped over the palisade, the chisel still in his hand, and ran. Then he looked back.

"All of the fort, and even the court, was visible. I saw there a horrible killing which was being made of our people and three ensigns of our adversaries planted upon the ramparts."

He made for the woods. Others swarmed down to the river and were taken aboard the *Pearl*, Jacques Ribaut, commander, who raised anchor and proceeded downstream, out of range.

Wandering in the woods, Le Moyne came across a soldier-tailor who had also escaped. Together they sought the sea, hoping to find Jean Ribaut's ships; but in the morning, after a night of trudging through flooded swamps and reeds—it was still raining—with the sea not yet in sight, the tailor decided to return. Perhaps, he reasoned, the Spaniards had had enough of killing; perhaps they could use him in his civilian capacity. Le Moyne accompanied him; but when he heard the sounds of revelry in the fort, he tried to persuade his companion to turn back.

"He embraced me," Le Moyne afterward recalled, "saying, 'I will go; so farewell.'

"In order to see what should happen to him, I got up to a height nearby and watched. As he came down from the high ground, the Spaniards saw him, and sent out a party. As they came upon him, he fell on his knees to beg for his life. They, however, in a fury, cut him to pieces, and carried off the dismembered fragments of his body on the points of their spears and pikes."

Le Moyne plunged back into the woods. He met, in his wanderings, several groups of refugees, and at length there shuddered by the Atlantic shore some twenty-six Frenchmen, and perhaps several women; Laudonnière's housekeeper was one. She escaped and saw her homeland again, as did Laudonnière. Le Challeux was also among those saved. They returned on two of the ships that had

DRAKE CAPTURES ST. AUGUSTINE

This, the first printed map of a city in the United States, shows the amphibious assault in every detail: the arrival of the English fleet; the landing by ships' boats; the march to a point opposite the Spanish fort, which was silenced by two cannon; pinnaces and ships' boats setting men ashore (upper left) to take the city—"which being won was at our departure burned to the ground." So was the fort. It was from St. Augustine that Drake proceeded to the rescue of the Virginia colonists under Lane. The decorative dolphin (lower left) is described as "very pleasant to behold in the sea by daylight, and in the night he seemeth to be of the color of gold. He taketh pleasure as other fishes do by swimming by the ship. He is excellent sweet to be eaten." From Walter Bigges's *A Summary and True Discourse of Sir Francis Drake's West Indian Voyage,* London, 1589, printed by Richard Field, who was to become Shakespeare's first publisher. Courtesy of the Prints Division, The New York Public Library.

crossed the river bar. Jacques Ribaut, who did not wait for his father's return, was in command of one.

In Fort Caroline, 132 French lay dead, many of the bodies mangled by the fury of the faithful. Fifty women and children, some mere infants, were prisoners. "There were, between women, infants, and boys of fifteen years and under, some fifty persons, whom it gives me the greater pain to see in the company of my men, by reason of their wicked sect, and I have feared that our Lord would chastise me if I should deal cruelly with them, for eight or ten children were born here" (Avilés to the king, October 15. He afterward sent them to Santo Domingo). Not a single Spaniard had been killed, and only one was wounded in the successful surprise assault, which had lasted an hour. In the storehouse the Spaniards found dry clothes and food—bread, lard and pork. There was a good amount of silver ore, and gold and pearls. The fort was renamed San Mateo, in honor of St. Matthew, on whose day it was taken.

Leaving a garrison of picked troops there, Avilés made the arduous journey back to St. Augustine, from which place he sent a vessel with supplies.

On September 28 Indians brought him the news that there were Frenchmen on a spit of land four or five leagues south of St. Augustine, cast ashore from two wrecked ships, and trapped between the sea, a river and an inlet. Avilés marched against them, reaching a point of land opposite the French, one of whom swam over to ask a safe-conduct to Fort Caroline. To this, Avilés replied:

> "We held their fort, having taken and put to death those who were in it for having erected it there without the leave of Your Majesty, and because they were planting their wicked Lutheran sect in Your Majesty's provinces, and that I made war with fire and blood as Governor and Captain-General of these provinces upon all who might come to these parts to settle and to plant this evil Lutheran sect, seeing that I came by Your Majesty's command to bring the gospel into these parts, to enlighten the natives thereof with that which is told and believed by the Holy Mother Church of Rome for the salvation of their souls; that therefore I should not give them passage, but, on the contrary, should pursue them by sea and by land until I had their lives." (Avilés to Philip II.)

It was the morning of September 29. The ominous reply was brought back. The next to come over were an officer and four gentlemen in a ship's boat. They brought an offer to surrender if their lives were spared.

"I answered," Avilés was to write, "that they might give up their arms and place themselves at my mercy; that I should deal with them as our Lord should command me."

The boat was permitted to return.

There were more than a hundred soldiers and sailors in the French encampment. Although many of them were armed, the land was bare, and they faced not only the prospect of starvation but attack by Indians. The decision was reached to surrender. In the ship's boat that had carried the officer and gentlemen to the parley with Avilés they now placed arquebuses, pistols, swords, shields, helmets, breastplates and several banners. It returned with twenty Spaniards who began to ferry the Frenchmen across in parties of ten.

Avilés, meanwhile, had stationed himself behind a dune. An arquebus-shot away, there was a line in the sand drawn by him with a pike. As the first unarmed Frenchmen arrived in his presence, he addressed them.

"Gentlemen," he said, "I have but a few soldiers with me, and you are many, and it would be an easy matter for you to overpower us and avenge yourselves upon us for your people which we killed in the fort. For this reason, it is necessary that you should march to my camp four leagues from here with your hands tied behind your backs."

This was the last moment of all in which the French still had a chance for life, or to go down fighting, bare hands being better than hands that were bound. It was not to be. One by one the groups of bound prisoners were marched to the line in the sand.

Avilés to the king: "They came and surrendered their arms to me, and I had their hands tied behind them, and put them all excepting ten to the knife." The ten were saved by the intercession of a priest, who asked Avilés to spare the lives of those who were Catholic; he consented, and they were examined on the spot.

The place where the executions took place did not have a name before September 29. It now had one—Matanzas, "Place of Slaughters."

Less than two weeks later Avilés received word from Indians that another party of Frenchmen was in the same area. Jean Ribaut's flagship, the *Trinity,* had broken up in a storm some miles below, in the neighborhood of Cape Kennedy, and the survivors, numbering some 350, had set out to reach Fort Caroline by land. Trapped on the same spit of land as the earlier group, they were living on roots and grass; the only water was from brackish pools.

Avilés sent troops overland, and went himself in one of two boats carrying additional men. On the morning of October 11, from his fortified position on the Matanzas River, he observed the French who had drawn up in battle array, banners flying, fifes and drums playing. As he made no response, Ribaut ordered a trumpet call for a parley, and again a sailor swam over to the Spanish side of the river. He was sent back in a canoe with the request to bring over an officer authorized to speak for the French.

The canoe returned with a sergeant major, who asked in the name of Jean Ribaut, Viceroy and Captain General of Florida for the King of France, for boats with which to reach Fort Caroline. To him, Avilés said:

"We are Spaniards. I, to whom you are speaking, am the Captain, and my name is Pedro Menéndez de Avilés. Tell your General that I have captured your fort, and killed your French there, as well as those who had escaped from the wreck of your fleet."

He then led the sergeant major to the bodies of those executed on September 29.

Asked to send an officer to Ribaut to discuss terms, Avilés said: "If your General wishes to talk with me, I give him my word that he can come in safety with five or six of his companions."

Eight accompanied Ribaut that afternoon. The Frenchman told Avilés: "What has happened to me may happen to you. Since our kings are brothers and friends, do you also play the part of a friend and give me ships with which to return to France."

Avilés merely repeated what he had told the others—"that they might give up their arms and place themselves at my mercy." With this ambiguous declaration Ribaut and his companions returned to the French camp. A night of councils followed. Less than half the Frenchmen, or about 150, were prepared to surrender to Avilés; the rest refused.

In the morning Ribaut rowed over with six of his officers. He brought with him the royal standard and his seal of office, which he surrendered with his arms, as did the others. Again the French were brought over in groups of ten; again Avilés made the same speech to them, and they allowed themselves to be bound. The fatal question was asked: "Are you Catholics or Lutherans, and are there any who wish to confess?"

Too late Ribaut realized what was in store. He is said to have repeated a passage from Genesis (in the King James version, 3:19, "dust thou art, and unto dust shalt thou return"), to which he appended his own exegesis: "Twenty years more or less, it was all the same thing." He also sang a portion of one of the Psalms, "Lord remember David, and all his afflictions" (Psalm 132:1; the Spanish accounts give "Domine, memento mei," which is obviously an error).

Ribaut was led to the line in the sand by Avilés' brother-in-law and biographer, Solis de Meras, who was armed with a pike, and a Captain San Vincente. The captain asked Ribaut for his felt hat, which was granted. Then he said: "You know how captains must obey their generals and execute their commands." He then stabbed Ribault in the stomach with a dagger, and Meras thrust him through the breast with his pike, after which they cut off his head.

Avilés to King Philip from St. Augustine:

"I put Jean Ribaut and all the rest of them to the knife, judging it to be necessary to the service of the Lord our God, and of Your Majesty. And I think it a very great fortune that this man is dead; for the King of France could accomplish more with him and fifty thousand ducats, than with other men and five hundred thousand ducats; and he could do more in one year, than another in ten, for he was the most experienced sailor and corsair known, very skillful in this navigation of the Indies and of the Florida coast."

Philip to Avilés: "We believe you have acted with entire justification and prudence, and we hold that we have been well served." Avilés to Philip:

"The other people with Ribaut, some seventy or eighty in all, took to the forest, refusing to surrender unless I grant them their lives. These and twenty others who escaped from the fort, and fifty who were captured by the Indians, from the ships that were wrecked, in all one hundred and fifty persons, rather less than more, are the French alive today in Florida, dispersed and flying through the forest, and captive with the Indians. And since they are Lutherans and in order that so evil a sect shall not remain alive in these parts, I will conduct myself in such wise, and will so incite my friends, the Indians, on their part, that in five or six weeks very few if any will remain alive."

The achievements of Avilés in the New World are soon told. He established two settlements, San Augustín and Fort San Mateo, in Florida; and a third, Fort San Felipe, in the region of France's Charlesfort, in South Carolina. There were also some blockhouses. He sent some Jesuit missionaries into Virginia. They were all killed. There were mutinies at Forts San Felipe and San Mateo, as well as Indian attacks on all the Spanish outposts. Like Ribaut before him,

Avilés was himself wrecked in the neighborhood of Cape Kennedy, and had to fight his way back to St. Augustine. The city that he founded was bombarded by French and English men-o'-war, and Drake sacked it.

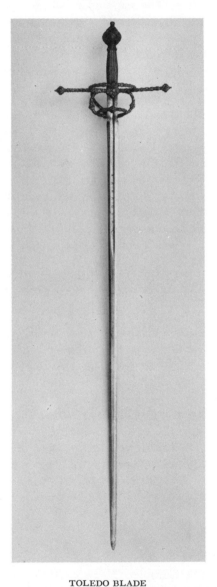

TOLEDO BLADE

A Spanish rapier, *circa* 1570. Over-all length: 46⅛ inches. Courtesy of the Metropolitan Museum of Art, Rogers Fund, 1904.

VI

ℛALEIGH'S
𝒱IRGINIA

Francis Drake commanded the *Judith,* a bark, when he sailed with
Hawkins on the latter's "third troublesome voyage made with the
Jesus of Lubeck, the *Minion,* and four other ships, to the parts of
Guinea and the West Indies" (that is, in the slave trade). One of
the things that made it so troublesome was the battle in the port
of San Juan de Ulua on the Mexican coast, in which the *Jesus of
Lubeck* took such a cannonading that it had to be abandoned.

> "The most part of the men that were left alive in the *Jesus*
> made shift and followed the *Minion* in a small boat, the rest
> which the little boat was not able to receive were enforced to
> abide the mercy of the Spaniards (which I doubt was very lit-
> tle); so with the *Minion* only and the *Judith* we escaped,"
> Hawkins wrote.

The battle was forced on the English, who had put in at San
Juan de Ulua for repairs and provisions, for which they offered to
pay. It is thought that the treachery of the Spaniards, who had
given their word in writing, and had even exchanged hostages as
evidence of good faith, made a lasting impression on Drake.

Drake was still plain Francis when he set out from Plymouth
November 15, 1577, with five vessels, his flagship the *Golden Hind,*

DRAKE CAPTURES A TREASURE SHIP
Caca Fogo: "The Chase—Fire." Caca Plata:
"The Chase—Silver." Engraving from Hulsius,
courtesy of the Rare Book Division, The New
York Public Library.

to circumnavigate the globe and plunder Spaniards. He had some
trouble on board before reaching the Strait of Magellan; one
Doughty was tried and sentenced to death. Before he was beheaded
Doughty asked for communion, and Drake took it with him, the
minister being Master Francis Fletcher.

The fleet continued down the Atlantic coast of South America,
pausing when it was safe to do so to refit and take on fresh water.
Two months were spent at Port Julian, which was left behind on
August 17, 1578; on the 20th, the fleet entered the Strait of Magellan.

The South Sea, which the Spaniards thought their own, lay open
to the English. Off Ecuador, Drake forced the surrender of a galleon laden with 26 tons of silver, 80 pounds of gold, a dozen or so
chests of coins and precious stones, and transferred the booty to
his own ships without a fight.

In March of 1579 the *Golden Hind* became separated from the

SIR FRANCIS DRAKE

"Most noble knight of England" is the heading of this engraving, thought to be by Jodocus Hondius. It was made when the sacker of cities on the Spanish Main and rescuer of Raleigh's colonists in Virginia was 43 years old. Reproduced by permission of the National Portrait Gallery, London.

other ships, and Drake proceeded alone up the North American coast.

It was on June 19 of that year that he reached a point—"in 30 degrees 30 minutes"—which is of abiding interest. He had discovered "a convenient and fit harbor" where he anchored. Was it San Francisco Bay? Or was it Drake's Bay, thirty miles to the north?

From *The World Encompassed by Sir Francis Drake, carefully collected out of the notes of Master Francis Fletcher, Preacher in this Employment, and divers other his followers:*

"The next day, after coming to anchor in the aforesaid harbor, the people of the country showed themselves, sending off a man with great expedition to us in a canoe; who being yet but a little from the shore, and a great way from our ship, spake to us continually as he came rowing on. And at last at a reasonable distance, staying himself, he began more solemnly a long and tedious oration, after his manner, using in his delivery thereof many gestures and signs, moving his hands, turning his head and body many ways; and after his oration ended, with great show of reverence and submission returned back to shore again.

"He shortly came again the second time in like manner, and so the third time, when he brought with him (as a present from the rest) a bunch of feathers, much like the feathers of a black crow, very neatly and artificially gathered upon a string, and drawn together into a round bundle, being very clean and finely cut, and bearing in length an equal proportion one with another, a special cognizance (as we afterwards observed) which they that guard their king's person wear on their heads. With this also he brought a little basket made of rushes, and filled with an herb which they called *Tabâh.* Both, being tied to a short rod, he cast into our boat."

More canoes put out, the Indians "wondering at us as at gods." They had not seen white men before.

"The third day following, *viz.,* the 21st, our ship, having received a leak at sea, was brought to anchor nearer the shore that her goods being landed, she might be repaired. But for that we were to prevent any danger that might chance against our safety, our General first of all landed his men, with all necessary provision, to build tents and make a fort for the defense of ourselves and goods, and that we might under the shelter of it with more safety (whatever should befall) end our business; which, when the people of the country perceived us doing, as men set on fire to war in defense of their country, in great haste and companies, with such weapons as they had, they came down unto us, and yet with no hostile meaning or intent to hurt us, standing, when they drew near, as men ravished in their minds, with the sight of such things as they never had seen or heard of before that time, their errand being rather with submission and fear to worship us as gods, than to have any war with us as with mortal men. Which thing, as it did partly show itself at that instant, so did it more and more manifest itself afterward, during the whole time of our abode among them. At this time, being willed by signs to lay from them their bows and arrows, they did as they were directed, and so did all the rest, as they came more and more by companies unto them, growing in a little while to a great number, both of men and women.

"To the intent, therefore, that this peace which they themselves so willingly sought might, without any cause of the breach thereof on our part given be continued, and that we might with more safety and expedition end our business in quiet, our General, with all his company, used all means possible gently to entreat them, bestowing upon each of them liberally good and necessary things to cover their nakedness; withal, signifying unto them we were no gods, but men, and had need of such things to cover our own shame, teaching them to use them to the same ends; for which cause, also, we did eat and drink in their presence, giving them to understand that without that we could not live, and therefore were but men as well as they.

"Notwithstanding, nothing could persuade them, nor remove that opinion which they had conceived of us, that we should be gods.

"In recompense of those things which they had received of us, as shirts, linen cloth, etc., they bestowed upon our General, and divers of our company, divers things, as feathers, cauls of network, the quivers of their arrows, made of fawn skins, and the very skins of beasts that their women wore upon their bodies."

California fashions are described:

"Their men for the most part go naked. The women take a kind of bulrushes, and combing it after the manner of hemp, make themselves thereof a loose garment, which being knit about their middles, hangs down about their hips, and so affords them a covering of that which Nature teaches should be hidden. About their shoulders they wear also the skin of a deer, with the hair upon it. They are very obedient to their husbands, and exceeding ready in all services, yet of themselves offering to do nothing without the consents, or being called, of the men."

An idyllic spot—an ideal arrangement. Their king was kingly. He arrived with a guard of "tall and warlike men," himself "a man of goodly stature and comely personage," wearing a coat of rabbit skins reaching to his waist.

There was now a multitude by the shore, the men dancing and singing, the women merely dancing.

"After that they had satisfied, or rather tired, themselves in this manner, they made signs to our General to have him sit down; unto whom both the king and divers others made several orations or rather indeed, if we had understood them, supplications, that he would take the province and kingdom into his hand and become their king and patron, making signs that they would resign unto him their right and title in the whole land and become his vassals in themselves and their posterities."

Thus urged, Drake took possession for Elizabeth, "by the grace

DRAKE'S PLATE

Inscription on brass, taking possession of California for Queen Elizabeth.

BE IT KNOWN UNTO ALL MEN BY THESE PRESENTS:

JUNE 17, 1579.

BY THE GRACE OF GOD AND IN THE NAME OF HER
MAJESTY QUEEN ELIZABETH OF ENGLAND AND HER
SUCCESSORS FOREVER I TAKE POSSESSION OF THIS
KINGDOM WHOSE KING AND PEOPLE FREELY RESIGN
THEIR RIGHT AND TITLE IN THE WHOLE LAND UNTO HER
MAJESTY'S KEEPING. NOW NAMED BY ME AN[D] TO BE
KNOWN TO ALL MEN AS NEW ALBION.

FRANCIS DRAKE.

The plate is approximately 5 inches wide, 8 inches long and ⅛ of an inch thick. It was probably fastened to the "great and firm post," mentioned in the text, by two spikes, top and bottom. The hole at right held the sixpence with Elizabeth's portrait. The letters appear to have been cut with a chisel. The plate was found on a hill near Greenbrae, Marin County, California, where a previous possessor had discarded it. It is now on display at the Bancroft Library, University of California, Berkeley.

of God of England, France and Ireland Queen, Defender of the Faith, etc."

It was June 26, 1579.

"This country our General named *Albion*, and that for two causes—the one in respect of the white banks and cliffs, which lie toward the sea, the other that it might have some affinity, even in name also, with our own country, which was sometimes so called.

"Before we went from thence, our General caused to be set up a monument of our being there, as also of Her Majesty's and successors' right and title to that kingdom: namely, a plate of brass, fast nailed to a great and firm post, whereon is engraven Her Grace's name, and the day and year of our arrival there, and of the free giving up of the province and kingdom, both by the king and people, in Her Majesty's hands; together with Her Highness's picture and arms, in a piece of sixpence current English money, showing itself by a hole made of purpose through the plate [in which the sixpence was set]. Underneath was likewise engraven the name of our General, etc."

(The brass plate, measuring 5 by 8 inches, is now at the University of California at Berkeley. It was found in 1936).

Drake sailed away on July 23, his friendly hosts watching the English departure "with sighs and sorrowings, with heavy hearts and grieved minds." The *Golden Hind*, after a stop in the Philippines, rounded the Cape of Good Hope and reached Plymouth September 26, 1580. It was afterward berthed at Deptford, then a little village across the Thames from London; there, in 1581, kneeling on its deck, Drake received the order of knighthood from his grateful queen.

Two years later, Sir Humphrey Gilbert, a half-brother of Sir Walter Raleigh by his mother, became (in the words of a fellow voyager) "the first of our nation that carried people to erect an habitation and government in those northerly countries of America"—that is, to Newfoundland; but he did not confine himself, for he also "intended to discover and to plant Christian inhabitants in place[s] convenient, upon those large and ample countries extended northward from the cape of Florida."

England's claims to these large territories were, of course, based on the voyages of the Cabots, which were thought to antedate all others:

"The first discovery of these coasts (never heard of before) was well begun by John Cabot the father, and Sebastian his son, an Englishman born, who were the first finders out of all that great tract of land stretching from the cape of Florida unto those Islands which we now call the Newfoundland, all which they brought and annexed unto the crown of England; since when, if with like diligence the search of inland countries had been followed, as the discovery upon the coast and outparts thereof was performed by those men, no doubt Her Majesty's territories and revenues had been mightily enlarged and advanced by this day." (From *A Report of the Voyage and success thereof, attempted in the year of our Lord 1583 by Sir Humphrey Gilbert, knight,* written by Edward Hayes, one of the commanders of the expedition.)

From Richmond, Raleigh wrote Gilbert, March 17:

"Brother—I have sent you a token from Her Majesty, an anchor guided by a lady as you see; and farther, Her Highness willed me to send you word that she wished you as great good hap, and safety to your ship, as if she herself were there in person; desiring you to have care of yourself, as of that which she tendereth; and therefore for her sake you must provide for it accordingly."

The token was a pendant, and Gilbert wore it around his neck.

Five ships started out—the *Delight,* 120 tons, Gilbert's flagship (called Admiral, for its position), William Winter, captain and part owner, Richard Clark of Weymouth, master; the *Raleigh,* a bark of 200 tons, vice admiral (owned and outfitted by Walter Raleigh, who was not permitted to go), one Butler, captain, Robert Davis, master; another *Golden Hind,* 40 tons, rear admiral, Edward Hayes, captain and owner, William Cox of Limehouse, master; the *Swallow,* 40 tons, Maurice Browne, captain, and the *Squirrel,* a frigate of 10 tons, William Andrews, captain, "and one Cade, master." They carried 260 men, among them being shipwrights, masons, carpenters, smiths and "mineral men and refiners." There was also a poet, Stephen Parmenius, a learned Hungarian who had been a roommate of Richard Hakluyt at Oxford, present aboard the *Delight* to compose a Latin poem celebrating the voyage.

In addition to the usual stores and weapons,

"for solace of our people and allurement of the savages we were provided of music in good variety, not omitting the least toys [trifles], as morris dancers, hobby horses [of wicker, used in morris dance], and Maylike conceits [from May Day; this was before the Puritans abolished its simple pleasures] to delight the savage people, whom we intended to win by all fair means possible. And to that end we were indifferently furnished of all petty haberdashery wares to barter with these people."

The fleet left Plymouth Tuesday, June 11, 1583, in good weather and a fair wind, "good all day, but a great storm of thunder and wind fell the same night." On Thursday the *Raleigh* signaled that its captain and many of its crew had fallen sick and it was turning back. Hayes wrote: "It was after credibly reported, that they were infected with a contagious sickness, and arrived greatly distressed at Plymouth." The weather continued bad: "From Saturday the 15th of June until the 28th, which was upon a Friday, we never had fair day without fog or rain, and winds bad."

In one of the fogs the *Swallow* was lost to view, and was not seen again until Gilbert and Hayes reached Conception Bay (the *Squirrel* also seems to have taken its own course, as will appear). The men on the *Swallow* were "altered into other apparel, whereof it seemed their store was so amended, that for joy and congratulation of our meeting they spared not to cast up into the air and overboard their caps and hats in good plenty."

It was soon learned how they had obtained these new clothes. They had met a bark (nationality not recorded) returning with a haul of fish;

"and because the men in the *Swallow* were very near scanted of victual, and chiefly of apparel, doubtful withal where or when to find and meet with their Admiral, they besought the captain they might go aboard this Newlander, only to borrow what might be spared, the rather because the same was bound homeward. Leave given, not without charge to deal favorably, they came aboard the fisherman, whom they rifled of tackle, sails, cables, victuals, and the men of their apparel—not sparing by torture (winding cords about their heads) to draw out else what they thought good.

"This done with expedition (like men skilful in such mischief) as they took their cockboat to go aboard their own ship, it was overwhelmed in the sea, and certain of these men were drowned. The rest were preserved even by those silly souls whom they had before [des]spoiled, who saved and delivered them aboard the *Swallow*. What became afterward of the poor Newlander, perhaps destitute of sails and furniture sufficient to carry them home (whither they had not less to run than 700 leagues) God alone knoweth, who took vengeance not long after of the rest that escaped at this instant."

The men, it seems, were "skilful in such mischief" because they were "such as had been by us surprised upon the narrow seas of England, being pirates [who] had taken at that instant certain Frenchmen laden, one bark with wines, and another with salt; both which we rescued, and took the man of war with all her men, which was the same ship now called the *Swallow*"—in other words, they had been impressed, ship and crew alike. Hayes holds Captain Maurice Browne blameless—"albeit himself was very honest and religious, yet was he not appointed of men to his humor and desert."

The *Delight, Golden Hind* and *Swallow* proceeded southward, and the same day—Saturday, August 3—came up with the *Squirrel* anchored off St. John's. Its entrance had been barred by an English fishing fleet; there were also other fishing vessels there, "of all nations to the number of 36 sails" (a marginal note by Hakluyt, who published Hayes' narrative, states: "English ships are the strongest and admirals of other fleets fishing upon the south parts of Newfoundland." In actuality, there was a little United Nations there, the "admirals" being chosen in rotation). Gilbert dispatched a ship's boat "to give them knowledge of his coming for no ill intent, having commission from Her Majesty for his voyage."

A parley followed aboard the *Delight*.

"The next morning, being Sunday and the fourth of August, the General and his company were brought on land by English merchants, who showed unto us their accustomed walks unto a place called 'The Garden.' But nothing appeared more than Nature itself without art, who confusedly hath brought forth roses abundantly, wild but odoriferous, and to sense very comfortable; also the like plenty of raspberries, which do grow in every place."

Some of the merchants had brought sheep with them, "and had them raised exceeding fat in less than three weeks." It was a lush land. The partridges were so fat they were unable to fly, and were killed with cudgels. There were bear and deer, otters, beavers and

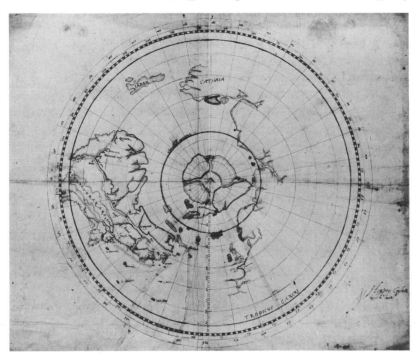

NORTH AMERICA AND THE ARCTIC REGIONS, *circa* 1582
Original owner's autograph signature, lower right: "Humfray Gylbert knight his charte." Verrazano's mythical inland sea is at left center; if it had existed, it would have provided a passage to the East. Also shown: a northeast passage through arctic waterways. The man who made the map for Gilbert was John Dee, mathematician and astrologer, as the learned saw him—a magician and sorcerer as seen by others for his chemical experiments (in 1604 he petitioned James I for formal clearance of these imputations). Dee was a friend and co-experimenter with Henry Percy, ninth Earl of Northumberland, the "Wizard Earl," into whose library the map found its way after Gilbert's death at sea. Present location: the Rare Book Department of The Free Library of Philadelphia.

martins. The waters teemed with fish. Hayes was indignant in recollection about

> "the fault and foolish sloth in many of our nation choosing rather to live indirectly, and very miserably to live and die within this realm pestered with inhabitants, than to adventure as becometh men to obtain an habitation in those remote lands, in which Nature very prodigally doth minister unto men's endeavors, and for art to work upon."

Losing no time, Gilbert took possession for Elizabeth and England.

"Monday following, the General had his tent set up, who being accompanied with his own followers, summoned the merchants and masters, both English and strangers [foreigners] to be present at his taking possession of those countries, before whom openly was read and interpreted unto the strangers his commission. By virtue whereof he took possession in the same harbor of St. John, and 200 leagues every way, invested the Queen's majesty with the title and dignity thereof [and] had delivered unto him (after the custom of England) a rod and a turf of the same soil, entering possession also for him, his heirs and assigns forever; and signified unto all men that from that time forward they should take the same land as a territory appertaining to the Queen of England, and himself authorized under Her Majesty to possess and enjoy it, and to ordain laws for the government thereof, agreeable (so near as conveniently might be) unto the laws of England, under which all people coming thither hereafter, either to inhabit or by way of traffic, should be subjected and governed.

"And especially at the same time for a beginning, he proposed and delivered three laws to be in force immediately— that is to say: the first for religion, which in public exercise should be according to the Church of England. The second for maintenance of Her Majesty's right and possession of those territories, against which if anything were attempted prejudicial, the party or parties offending should be adjudged and executed as in case of high treason, according to the laws of England. The third, if any person should utter words sounding to the dishonor of Her Majesty, he should lose his ears, and have his ships and goods confiscate.

"These contents published [declared in public], obedience was promised by general voice and consent of the multitude, as well of Englishmen as strangers, praying for continuance of this possession and government begun. After this, the assembly was dismissed. And afterward were erected not far from that place the arms of England engraven in lead and enfixed upon a pillar of wood. Yet further and actually to establish this possession taken in the right of Her Majesty, and to the behoof of Sir Humphrey Gilbert, knight, his heirs and assigns forever, the General granted in fee farm divers parcels of land lying by the waterside, both in this harbor of St. John and elsewhere, which was to the owners a great commodity, being thereby assured (by their proper inheritance) of grounds convenient to dress and to dry their fish, whereof many times before they did fail, being prevented by them that came first into the harbor. For which grounds they did covenant to pay a certain rent and service unto Sir Humphrey Gilbert, his heirs or assigns forever, and yearly to maintain possession of the same, by themselves or their assigns.

"Now remained only to take in provision granted."

This had been arranged at the parley on the *Delight,* when

"it was further determined that every ship of our fleet should deliver unto the merchants and masters of that harbor a note of all their wants; which done, the ships, as well English as strangers, were taxed at an easy rate to make supply. And besides, commissioners were appointed, part of our own company and part of theirs, to go into other harbors adjoining (for our English merchants command all there) to levy our provision, whereunto the Portugals (above other nations) did most willingly and liberally contribute. Insomuch as we were presented (above our allowance) with wines, marmalades, most fine rusk or biscuit, sweet oils and sundry delicacies [including figs, and "lemons barreled"]. Also, we wanted not of fresh salmons, trouts, lobsters and other fresh fish brought daily unto us.

"Moreover, as the manner is in their fishing every week to choose their admiral anew, or rather they succeed in orderly course, and have weekly their admiral's feast solemnized, even so the General, captains and masters of our fleet were continually invited and feasted."

Not only was there present plenty; one of the Portuguese confided that some thirty years before—he had himself been present—cattle and swine had been put ashore on Sable Island to breed, "which were since exceedingly multiplied." Hayes commented: "This seemed unto us very happy tidings, to have an island lying so near unto the main, which we intended to plant upon [colonize], such store of cattle, whereby we might at all times conveniently be relieved of victual."

It was a pleasant time for all, but chiefly for Gilbert and his officers. One Daniel, "a Saxon born," albeit from Hungary, who had gone prospecting, brought back some ore confidently believed to be silver. It was secretly conveyed aboard the *Delight.* Hayes demanded to see it, and Gilbert replied:

"Content yourself, I have seen enough, and were it but to satisfy my private humor, I would proceed no further. The promise unto my friends, and necessity to bring also the south countries within compass of my patent, near expired, as we have already done these north parts, do only persuade me further. And touching the ore, I have sent it aboard, whereof I would have no speech to be made so long as we remain within harbor, here being both Portugals, Biscayans and Frenchmen not far off, from whom must be kept any bruit or muttering of such matter. When we are at sea proof [demonstration] shall be made; if it be to our desire, we may return the sooner hither again."

Hayes was content. But

"others of another sort and disposition were plotting of mischief, some casting to steal away our shipping by night, watching opportunity by the General's and captains' lying on the shore, whose conspiracies discovered, they were prevented. Others drew together in company and carried away out of the harbors adjoining a ship laden with fish, setting the poor men on shore. A great many more of our people stole into the woods to hide themselves, attending time and means to return home by such shipping as daily departed from the coast.

"Some were sick of fluxes [dysentery?], and many dead; and, in brief, by one means or other our company was diminished, and many by the General licensed to return home. Insomuch as after we had reviewed our people, resolved to see an end of our voyage [that is, bring it to a proper conclusion by further exploration], we grew scant of men to furnish all our shipping. It seemed good, therefore, unto the General to leave the *Swallow* with such provision as might be spared for transporting home the sick people."

Captain William Winter of the *Delight* was put in command of the *Swallow*, his place being taken by Captain Browne. Captain William Andrews of the frigate *Squirrel* elected to return with Winter, and Gilbert took his place, "the same frigate being most convenient to discover upon the coast, and to search into every harbor or creek, which a great ship could not do." It was converted into a fighting ship; Hayes says it was "overcharged with bases and such small ordnance, more to give a show, than with judgment to foresee unto the safety of her and the men."

Loaded down with provisions and delicacies, the *Delight, Golden*

Hind and *Squirrel* put out from St. John's, Tuesday, August 20, reaching Cape Race the next day at nightfall. Becalmed, the sailors fished for cod with hook and line, "and drew in less than two hours fish so large, and in such abundance, that many days after we fed upon no other provision. From hence we shaped our course unto the Island of Sablon [Sable Island], if conveniently it would so fall out, also directly to Cape Breton." Eight days were spent "trending" the coast, "yet could we never attain sight of any land all that time, seeing we were hindered by the current. At last we fell into such flats and dangers, that hardly any of us escaped."

It is Wednesday night, August 28, off Cape Breton Island, perhaps its southeasterly coast. Sailors aboard the *Golden Hind* caught "a very mighty porpoise" with a harping iron; other porpoises had been harpooned, but had got away. Hayes commented that, "passing through the ocean in herds, they portended storm." The *Delight*, with almost a hundred men aboard, was in the lead. A concert was in progress on her deck.

"The evening was fair and pleasant," Hayes wrote, "yet not without token of storm to ensue, and most part of this Wednesday night—like the swan that singeth before her death—they in the Admiral, or *Delight*, continued in sounding of trumpets, with drums and fifes, also winding the cornets [and] hautboys.

"Thursday the 29th of August the wind rose and blew vehemently at south and east, bringing withal rain and thick mist, so that we could not see a cable length before us. And betimes in the morning we were altogether run and folded in amongst flats and sands, amongst which we found shoal and deep in every three or four ship's length after we began to sound; but first we were upon them unawares, until Master Cox, looking out, discerned (in his judgment) white cliffs, crying 'Land!' withal, though we could not afterward descry any land, it being very likely the breaking of the sea white, which seemed to be white cliffs through the haze and thick weather.

"Immediately tokens [signals] were given unto the *Delight* to cast about to seaward, which, being the greater ship, and of burden 120 tons, was yet foremost upon the breach, keeping so ill watch, that they knew not the danger before they felt the same, too late to recover it. For presently the Admiral struck aground, and had soon after her stern and hinder parts beaten in pieces. Whereupon the rest—that is to say, the frigate in which was the General and the *Golden Hind*—cast about east-

southeast, bearing to the south, even for our lives, into the
wind's eye, because that way carried us to seaward. Making out
from this danger, we sounded one while seven fathom, then
five fathom, then four fathom and less, again deeper, immediately four fathom, then but three fathom, the sea going
mightily and high. At last we recovered (God be thanked) in
some despair to sea room enough."

Of the five ships that had left Plymouth so short a time before,
only two were left, and these of the smallest, 40 and 10 tons, respectively. Captain Browne perished with the *Delight*, refusing to
leave it while there was time—some of his men got into a pinnace
at the stern and called to him to join them. (They were adrift six
days and nights, two dying before French fishermen found them
and carried them to France.) Also lost were the learned Hungarian, Stephen Parmenius, whom Hayes eulogizes, and Daniel,
"our Saxon refiner and discoverer of inestimable riches, as it was
left amongst some of us in undoubted hope." His ore samplings
went down with the ship.

Hayes says:

"Our people lost courage daily after this ill success, the weather
continuing thick and blustering, with increase of cold, winter
drawing on, which took from them all hope of amendment,
settling an assurance of worse weather to grow upon us every
day. The lee side of us lay full of flats and dangers inevitable,
if the wind blew hard at south. Some again doubted [thought]
we were engulfed in the Bay of St. Lawrence, the coast full of
dangers and unto us unknown. But above all, provision waxed
scant, and hope of supply was gone, with loss of our Admiral.
    "Those in the frigate were already pinched with spare allow-
ance, and want of clothes chiefly; whereupon they besought the
General to return to England before they all perished. And to
them of the *Golden Hind* they made signs of their distress,
pointing to their mouths, and to their clothes, thin and ragged.
Then immediately they also of the *Golden Hind* grew to be of
the same opinion and desire to return home."

Saturday, August 31, the decision was reached.
"The wind was large for England."
On Monday, September 2, Gilbert went aboard the *Golden Hind*
to have that ship's surgeon attend to his foot; he had stepped on a
nail. Captain Hayes begged him to remain, but Gilbert replied: "I
will not forsake my little company going homeward, with whom I

have passed so many storms and perils." He returned to the *Squirrel* with provisions.

A week later:

"Monday the 9th of September, in the afternoon, the frigate was near cast away, oppressed by waves, yet at that time recovered; and giving forth signs of joy, the General, sitting abaft with a book in his hand, cried out unto us in the *Hind* (so oft as we did approach within hearing): 'We are as near to heaven by sea as by land!'"

He was nearer than he knew.

"The same Monday night, about twelve of the clock, or not long after, the frigate being ahead of us in the *Golden Hind,* suddenly her lights were out whereof, as it were in a moment, we lost the sight; and withal our watch cried: 'The General was cast away!'—which was too true. For in that moment, the frigate was devoured and swallowed up of the sea."

Three months and eleven days after leaving England, the *Golden Hind,* alone of the five ships commanded by Sir Humphrey Gilbert, arrived home, September 22, 1583.

As William Shakespeare reached manhood—he was born the year Hawkins set out on the voyage that took him to Fort Caroline—the stir and bustle in England's ports mounted. At the center of things was London, "the flower of cities all," and at the center of London was the queen who ruled like a king.

"She was of personage tall, of hair and complexion fair, and therewith well-favored, but high-nosed, of limbs and feature neat, and which added to the lustre of those exterior graces, of stately and majestic comportment." (Sir Robert Naunton, *Fragmenta Regalia.*)

Her tutor had been the renowned Roger Ascham. She could dispute with bishops, and make up a verse in English or Latin extemporaneously. She liked handsome men around her; but as Naunton observes, she "never took into her favor a mere new man, or a mechanic," as did Louis XI, who made his barber a duke. Of her favorite, Sir Walter Raleigh, "well descended and of good alliance, but poor in his beginnings," Naunton wrote:

ELIZABETH I

The great queen (at 60) with England at her feet. Painted by an unknown artist *circa* 1593. Reproduced by permission of the National
Portrait Gallery, London.

"He had in the outward man a good presence, in a handsome
and well compacted person, a strong natural wit, and a better
judgment, with a bold and plausible tongue, whereby he could
set out his parts to the best advantage; and to these he had the

adjuncts of some general learning, which by diligence he enforced to a great augmentation and perfection, for he was an indefatigable reader, whether by sea or land, and none of the least observers both of men and the times. And I am confident, that among the second causes of his growth, that variance between him and my Lord Grey [de Wilton, Lord Deputy of Ireland, under whom Raleigh served], in his descent into Ireland, was a principal; for it drew them both over the Council table, there to plead their cause, where (what advantage he had in the cause, I know not) but he had much better in the telling of his tale; and so much, that the Queen and the Lords [of the Privy Council] took no slight mark of the man and his parts, for from thence he came to be known and to have access to the Queen and the Lords, and then we are not to doubt how such a man would comply and learn the way of progression.

"And whether [the Earl of] Leicester had then cast in a good word for him to the Queen, which would have done no harm, I do not determine; but true it is, he had gotten the Queen's ear at a trice, and she began to be taken with his elocution, and loved to hear his reasons to her demands. And the truth is, she took him for a kind of oracle, which nettled them all."

As important posts fell vacant she let Raleigh fill them, which nettled them some more. There was also a vacant house.

On the Strand, near Whitehall, was the riverside palace called Durham House, once the town house of the Bishops of Durham, sequestered by Henry VIII, seized in turn by Mary, and presented to Elizabeth by her half-brother, Edward VI. It had served the queen as a guest house, but now she had another use for it—she gave it to Raleigh. It had great round towers, and was battlemented like a castle on its river side; John Aubrey, who appears to have known it, speaks of it in his account of Raleigh as "a noble palace."

"I well remember his study, which was a little turret that looked into and over the Thames, and had the prospect which is pleasant perhaps as any in the world" (*Brief Lives*).

Raleigh's court attire was a combination of white with black and silver. Under a fur-collared black velvet cape rayed with silver beads he wore a doublet of pinked white silk with turned-down collar which matched the cuffs and shoulder caps; the buttons were studded with pearls (Aubrey, who saw the original of the portrait here described, says that some "old servants have told me that the pearls were near as big as the painted ones"). The sword belt worn with this outfit was trimmed in silver to match the paned slops (breeches). A single earring hung from Raleigh's left ear.

"He was a tall, handsome and bold man; but his *naeve* was that he was damnable proud," Aubrey commented. (Naeve: distinguishing mark, or stigma.)

SIR WALTER RALEIGH

Courtier, poet, foe of Spain and colonizer of Virginia. Painted by an unknown artist when Raleigh was 34 years old. Reproduced by permission of the National Portrait Gallery, London.

Such were the sovereign and subject who were to plant England in the New World. Undaunted by the disasters of the previous year, the queen granted Raleigh a royal patent empowering him "to discover, search, find out, and view such remote, heathen and barbarous lands, countries and territories not actually possessed of any Christian prince, nor inhabited by Christian people," although Elizabeth had no intention of letting him risk his life in the enterprise. Settlers were to have "all the privileges of free denizens, and persons native of England." The patent, or charter, was signed by her at Westminster, "the 25th day of March, in the six and twentieth year of our reign," 1584, two vessels being ready to depart on an exploratory voyage at Raleigh's "charge and direction," and expense as well, the queen reserving to herself, her heirs and successors, "for all services, duties, and demands, the fifth part of all the ore of gold and silver" which, hopefully, would be found.

The vessels were two barks, "well furnished with men and victuals," which left England April 27 under the commands of Captain Philip Amadas and Captain Arthur Barlowe, one Simon Ferdinando, a Spaniard, going as pilot and master of the flagship. On May 10 they reached the Canaries, on June 10 the West Indies where, at one of the islands, they took on fresh water and provisions and proceeded northward. From Captain Barlowe's narrative (probably written at the request of Raleigh after the return of the ships and the delivery to him of the record of possession taken in the name of Elizabeth):

> "The second of July we found shoal water, where we smelt so sweet and so strong a smell, as if we had been in the midst of some delicate garden abounding with all kind of odoriferous flowers, by which we were assured that the land could not be far distant; and keeping good watch and bearing but slack sail, the fourth of the same month we arrived upon the coast, which we supposed to be a continent and firm land, and we sailed along the same a hundred and twenty English miles before we could find any entrance or river issuing into the sea.
>
> "The first that appeared unto us we entered, though not without some difficulty, and cast anchor about three arquebusshot within the haven's mouth, on the left hand of the same; and after thanks given to God for our safe arrival thither, we manned our boats and went to view the land next adjoining and to take possession of the same in the right of the Queen's most excellent Majesty, as rightful Queen and Princess of the same, and after delivered the same over to your use, according to Her Majesty's grant and letters patent, under Her Highness's great seal."

RALEIGH'S VIRGINIA: CAPE LOOKOUT TO CHESAPEAKE BAY
Drawn by John White, assisted by the astronomical obser-
vations of Thomas Hariot. The map has been called "the
most careful detailed piece of cartography for any part of
North America to be made in the sixteenth century."
Roanoke and Hatorask are at right center. In addition to
the English ships inside and outside the Carolina banks—
at least one of them a pinnace—there are eleven canoes.
The Indians in them appear to be fishing. Courtesy of the
Trustees of the British Museum. Copyright 1964.

A marginal note by Hakluyt gives the date: "July 13, possession
taken." Barlowe says "the particular gentlemen and men of account
who then were present as witnesses of the same" were himself, Captain Amadas, William Grenvile, John Wood, James Browewich,
Henry Greene, Benjamin Wood, Nicholas Petman, John Hewes,
and Simon Ferdinando, the Spanish pilot.

"Which being performed," Barlowe wrote, "according to the ceremonies used in such enterprises, we viewed the land about us, being whereas we first landed very sandy and low toward the water's side, but so full of grapes as the very beating and surge of the sea overflowed them, of which we found such plenty, as well there as in all places else, both on the sand and on the green soil on the hills, as in the plains as well on every little shrub, as also climbing toward the tops of high cedars, that I think in all the world the like abundance is not to be found. And myself, having seen those parts of Europe that most abound, find such difference as were incredible to be written.

"We passed from the sea side toward the tops of those hills next adjoining, being but of mean height, and from thence we beheld the sea on both sides, to the north and to the south finding no end any of both ways. This land lay stretching itself to the west, which after we found to be but an island of twenty miles long and not above six miles broad [see John White's chart, Wocokon Island, Pamlico Sound]. Under the bank or hill whereon we stood we beheld the valleys replenished with goodly cedar trees, and having discharged our arquebus-shot, such a flock of cranes (the most part white) arose under us, with such a cry redoubled by many echoes, as if an army of men had shouted all together [they were probably American egrets].

"This island had many good woods full of deer, conies [rabbits], hares and fowl, even in the middest of summer in incredible abundance. The woods are not such as you find in Bohemia, Moscovia, or Hyrcania, barren and fruitless, but the highest and reddest cedars of the world, far bettering the cedars of the Azores, of the Indies or Lebanon; pines, cypress, sassafras, the lentisk, or the tree that beareth the mastic [gum or resin], the tree that beareth the rind of black cinnamon, of which Master Winter [John Winter, who went with Drake in his voyage around the world] brought from the Straits of Magellan, and many other of excellent smell and quality.

"We remained by the side of this island two whole days before we saw any people of the country. The third day we espied one small boat rowing toward us, having in it three persons. This boat came to the island side, four arquebus-shot from our ships, and there two of the people remaining, the third came along the shore side toward us, and we being then all within board, he walked up and down upon the point of

AN EARTHLY PARADISE

"It is a pleasant sight to see the people, sometimes wading, and going sometimes sailing in those rivers, which are shallow and not deep, free from all care of heaping up riches for their posterity," wrote Thomas Hariot in *A briefe and true report of the new found land of Virginia*. Actually, the scene he was describing was inside the Carolina Outer Banks. A dugout, heaped with shad, is being paddled by a Carolina Algonquin, while another is fishing with a net. In the background, two more are spearing fish. Visible are shad, sturgeon, catfish, hammerhead sharks, king crabs and hermit crabs (in conches). Left: fish-weir and trap. Top left: pelican and a brace of swans. Top right: nine ducks. This watercolor by White is thought by connoisseurs to be his finest. Courtesy of the Trustees of the British Museum. Copyright 1964.

the land next unto us. Then the master and the pilot of the Admiral, Simon Ferdinando, and the captain, Philip Amadas, myself and others rowed to the land, whose coming this fellow attended, never making any show of fear or doubt. And after he had spoken of many things not understood by us, we brought him, with his own good liking, aboard the ships, and gave him a shirt, a hat and some other things, and made him taste of our wine and our meat, which he liked very well. And after having viewed both barks, he departed and went to his own boat again, which he had left in a little cove or creek adjoining. As soon as he was two bow-shot into the water, he fell to fishing, and in less than half an hour he had laden his boat as deep as it could swim, with which he came again to the point of land, and there he divided his fish into two parts, pointing one part to the ship and the other to the pinnace; which, after he had (as much as he might) requited the former benefits received, departed out of our sight.

"The next day there came unto us divers boats, and in one of them the king's brother, accompanied with forty or fifty men, very handsome and goodly people, and in their behavior as mannerly and civil as any of Europe. His name was Granganimeo, and the king is called Wingina, the country Wingandacoa, and now by Her Majesty, Virginia. The manner of his coming was in this sort: He left his boats all together as the first man did a little from the ships by the shore, and came along to the place over against the ships, followed with forty men. When he came to the place his servants spread a long mat upon the ground on which he sat down, and at the other end of the mat four others of his company did the like; the rest of his men stood round about him, somewhat afar off. When we came to the shore to him with our weapons he never moved from his place, nor any of the other four, nor ever mistrusted any harm to be offered from us, but sitting still he beckoned us to come and sit by him, which we performed; and being set he made all signs of joy and welcome, striking on his head and his breast, and afterwards on ours, to show we were all one, smiling and making show the best he could of all love and familiarity. After he had made a long speech unto us, we presented him with divers things, which he received very joyfully and thankfully. None of the company durst speak one word all the time, only the four which were at the other end spake one in the other's ear very softly."

Wingina did not appear during the visit of the two barks; he was recovering from wounds received in battle with a neighboring tribe, and was said to be at a village six days' journey away. His brother was as jealous of his prerogatives as though he had been king himself.

"After we had presented this his brother with such things as we thought he liked, we likewise gave somewhat to the others that sat with him on the mat; but presently he arose and took all from them and put it into his own basket, making signs and tokens that all things ought to be delivered unto him, and the rest were but his servants and followers.

"A day or two after this we fell to trading with them, exchanging some things that we had for chamois, buff and deer skins. When we showed him all our packet of merchandise, of all things that he saw a bright tin dish most pleased him, which he presently took up and clapped it before his breast, and after made a hole in the brim thereof and hung it about his neck, making signs that it would defend him against his enemy's

OUTDOOR GRILL

Bluefish on rack, mackerel transfixed. "They stick up in the ground four stakes in a square . . . and lay four posts upon them, and others overthwart the same . . . . and laying their fish upon this hurdle, they make a fire underneath to broil the same . . . . And whenas the hurdle cannot hold all the fishes, they hang the rest by the fires on sticks set up in the ground against the fire." Text by Hariot. Drawing by White. Courtesy of the Trustees of the British Museum. Copyright 1964.

The broyling of their fish ouer the flame of fier.

DRESSED FOR THE KILL OR THE CATCH
A Carolina Indian in body paint. White's own note on the
drawing reads: "The manner of their attire and painting
themselues when they goe to their generall huntings, or at
theire solemne feasts." Courtesy of the Trustees of the
British Museum. Copyright 1964.

arrows: for those people maintain a deadly and terrible war
with the people and king adjoining. We exchanged our tin dish
for twenty skins worth twenty crowns or twenty nobles, and a
copper kettle for fifty skins worth fifty crowns [crown: 5 shillings; noble, obsolete: 6 shillings eightpence]. They offered us
good exchange for our hatchets and axes and for knives, and

would have given anything for swords, but we would not part with any."

Granganimeo was ready to swap a box full of pearls for armor and a sword: "but we refused it for this time because we would not make them know that we esteemed thereof until we had understood in what places of the country the pearl grew, which now Your Worship doth very well understand," as will the reader.

Barlowe continues:

"After two or three days the king's brother came aboard the ships and drank wine and ate of our meat and of our bread, and liked exceedingly thereof; and after a few days overpassed, he brought his wife with him to the ships, his daughter and two or three children. His wife was very well favored, of mean stature, and very bashful. She had on her back a long cloak of leather, with the fur side next to her body, and before her a piece of the same. About her forehead she had a band of white coral, and so had her husband many times [over]. In her ears she had bracelets of pearls hanging down to her middle (whereof we delivered Your Worship a little bracelet) and those were of the bigness of good peas. The rest of her women of the better sort had pendants of copper hanging in either ear, and some of the children of the king's brother and other noblemen have five or six in either ear; he himself had upon his head a broad plate of gold or copper, for being unpolished we knew not what metal it should be, neither would he by any means suffer us to take it off his head; but feeling it, it would bow [bend] very easily. His apparel was as his wife's, only the women wear their hair long on both sides, and the men but on one. They are of color yellowish, and their hair black for the most part, and yet we saw children that had very fine auburn and chestnut-colored hair."

(Barlowe refers later to a ship wrecked on the Carolina coast, "whereof some of the people were saved, and those were white people, whom the country people preserved.")

Trading went on for as long as the two barks remained, tin wares and gewgaws for skins and produce of the land, and some pearls. Granganimeo was

"very just of his promise, for many times we delivered him merchandise upon his word; but ever he came within the day and performed his promise. He sent us every day a brace or two of fat bucks, conies, hares, fish—the best of the world. He sent us divers kinds of fruits—melons, walnuts, cucumbers, gourds, peas—and divers roots and fruits very excellent good, and of their country corn, which is very white, fair and well tasted, and groweth three times in five months. In May they sow, in July they reap; in June they sow, in August they reap; in July they sow, in September they reap. They only cast the corn into the ground, breaking a little of the soft turf with a wooden mattock or pickaxe. Ourselves proved [tried] the soil, and put some of our peas in the ground, and in ten days they were of fourteen inches high. They have also beans very fair, of divers colors and wonderful plenty, some growing naturally, and some in their gardens; and so have they wheat and oats. The soil is the most plentiful, sweet, fruitful and wholesome of all the world."

INDIANS WITH CORN NIBLETS

"Their manner of feeding is in this wise. They lay a mat made of bents [reeds or rushes] on the ground and set their meat on the midst thereof, and then sit down around, the men upon one side, and the women on the other. Their meat is maize sodden . . . deer's flesh . . . and fish." In this drawing by White the meat [dish] appears to be corn niblets which have been boiled [sodden]. Text by Hariot. Courtesy of the Trustees of the British Museum. Copyright 1964.

One day, taking seven men with him in a ship's boat, Captain Barlowe explored another island about twenty miles off, at the confluence of Pamlico and Albemarle Sounds. At its northern end there was an Indian village of nine houses, built of cedar wood, with a palisade around it.

"The wife of Granganimeo, the king's brother, came running out to meet us very cheerfully and friendly; her husband was not then in the village. Some of her people she commanded to draw our boat on shore for the beating of the billow, others she appointed to carry us on their backs to the dry ground, and others to bring our oars into the house for fear of stealing. When we were come into the outer room, having five rooms in her house, she caused us to sit down by a great fire, and after took off our clothes and washed them and dried them again. Some of the women plucked off our stockings and washed them, some washed our feet in warm water, and she herself took great pains to see all things ordered in the best manner she could, making great haste to dress some meat for us to eat.

"After we had thus dried ourselves, she brought us into the inner room, where she set on the board standing along the house some wheat like frumenty [hulled wheat boiled in milk and sweetened with cinnamon or sugar]; sodden venison and roasted; fish, sodden, boiled and roasted; melons raw and sodden; roots of divers kind and divers fruits. Their drink is commonly water, but while the grape lasteth they drink wine, and for want of casks to keep it, all the year after they drink water, but it is sodden with ginger in it and black cinnamon, and sometimes sassafras and divers other wholesome and medicinable herbs and trees.

"We were entertained with all love and kindness, and with as much bounty (after their manner) as they could possibly devise. We found the people most gentle, loving, and faithful, void of all guile and treason, and such as live after the manner of the Golden Age. The people only care how to defend themselves from the cold in their short winter, and to feed themselves with such meat as the soil affordeth. Their meat is very well sodden and they make broth very sweet and savory. Their vessels are earthen pots, very large, white and sweet; their dishes are wooden platters of sweet timber. Within the place where they feed was their lodging, and within that their idol, which they worship, of whom they speak incredible things.

"While we were at meat, there came in at the gates two or

A chiefe Herowan

A ROANOKE CHIEF

The Carolina Algonquin word for chief is variously given as "herowan," "herowance" or "werowance." Hariot says the "cheefe men" of the island of Roanoke wear their hair "cut like a cock's comb." But it was allowed to grow long on one side, and this was trussed up in a knot. Plates of copper were much prized as ornament. "Moreover, they fold their arms together as they walk, or as they talk one with another in sign of wisdom." Drawn by White from life. Courtesy of the Trustees of the British Museum. Copyright 1964.

three men with their bows and arrows from hunting, whom when we espied, we began to look one towards another, and offered to reach our weapons; but as soon as she espied our mistrust, she was very much moved, and caused some of her men to run out and take away their bows and arrows and break them, and withal beat the poor fellows out of the gate again.

"When we departed in the evening and would not tarry all night she was very sorry, and gave us into our boat our supper half dressed, pots and all, and brought us to our boat side, in which we lay all night, removing the same a pretty distance from the shore. She, perceiving our jealousy [suspicion; also, vigilance], was much grieved, and sent divers men and thirty women to sit all night on the bankside by us, and sent us into our boat five mats to cover us from the rain, using very many words to entreat us to rest in their houses; but because we were few men, and if we had miscarried, the voyage had been in very great danger, we durst not adventure anything, although there was no cause of doubt, for a more kind and loving people there cannot be found in the world, as far as we have hitherto had trial."

Captain Barlowe thought this island "a most pleasant and fertile ground, replenished with goodly cedars, and divers other sweet woods, full of currants, of flax, and many other notable commodities." It was sixteen miles long, not far from the mainland, where flowed several great rivers, by one of which stood the town of Pomeiooc; while in another, which emptied into the first, "there is found great store of mussels in which there are pearls."

The island has since greatly diminished in size, as though the sea itself were striving to wash away that scene of earliest national mourning. Its name continues to dwell in the American consciousness like some undispelled grief.

It was Roanoke.

Granganimeo did not say his country was called Wingandacoa. He merely told the English captains, who had put on their finery, "You wear pretty clothes" or "What pretty clothes you are wearing," which is what "Wingandacoa" signifies in Algonquin. As for the name Virginia, it was in fact so designated by Elizabeth, perhaps at the suggestion of Raleigh, it being so fit a symbol of her maiden life, and he a courtier. The queen, overjoyed by the success of the exploratory voyage, promptly knighted him, which enabled him to discard his old seal and order a new one with this legend: *Propria insignia Walteri Raleigh, militis, Domini et Gubernatoris Virginiae* ("Seal of Walter Raleigh, knight, Lord and Governor of Virginia"). But still she kept him close.

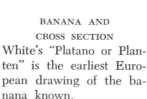

BANANA AND CROSS SECTION
White's "Platano or Planten" is the earliest European drawing of the banana known.

PINEAPPLE
"The Pyne frute," drawn by John White in the West Indies.

FLAMINGO
Bright pink in their natural habitat, flamingos lose their color in captivity.

FIREFLIES AND GADFLY
John White's renderings of "A flye which in the night semeth a flame of fyer" and "A dangerous byting flye." Phenomena observed—and felt—when voyagers paused in the West Indies for fresh water and other supplies. Courtesy of the Trustees of the British Museum. Copyright 1964.

IGUANA
"Some of thes are 3. fote in length, and lyue on land." Drawn by White during a stopover in the West Indies en route to "Virginia."

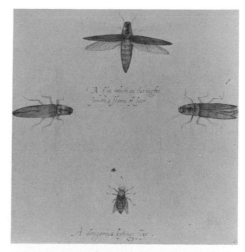

No time was lost in outfitting the new expedition, which was carried to Virginia on seven vessels. A Grenville kinsman had been with the first; the second was commanded by Sir Richard Grenville, Raleigh's cousin. Grenville's deputy—who became, in effect, the first royal governor of an English colony in America—was one Master Ralph Lane, who had been recalled from Ireland "in consideration of his ready undertaking the voyage to Virginia." He has been termed "a projecting man." He was a tough leader but a poor manager; and as a narrator, one with an indifferent style. With him were "two of the savages, being lusty men, whose names were Wanchese and Manteo," as Barlowe, who brought them to England, put it. He did not say whether they had come along willingly, but it is unlikely that they stowed away.

The expedition numbered some six hundred persons, including seamen, soldiers, settlers, and some specialists, Thomas Hariot, Raleigh's mathematical tutor, whose inventions gave algebra its modern form and who used a telescope as early as Galileo, went along to make a scientific survey; he afterward published *A brief and true report of the new found land of Virginia: of the commodities there found and to be raised, as well merchantable as others.*

John White was the artist of the expedition. By a coincidence, he appears to have been influenced by Jacques Le Moyne, the Huguenot artist who escaped from Fort Caroline and later was forced to flee from France to England after the Massacre of St. Bartholomew. Le Moyne was employed by Raleigh and knew Hakluyt, and had for patron Mary, Countess of Pembroke, the sister of Sir Philip Sidney.

Grenville's fleet left Plymouth April 9, 1585, reached the Canaries on the 14th, and steered for Puerto Rico where—as the log of the *Tiger*, Grenville's flagship, reveals—the English went ashore in May and built a fortified camp by the sea not far from St. German, which was occupied by Spaniards. Their object was to take on fresh water, buy provisions and build a pinnace. The English sent armed expeditions three miles inland to bring back timber, without meeting any resistance. They also marched to St. German to get the provisions promised by the Spaniards who "keeping their old customs for perjury and breach of promise came not."

On May 26 Lane went in a captured frigate to Roxo Bay "to fetch salt, being thither conducted by a Spanish pilot." Landing with twenty men, Lane entrenched himself, "compassing one of their salt hills within the trench." The Spaniards replied by sending troops of horsemen and foot soldiers, "who gave him the looking and gazing on, but darst not come nearer." The salt was brought back on

SIR RICHARD GRENVILLE
The renowned sea-fighter and naval commander "in the
29th year of his age." He died in combat with the Spaniards in the celebrated action off Flores in the Azores.
Painted by an unknown artist in 1571. Reproduced by
permission of the National Portrait Gallery, London.

the frigate. White made drawings of these exploits, and of the
banana and pineapple, tropical birds, fish, reptiles and insects, including the gadfly and fireflies.

There were other stopovers, in Hispaniola and the Bahamas. The
Carolina coast was sighted June 20, and Grenville records that "the
23rd, we were in great danger of wreck on a breach [nautical:
breaking of waves] called the Cape of Fear." After rounding the
cape, the *Tiger* ran aground on the Carolina Banks and her stores
were spoiled by sea water. The fleet finally came to anchor at
Wocokon on June 26, and the new pinnace reached Roanoke July 3.
The fateful decision was made to establish a fort and settlement at
its northwestern end. One hundred and seven men were put ashore
there.

Surveys of the coast and interior got under way July 11, when
Grenville, accompanied by White, Hariot and others, crossed Pamlico Sound and visited Pomeiooc, Aquascogoc and Secotan. At

Pomeiooc, White drew not only the village itself, but its inhabitants. One of the Indian children who posed for him is holding an Elizabethan doll (see illustration).

White also made a water-color map of Virginia from Cape Lookout to Chesapeake Bay; in this, he was assisted by the surveying and astronomical observations of Hariot, there being no other way to account for its accuracy; its beauty is apparent. The map has been praised as "the most careful detailed piece of cartography for any part of North America to be made in the sixteenth century" (D. B. Quinn, Professor of Modern History at the University of Liverpool). White also enlarged a map which Le Moyne had given Raleigh; it shows the Florida coastline extended to include Virginia. What it lacks as cartography is more than made up (for the non-explorer or -seafarer) by its pictorial value, it being embellished with exquisite drawings of ships, whales, dolphins and flying fish.

In addition to White, there were such specialists as a master of the victuals, keeper of the store, and various commanders, including one Captain Stafford, of whom Lane says: "I must truly report of him from the first to the last he was the gentleman that never spared labor or peril either by land or water, fair weather or foul, to perform any service committed unto him."

GRENVILLE'S SHIPS OFF THE NORTH CAROLINA COAST,
1585

The expedition under Lane probes Pamlico Sound in a pinnace (center) for a landing place; to the left, Roanoke. "The sea coasts of Virginia are full of islands, whereby the entrance into the mainland is hard to find" (Hariot, *A brief and true report*). Engraving by De Bry after a drawing by White, artist of the expedition. From De Bry's *Voyages*, Part I, Virginia. Courtesy of the Rare Book Division, The New York Public Library.

THE FIRST ENGLISH FORT ON ROANOKE, 1585–1586
Governor Ralph Lane's fort at the north end of
the island from the air. A reconstruction. Courtesy of the National Park Service.

Thus far, relations with the Indians appear to have been friendly.
Trading was carried on with copper as a medium of exchange. The
metal, being malleable, could be hammered into prized ornaments.
Grenville sailed to England on August 25, promising to return with
men and supplies by Easter, 1586. The fate of the colony was in the
hands of Lane, whose account of his stewardship "sent and directed
to Sir Walter Raleigh" on his return, begins bravely enough with
explorations made and planned:

"The uttermost place to the southward of any discovery was
Secotan, being by estimation fourscore miles distant from
Roanoke. The passage from thence was through a broad sound
within the main, the same being without kenning of land, and
yet full of flats and shoals. We had but one boat with four
oars to pass through the same, which boat could not carry
above fifteen men with their furniture, baggage and victual for
seven days at the most, and for our pinnace, besides that she
drew too deep water for that shallow sound, she would not stir
for an oar. For these and other reasons (winter also being at
hand) we thought good wholly to leave the discovery of those
parts until our stronger supply.

"To the northward our furthest discovery was to the Chesapians, distant from Roanoke about 130 miles. The passage to it
was very shallow and most dangerous, by reason of the breadth
of the sound, and the little succor that upon any flaw [squall]

was there to be had. But the territory and soil of the Chesapians (being distant fifteen miles from the shore) was—for pleasant-ness of seat, for temperature of climate, for fertility of soil and for the commodity of the sea, besides multitude of bears (being an excellent good victual), with great woods of sassafras and walnut trees—not to be excelled by any whatsoever."

Lane also explored to the northwest. He terms Chawanook

"the greatest province and seignory lying upon that river [the Chowan], and the very town itself is able to put 700 fighting men into the field, besides the force of the province itself. The king of the said province is called Menatonon, a man impotent in his limbs but otherwise, for a savage, a very grave and wise man, and of a very singular good discourse in matters concern-ing the state not only of his own country, and the disposition of his own men, but also of his neighbors round about him, as well far as near, and of the commodities that each country yieldeth."

POMEIOOC

A palisaded village. Engraving by De Bry from White, who spaced the poles out for a better view. (A) Temple. "They think that all the gods are of human shape, and therefore they represent them by images in the forms of men, which they call *Kewasowok;* one alone is called *Kewás.* Them they place in houses appropriate, or temples, which they call *Mathicómuck"* (Hariot). (B) Chief's long-house. (C) Fresh-water pond. There is a stand of corn outside the palisade (upper left). From the Rare Book Division, The New York Public Library.

Lane held onto him—"I had him prisoner with me, for two days."
This, no doubt, made Menatonon graver and called forth his wisdom. He told Lane what Lane wished to hear—where there were
pearls. It turned out to be "three days' journey in a canoe up his
river of Chawanook, and then descending to the land, you are
within four days' journey to pass overland northeast to a certain
king's country, whose province lieth upon the sea."

Lane next inquired about gold. Up the river of Moratoc [the
Roanoke] there was a mine, "so notorious amongst them, as not only
to the savages dwelling up the said river, and also to the savages of

A CAROLINA ALGONQUIN GIRL WITH ELIZABETHAN DOLL
This White drawing was made at Pomeiooc, and represents
the wife and daughter of a chief. The woman's face and
arms are "pounced" (tattooed), and she is wearing a
fringed deerskin skirt edged with beads. Her daughter has
on a girdle of deerskin, and is holding a fully clothed
Elizabethan doll; Hariot says the Indian children were
"greatly delighted with puppets and babes [dolls] which
were brought out of England." Courtesy of the Trustees of
the British Museum. Copyright 1964.

Chawanook, and all them to the westward, but [known] also to all
them of the main. The country's name is of fame, and is called
Chaunis Temoatan."

Old Menatonon was released "upon a ransom agreed for," perhaps
pearls, and his son Skiho was sent by pinnace to Roanoke, prisoner

in his stead. Lane and about forty men now set out to explore the river, taking Manteo, some other Indians, and two mastiffs: "but it fell out very contrary to all expectations, for after two days' travel, and our whole victual spent, lying on shore all night, we could never see man, only fires we might perceive made along the shore where we were to pass, and up into the country, until the last day." They made "dogges porredge"—the mastiffs boiled with sassafras leaves—and fought their way back.

By the spring of 1586 Lane had committed all the blunders of the earlier explorers and discoverers. Granganimeo was dead; in his place, on Roanoke, was his brother Wingina, plotting with Wanchese the overthrow of the English and the destruction of their settlement.

Wingina had given orders to his followers that

"they should not for any copper sell us any victuals whatsoever, besides, that in the night they should send to have our weirs robbed, and also cause them to be broken, and once being broken, never to be repaired again by them. By this means the king stood assured that I must be enforced by lack of sustenance there to disband my company into sundry places to live upon shellfish, for so the savages themselves do, going to Hatorask, Croatoan, and other places, fishing and hunting, while their grounds be in sowing and their corn growing: which failed not his expectation. For the famine grew so extreme among us, our weirs failing us of fish, that I was enforced to send Captain Stafford with 20 with him to Croatoan."

Other men were sent to Hatorask, and "also I sent every week 16 or 20 of the rest of the company to the main over against us, to live off cassava and oysters."

At this juncture, Wingina crossed over to Dasamonquepeio—Lane says for three reasons:

"The one to see his grounds there broken up, and sowed for a second crop. The other to withdraw himself from my daily sending to him for supply of victual for my company, for he was afraid to deny me anything, neither durst he in my presence but by color and with excuses, which I was content to accept for the time, meaning in the end, as I had reason, to give him the jump once for all."

The third was ominous: it was to send messages to other tribes for help.

On the night of May 31 Lane's mind was made up:

"I meant to give them in the island a *camisado* [surprise: from the white shirts worn by an attacking force in order to recognize friend from foe] and at the instant to seize upon all the canoes about the island to keep him from advertisements. But the town took the alarm before I meant it to them."

The next morning Lane went ashore at Dasamonquepeio with soldiers and friendly Indians, transported by gig and canoe. He wrote:

"The king did abide my coming to him, and finding myself amidst seven or eight of his principal weroances [or werowances: elders and chiefs] and followers (not regarding any of the common sort), I gave the watchword agreed upon, which was 'Christ our victory.'"

Wingina was killed by a shot from a cavalry pistol. A week later, on June 8, word reached Lane from Croatoan that twenty-three sails had been descried on the horizon; but whether of friends or foes was as yet unknown. The next day Stafford arrived with a letter from the fleet's commander offering Lane victuals, munitions, clothing—and barks, pinnaces and boats, together with men to man them.

The commander was El Draque—the Dragon, or devil himself—in real life a short, thickset man with a fresh complexion, trim beard, and bright, intelligent eyes: Sir Francis Drake.

The Spaniards had reason to call him that, for in addition to past injuries given, he had just completed a kind of Elizabethan tour of Spanish towns in the New World, bombarding, sacking and razing them. Together with spoils from the land he had taken prizes on the sea—Spanish ships, surrendered or overpowered; now, as the narrator in Hakluyt put it, "in his prosperous return from the sacking of Santo Domingo, Cartagena, and Saint Augustine [he] determined in his way homeward to visit his countrymen, the English colony then remaining in Virginia."

The fleet anchored off Hatorask on June 10; on the 11th Lane went aboard Drake's flagship and found him ready "to perform that which in writing and message he had most courteously offered, he having aforehand propounded the matter to all the captains of his fleet, and got their liking and consent thereto." A bark of 70 tons, called the *Francis*, was loaded with provisions for a hundred men for four months; in addition, Lane was given two pinnaces and four small boats. Drake also agreed to carry back with him "a number of weak and unfit men." Lane's plan was to stay on while the new provisions lasted, and if relief did not come from England, to return in the bark.

On June 13 "an unwonted storm" broke. It continued for four days and "had like to have driven all on shore," and drove some of the ships to sea, including the *Francis*. Drake offered another ship, together with a master and pilot; but Lane and his officers appear to have had enough, and elected to return with the fleet. Pinnaces were sent to the island to take the colonists off.

"The weather was so boisterous, and the pinnaces so often on ground, that the most of all we had, with all our cards [sea charts], books and writings were by the sailors cast overboard, the greater number of the fleet being much aggrieved with their long and dangerous abode in that miserable road."

Hakluyt says: "For fear they should be left behind they left all things confusedly, as if they had been chased from thence by a mighty army; and no doubt they were, for the hand of God came upon them for the cruelty and outrages committed by some of them against the native inhabitants of that country" (*The third voyage made by a ship sent in the year 1586, to the relief of the Colony planted in Virginia, at the sole charges of Sir Walter Raleigh*).

The ship sent by Raleigh was "freighted with all manner of things in most plentiful manner for the supply and relief of his colony then remaining in Virginia; but before they set sail from England it was after Easter."

Hakluyt wrote:

"Immediately after the departing of our English colony out of this paradise of the world, the ship above mentioned sent and set forth at the charges of Sir Walter Raleigh and his direction, arrived at Hatorask; who after some time spent in seeking our colony up in the country, and not finding them, returned with all the aforesaid provision into England.

"About fourteen or fifteen days after the departure of the aforesaid ship, Sir Richard Grenville, General of Virginia, accompanied with three ships well appointed for the same voyage, arrived there; who not finding the aforesaid ship according to his expectation, nor hearing any news of our English colony there seated, and left by him Anno 1585, himself traveling up into divers places of the country, as well to see if he could hear any news of the colony left there by him the year before under the charge of Master Lane, his deputy, as also to discover some places of the country; but after some time spent therein, not hearing any news of them, and finding the places which they inhabited desolate, yet unwilling to lose the possession of the country which Englishmen had so long held, after good deliberation he determined to leave some men behind to retain possession of the country; whereupon he landed fifteen men in the Isle of Roanoke, furnished plentifully with all manner of provision for two years, and so departed for England."

The theme of the search for the settlers was to have a melancholy reprise.

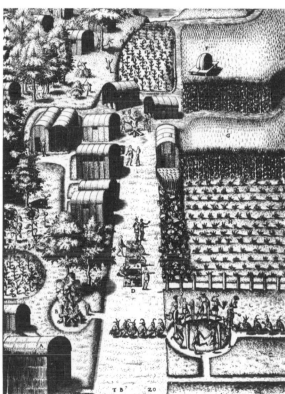

A PANORAMIC VIEW OF SECOTAN

From the drawing of White as engraved by De Bry. (A) Resting place of dead chiefs and elders. (B) Sacred fire for rituals. (3) Carved posts for ritual dances before a solemn feast. (D) Feasting place. (E) Tobacco plots (lower left and top center). (F) Platform and hut for watcher to scare off birds and beasts from ripe corn. (G) A later planting. (H) Another. The Carolina Algonquins planted three crops in the course of the year. (I) Pumpkins—alongside H ("I" is also "J" in Elizabethan English). (K) Another sacred fire. (L) Pamlico River. Upper left hand: "They have also groves wherein they take deer" (Hariot). From the Rare Book Division, The New York Public Library.

"In the year of our Lord 1587 Sir Walter Raleigh, intending to persevere in the planting of his Country of Virginia, prepared a new colony of one hundred and fifty men to be sent thither under the charge of John White, whom he appointed governor and also appointed unto him twelve assistants, unto whom he gave a charter, and incorporated them by the name of Governor and Assistants of the City of Raleigh in Virginia." Hakluyt, *The fourth voyage made to Virginia with three ships, in the year 1587. Wherein was transported the second Colony.*)

There were thirty-two incorporators of the new venture, of whom nineteen were London merchants. The ships were the *Lion,* a bark of 120 tons; a flyboat (Dutch: *vlieboot,* a fast-sailing vessel), and a pinnace. Not counting soldiers, among them the trusty Captain Stafford, and seamen, there were 89 men, 17 women, some unmarried, and 9 "boys and children." Among the married couples were White's son-in-law and daughter, Ananias and Elinor Dare, Dare being one of the "assistants." Under "savages that were in England and returned home into Virginia" we find Manteo once more, and Towaye; Manteo, and presumably Towaye, had sailed away with Drake. The master and pilot of the *Lion,* or admiral, was Simon Ferdinando, who behaved oddly.

White's instructions were to bring relief to the fifteen men left on Roanoke, then seek a new site for a colony on Chesapeake Bay. The three ships left Portsmouth April 26, 1587, reached Plymouth May 5, "and departed thence for Virginia" on the 8th. There were the usual stopovers in the West Indies; on June 22 "we came to anchor at an island called Santa Cruz, where all the planters were set on land, staying there till the 25th of the same month," which must have been a relief.

A battle of wills between Ferdinando and White makes strange reading.

Roxo Bay.

"At this place Ferdinando had promised we should take in salt, and had caused us before to make and provide as many sacks for that purpose as we could. The Governor also, for that he understood [knew] there was a town in the bottom of the bay, not far from the salt hills, appointed thirty shot [musketeers], ten pikes and ten targets to man the pinnace and to go aland for salt. Ferdinando perceiving them in a readiness, sent to the Governor, using great persuasions with him not to take in salt there, saying that he knew not well whether the same were the place or not; also, that if the pinnace went into the bay, she could not without great danger come back till the next day at night, and that if in the meantime any storm should rise, the admiral were in danger to be cast away.

"While he was thus persuading, he caused the lead to be cast, and having craftily brought the ship in three fathom and a half water, he suddenly began to swear and tear God in pieces, dissembling great danger, crying to him at the helm: 'Bear up hard! Bear up hard!' So we went off, and were disappointed of our salt by this means."

It was not the only instance; Ferdinando said there would be sheep on a certain island; as for the salt not fetched at Roxo Bay, there would be some at Caicos. White's comment on the latter: "It proved as true as finding of sheep."

More serious was the situation when the American coast was reached.

"The two and twentieth of July we arrived safe at Hatorask, where our ship and pinnace anchored. The Governor went aboard the pinnace accompanied by forty of his best men, intending to pass up to Roanoke forthwith, hoping there to find those fifteen Englishmen which Sir Richard Grenville had left there the year before; with whom he meant to have conference concerning the state of the country and savages, meaning after he had done so to return again to the fleet and pass along the coast to the Bay of Chesapeake where we intended to make our seat and fort, according to the charge given us, among other directions, in writing under the hand of Sir Walter Raleigh.

"But as soon as we were put with our pinnace from the ship, a gentleman by the means of Ferdinando, who was appointed to return for England, called to the sailors in the pinnace, charging them not to bring any of the planters back again, but to leave them in the island, except the Governor and two or three such as he approved, saying that the summer was far spent, and wherefore he would land all the planters in no other place. Unto this were all the sailors, both in the pinnace and ship, persuaded by the master; wherefore it booted not the Governor to contend with them, but passed to Roanoke."

At sunset that first day White went to the spot where the fifteen men had been left by Grenville, "but we found none of them nor any sign that they had been there, saving only we found the bones of one of those fifteen, which the savages had slain long before." It was too late to explore farther that night.

"The three and twentieth of July the Governor with divers of his company walked to the north end of the island where Master Ralph Lane had his fort, with sundry necessary and decent dwelling houses made by his men about it the year before, where we hoped to find some signs or certain knowledge of our fifteen men. When we came thither we found the fort razed down, but all the houses standing unhurt, saving that the nether rooms of them, and also of the fort, were overgrown with melons of divers sorts, and deer within them feeding on those melons; so we returned to our company, without hope of ever seeing any of the fifteen men living.

"The same day order was given that every man should be employed for the repairing of those houses which we found standing, and also to make other new cottages for such as should need."

This, however, was a temporary measure, for White fully intended to carry out Raleigh's wishes and move to the mainland some fifty miles farther up the coast.

On July 25 the flyboat, carrying the remaining colonists, "arrived all safe at Hatorask, to the great joy and comfort of the whole company." It had become separated from the admiral and pinnace; White blamed it on Ferdinando who, he says,

"purposely left them in the Bay of Portugal and stole away from them in the night, hoping that the master thereof, whose name was Edward Spicer, for that he had never been in Virginia, would hardly find the place, or else being left in so dangerous a place as that was, by means of so many men of war as at the time were abroad, they should surely be taken or slain. But God disappointed his wicked pretenses."

Ferdinando underestimated Spicer's talents. He had several. Nevertheless, the Spaniard had his will and his way: for the present, at least, the site of the colony was to be Roanoke once more, despite Raleigh's wishes or White's chagrin. That it was perilous for the English was shortly revealed:

"The eight and twentieth, George Howe, one of our twelve

Assistants, was slain by divers savages, which were come over
to Roanoke either of purpose to espy our company, and what
we were, or else to hunt deer whereof were many in the island.
These savages, being secretly hidden among high reeds, where
oftentimes they find the deer asleep and so kill them, espied
our man wading in the water alone, almost naked, without any
weapon save only a small forked stick, catching crabs therewithal, and also being strayed two miles from his company, and
shot at him in the water, where they gave him sixteen wounds
with their arrows."

TRIBAL INSIGNIA

Hariot labeled this engraving by De Bry "The marks of
sundry of the chief men of Virginia." These were
"raised on their backs"—that is, tattooed—"whereby it
may be known what Prince's subjects they be." *A* signified followers of Wingina, "the chief lord" of Roanoke.
B, Wingina's sister's husband. *C* and *D* "belong unto
divers chief lords in Secotan." *E, F* and *G* "are certain
chief men of Pomeiooc, and Aquascogoc." From the
folio of Hariot's *Virginia,* courtesy of the William and
Mary College Library, Williamsburg, Va.

He left a young son, likewise named George.
Two days later Captain Stafford landed on Croatoan with twenty
men; with him was Manteo, whose mother and kindred dwelt there,
and of whom

"we hoped to understand some news of our fifteen men, but
especially to learn the disposition of the people of the country
toward us, and to renew our old friendship with them.

"At our first landing they seemed as though they would fight with us, but perceiving us begin to march with our shot toward them, they turned their backs and fled. Then Manteo, their countryman, called to them in their own language whom, as soon as they heard, they returned and threw away their bows and arrows, and some of them came to us, embracing and entertaining us friendly, desiring us not to gather or spill any of their corn, for that they had but little."

Here, White learned that Howe had been killed by Wingina's men, and that Wanchese was with them. The fifteen Englishmen left at Roanoke the year before had been attacked by Indians from Secotan, Aquascogoc and Dasamonquepeio. White "thought to defer the revenge thereof no longer," and the night of August 8

"passed over the water, accompanied with Captain Stafford and twenty-four men, whereof Manteo was one, whom we took with us to be our guide to the place where those savages dwelt, where he behaved himself toward us as a most faithful Englishman.

"The next day, being the 9th of August, in the morning—so early that it was yet dark—we landed near the dwelling place of our enemies and very secretly conveyed ourselves through the woods to that side where we had their houses between us and the water. And having espied their fire, and some sitting about it, we presently set on them. The miserable souls, herewith amazed, fled into a place of thick reeds growing fast by, where our men perceiving them shot one of them through the body with a bullet, and therewith we entered the reeds, among which we hoped to acquit their evil doing towards us; but we were deceived, for those savages were our friends, and were come from Croatoan to gather the corn and fruit of that place because they understood our enemies were fled immediately after they had slain George Howe, and for haste had left all their corn, tobacco and pumpkins standing in such sort that all had been devoured of the birds and deer if it had not been gathered in time."

The narrative mentions two notable events that month:

"The 13th of August our savage Manteo, by the commandment of Sir Walter Raleigh, was christened in Roanoke, and called Lord thereof and of Dasamonquepeuk, in reward of his faithful services.

"The 18th Elinor, daughter to the Governor and wife to

Ananias Dare, one of the Assistants, was delivered of a daughter in Roanoke, and the same was christened there the Sunday following; and because this child was the first Christian born in Virginia, she was named Virginia."

Two of the assistants were to go back "as factors for the company," but all refused, and on August 22 not only they but the colonists as well, asked Governor White to go, "for the better and sooner obtaining of supplies and other necessaries." White went— going on board the flyboat, Edward Spicer, master, in haste at midnight, August 27; he had had enough of Ferdinando. His voyage was long, arduous, and unlucky; but he seems to have been unlucky for Spicer, too.

> "The ships weighed anchor and set sail for England. At this weighing their anchors, twelve of the men which were in the flyboat were thrown from the capstan which, by means of a bar breaking, came so fast about them that the other two bars thereof struck and hurt most of them so sore that some of them never recovered it; nevertheless, they essayed presently again to weigh their anchor, but being so weakened with the first fling, they were not able to weigh it, but were thrown down and hurt the second time.
> "Wherefore, having in all but fifteen men aboard, and most of them by this unfortunate beginning so bruised and hurt, they were forced to cut their cable and lose their anchor. Nevertheless, they kept company with the admiral until the seventeenth of September, at which time we fell with Corvo, and saw Flores."

Ferdinando's impatience to get to Roanoke and go no further, and haste back again without loss of time, now became clear: he had the ship, the guns and the men, and says White, he "meant not to make any haste for England but to linger about the Island of Terceira for purchase" [Middle English: hunt, seize, plunder—in this case, Spanish ships].

The flyboat proceeded alone; of its crew of fifteen, only five were fit for labor. When it reached Smerwick it was necessary for White to transfer to another vessel, which sailed from nearby Dingen a Cushe (now Dingle, County Kerry). He arrived in Southampton on November 8, almost three and a half months after setting out from Roanoke.

He could not have arrived at a worse time for himself and his cause—and, for that matter, for England. It was the eve of the signal year 1588. But busy as Raleigh was with preparations for the Armada he yet found time to receive White on November 20, and while White assembled some additional settlers, a squadron under Sir Richard Grenville prepared to sail for the relief of the colony. At this juncture, the Privy Council instructed Grenville to bring the larger ships to join Drake at Plymouth.

That left the smaller ships. These were two, the *Brave*, thirty tons, and the *Roe*, which sailed from Bideford on April 22, White aboard the former, Arthur Facy, captain. Captain Facy could not resist the national pastime at sea—he pursued and robbed other ships; but taking on a Frenchman he overreached himself, and was shot up and overpowered. White himself was wounded twice in the head, once by the blow of a sword, the other with a pike; "and hurt also in the side of the buttock with a shot." Some of the settlers he was taking with him were also wounded, and their furnishings and stores looted. The *Brave* limped back into Bideford on May 22. The *Roe* turned up soon after. By now, of course, the Armada had left the Tagus; by the end of the month it was approaching Finisterre.

ELIZABETH PRAISED
Dux femina facti—"The leader of the deed was a woman."
The leader: Elizabeth. The deed: defeat of the Armada.
Detail from frontispiece to *Purchas his Pilgrims*.

Of the ships that took part in the fighting that year two may be mentioned: the swift, well-equipped bark, *Raleigh*, was now the *Ark Royal*, flagship of Charles, Lord Howard of Effingham, the Lord Admiral; and the *Margaret and Rose*, 200 tons, owned by one John Watts, merchant of London, afterward its Lord Mayor. Both were in an action at Calais, when the great galleass *San Juan de Sicilia* was driven ashore. Lord Howard told some of his officers to take the longboat "and have their pillage of her." The same idea occurred to Master Watts, who raced shoreward in his own longboat, or pinnace.

Watts was patriotic—as seen here, brave or bold; but he was also a high-handed, tough-minded merchant, or businessman, first.

It was not until 1590 that John White was able to return to Virginia. He told Richard Hakluyt in a letter:

"I was by the owner and commanders of the ships denied to have any passengers, or anything else transported in any of the said ships, saving only myself and my chest; no, not so much as a boy to attend upon me, although I made great suit and earnest entreaty as well to the chief commanders as to the owner of the said ships. Which cross and unkind dealing, although it very much discontented me, notwithstanding, the scarcity of time was such that I could have no opportunity to go unto Sir Walter Raleigh with complaint, for the ships being then all in readiness to go to the sea, would have been departed before I could have made my return."

The owner was John Watts. The ships were the *Hopewell, John the Evangelist,* and *Little John,* which set out from Plymouth on March 20, 1590. Off the Canaries they "gave chase to a double fly-boat, the which we also the same day fought with, and took her, with loss of three of their men slain and one hurt," which suggests the nature of Watts' enterprise. So does the following: "The 2nd of May our admiral and our pinnace departed from Dominica, leaving the *John,* our vice-admiral, playing off and on about Dominica, hoping to take some Spaniard outward bound to the Indies." On May 7, at night, "we took a frigate of ten ton coming from Gwathanelo [Guatemala]." More ships were taken: one of them "proved not so rich a prize as we hoped for, for that a French man-of-war had taken and spoiled her before we came." There were also sea fights.

"The second of July Edward Spicer, whom we left in England, came to us at Cape Tiburon [Haiti], accompanied with a small pinnace whereof one Master Harps was captain." Spicer was in command of a ship named *Moonlight* which, together with the *Hopewell* and the other ships, created havoc among Spanish shipping. Captain Harps took two small frigates, which shows he had joined the right company. The *Hopewell,* Captain Abraham Cooke, and the *Moonlight* proceeded to Virginia, coming to anchor off Hatorask on August 15.

"At our first coming to anchor on this shore we saw a great smoke rise in the Isle Roanoke near the place where I left our colony in the year 1587, which smoke put us in good hope that some of the colony were there, expecting my return out of England.

"The 16th and next morning our two boats went ashore, and Captain Cooke and Captain Spicer and their company with me, with intent to pass to the place at Roanoke where our countrymen were left. At our putting from the ship we commanded our master gunner to make ready two minions and a falcon [pieces of ordnance] well loaden, and to shoot them off with reasonable space between every shot, to the end that their reports might be heard to the place where we hoped to find some of our people."

But now they saw another smoke, which was either a signal or a lure:

"we therefore thought good to go to that second smoke first, but it was much further from the harbor where we landed than we supposed it to be, so that we were very sore tired before we came to the smoke. But that which grieved us more was that when we came to the smoke, we found no man nor sign that any had been there lately, nor yet any fresh water in all this way to drink. Being thus wearied with this journey we returned to the harbor where we left our boats."

The next day, while attempting to pass the breach, Spicer's boat overturned; of the eleven men in it, seven drowned, including Spicer. The others were saved by the men in Cooke's boat. It was all Cooke and White could do to persuade the remaining seamen to continue the search. Perhaps nothing in the story of discovery can match the poignancy of the scene in the darkness off Roanoke as White related it:

"We let fall our grapnel near the shore and sounded with a trumpet a call, and afterwards many familiar English tunes of songs, and called to them friendly; but we had no answer."

The colonists were never found.

It was Hakluyt who asked White to write the account of his last voyage, and with this, and his covering letter, dated from Newtown, County Cork, February 4, 1593, he fades from men's sight. His memorial is the art he has left us, depicting the Carolina Algonquins of the sixteenth century, together with their homes, their crafts and vanished way of life, and the flora and fauna of "Virginia."

Raleigh's Virginia, like de Soto's Florida, was an elastic land, stretching whithersoever its explorers went. They went next to New England, as revealed by *A Brief and True Relation of the Discovery of the North Part of Virginia, being a most pleasant, fruitful and commodious soil. Made this present year 1602, by Captain Bartholomew Gosnold, Captain Bartholomew Gilbert, and divers other gentlemen their associates, by the permission of the honorable knight, Sir Walter Raleigh, etc.* What the "etc." stood for is set forth in the dedication: "To the honorable Sir Walter Raleigh, knight, Captain of Her Majesty's Guards, Lord Warden of the Stanneries, Lieutenant of Cornwall and Governor of the Isle of Jersey." The author was John Brereton, "one of the voyage." Bartholomew Gilbert was the son of Sir Humphrey Gilbert.

The voyage was made in the bark *Concord*, which sailed from Falmouth with thirty-two passengers on March 26, 1602, "holding a course for the north part of Virginia"—that is, straight across the Atlantic without resort to Newfoundland or the West Indies. It made a landfall May 14 north of Massachusetts Bay: "the land somewhat low, certain hummocks or hills lying into the land, the shore full of white sand, but very stony or rocky."

Another member of the voyage says that the place where the landfall was made "we called Savage Rock, because the savages first showed themselves there." At noon that day, as the bark rode at anchor offshore, a Biscayan shallop (open boat with mast and sail) approached. Brereton says it had "an iron grapple," and that its crew "came boldly aboard us," one carrying a copper kettle. The crewmen—there were six—were Indians, "one of them apparelled with a waistcoat and breeches of black serge, made after our sea-fashion, hose and shoes on his feet; all the rest (saving one that had a pair of breeches of blue cloth) were all naked." Some of them knew French words, chiefly Newfoundland place names.

How the Indians got hold of this particular shallop made the Englishmen thoughtful. So did their appearance: "These people are of tall stature, broad and grim visage, of a black swart complexion, their eyebrows painted white. Their weapons are bows and arrows." The *Concord* parted company three hours later.

"Standing southerly off into sea the rest of that day and the night following with a fresh gale of wind, in the morning we found ourselves embayed with a mighty headland."

Captain Gosnold, Brereton and three others went ashore.

"And marching all that afternoon with our muskets on our necks on the highest hills which we saw (the weather was very hot), at length we perceived this headland to be a parcel of the main, and sundry islands lying almost round about it."

Returning, they found that

"in five or six hours' absence we had pestered our ship so with cod fish that we threw numbers of them overboard again. And surely I am persuaded that in the months of March, April and May there is upon this coast better fishing and in as great plenty as in Newfoundland. For the schools of mackerel, herrings, cod and other fish that we daily saw as we went and came from the shore were wonderful; and besides, the places where we took these cods (and might in a few days have laden our ship) were but in seven fathom water and within less than a league of the shore, where in Newfoundland they fish in forty or fifty fathom water and far off."

They called it "Cape Cod."

"From this place we sailed round about this headland almost all the points of the compass, the shore very bold; but as no coast is free from dangers, so I am persuaded this is as free as any, the land somewhat low, full of goodly woods, but in some places plain.

"At length we were come amongst many fair islands, which we had partly discerned at our first landing, all lying within a league or two one of another, and the outermost not above six or seven leagues from the main. But coming to an anchor under one of them [marginal note: "The first island called Martha's Vineyard"], which was about three or four leagues from the main, Captain Gosnold, myself, and some others, went ashore, and going round about it we found it to be four English miles in compass, without house or inhabitant, saving a little old house made of boughs, covered with bark; an old piece of a weir of the Indians to catch fish, and one or two places where they had made fires.

"The chiefest trees of the island are beeches and cedars, the outward parts all overgrown with low, bushy trees three or four feet in height which bear some kinds of fruits, as appeared by their blossoms; strawberries, red and white, as sweet and much bigger than ours in England; raspberries, gooseberries, hurtleberries [whortleberries: the bilberry, or something American resembling it], and such; an incredible store of vines, as well in the woody part of the island where they run upon every tree as on the outward parts, that we could not go for treading upon them. Also, many springs of excellent sweet water, and a great standing lake of fresh water near the sea side an English mile in compass, which is maintained with the springs running exceeding pleasantly through the woody grounds, which are very rocky.

"Here are also in this island great store of deer, which we saw, and other beasts, as appeared by their tracks; as also divers fowls, as cranes, hernshaws, bitterns, geese, mallards, teals and other fowls in great plenty. Also, great stores of peas, which grow in certain plots all the island over."

On another island "to the northward" they saw Indians—

"tall, big-boned men, all naked, saving they cover their privy parts with a black, thewed skin much like a blacksmith's apron tied about their middle and between their legs behind. They gave us their fish ready boiled (which they carried in a basket made of twigs, not unlike our osier), whereof we did eat and judged them to be freshwater fish; they gave us also of their tobacco, which they drink [suck] green, but dried into powder, very strong and pleasant, and much better than any I have tasted in England. The necks of their pipes are made of clay hard dried (whereof in that island is great store both red and white); the other part is a piece of hollow copper, very finely closed and cemented together."

The English gave them knives and trinkets.

The next island explored may have been Cuttyhunk, which Gosnold named Elizabeth's Island. Brereton says it was "within a league or two of the main" and sixteen English miles in compass, but perhaps there was no strait between it and the next island to the north as there is now, and in fact he says: "it containeth many pieces or necks of land which differ nothing from several islands, saving that certain banks of small breadth do, like bridges, join them to this island." .

It seemed like a good place for a colony, and the *Concord* lingered.

"In mid-May we did sow in this island (as for trial) in sundry places wheat, barley, oats and peas, which in fourteen days were sprung up nine inches and more. The soil is fat and lusty, the upper crust of gray color; but a foot or less in depth, of the color of our hemplands in England; and being this apt for these and the like grains. The sowing or setting (after the ground is cleansed) is no greater labor than if you should set or sow in one of our best prepared gardens in England."

The paradise unfolds:

"This island is full of high timbered oaks, their leaves thrice so broad as ours; cedars, straight and tall; beech, elm, holly; walnut trees in abundance, the fruit as big as ours, as appeared by those we found under the trees which had lain all the year ungathered; hazelnut trees, cherry trees (the leaf, bark and big-ness not differing from ours in England, but the stalk beareth the blossoms or fruit at the end like a cluster of grapes, forty or fifty in a bunch); sassafras trees plenty all the island over, a tree of high price and profit; also divers other fruit trees, some of them with strange barks of an orange color, in feeling, soft and smooth like velvet. In the thickest part of the woods you may see a furlong or more round about.

"On the northwest side of this island, near to the sea side, is a standing lake of fresh water, almost three English miles in compass, in the middest whereof stands a plot of woody ground an acre in quantity, or not above. This lake is full of small tor-toises, and exceedingly frequented with all sorts of fowls, be-fore rehearsed, which breed some low on the banks, and others on low trees about this lake in great abundance, whose young ones of all sorts we took and ate at our pleasure; but all these fowls are much bigger than ours in England.

"Also, in every island, and almost in every part of every island, are great store of ground nuts, forty together on a string, some of them as big as hens' eggs; they grow not two inches

underground, the which nuts we found to be as good as pota-
toes. Also, divers sorts of shellfish, as scallops, mussels, cockles,
lobsters, crabs, oysters and whelks, exceeding good and very
great."

But Elizabeth's Island (Cuttyhunk) was as nothing compared to
the mainland:

"We went in our light horseman [gig] from this island to the
main, right against this island some two leagues off, where
coming ashore we stood a while like men ravished at the beauty
and delicacy of this sweet soil. For besides divers clear lakes of
fresh water (whereof we saw no end), meadows very large and
full of green grass [here, Brereton not only lost his senses, but
his syntax]; even the most woody places (I speak only of such
as I saw) do grow so distinct and apart, one tree from another,
upon green grassy ground, somewhat higher than the plains,
as if Nature would show herself above her power, artificial.

"Hard by, we espied seven Indians, and coming up to them,
at first they expressed some fear; but being emboldened by our
courteous usage, and some trifles which we gave them, they
followed us to a neck of land which we imagined had been
severed from the main, but finding it otherwise, we perceived
a broad harbor or river's mouth which ran up into the main.
But because the day was far spent we were forced to return to
the island from whence we came, leaving the discovery of this
harbor for a time of better leisure. Of the goodness of which
harbor, as also of many others thereabouts, there is small doubt,
considering that all the islands, as also the main (where we
were) is all rocky grounds and broken lands.

"Now the next day we determined to fortify ourselves in the
little plot of ground in the midst of the lake above mentioned,
where we built an house and covered it with sedge, which grew
about this lake in great abundance; in building whereof we
spent three weeks and more. But the second day after our coming from the main we espied nine canoes or boats with fifty
Indians in them coming towards us from this part of the main
where we, two days before, landed; and being loath they should
discover our fortification, we went out on the sea side to meet
them, and coming somewhat near them they all sat down upon
the stones, calling aloud to us (as we rightly guessed) to do the
like a little distance from them.

"Having sat a while in this order, Captain Gosnold willed me
to go unto them to see what countenance they would make, but

as soon as I came up unto them, one of them, to whom I had
given a knife two days before in the main, knew me (whom I
also very well remembered) and, smiling upon me, spake somewhat unto their lord or captain, which sat in the midst of them;
who presently rose up and took a large beaver skin from one
that stood about him and gave it unto me, which I requited for
that time the best I could. But I, pointing towards Captain
Gosnold, made signs unto him that he was our captain and
desirous to be his friend and enter league with him, which (as
I perceived) he understood and made signs of joy. Whereupon
Captain Gosnold with the rest of his company, being twenty
in all, came up unto them; and after many signs of gratulations,
Captain Gosnold presenting their lord with certain trifles which
they wondered at and highly esteemed, we became very great
friends and sent for meat aboard our shallop and gave them
such meats as we had then ready dressed, whereof they mis-
liked nothing but our mustard whereat they made many a
sour face.

"While we were thus merry, one of them had conveyed a
target of ours into one of their canoes, which we suffered only
to try whether they were in subjection to this lord, to whom
we made signs (by showing him another of the same likeness
and pointing to the canoe) what one of his company had done;
who suddenly expressed some fear, and speaking angrily to one
about him (as we perceived by his countenance) caused it
presently to be brought back again.

"So the rest of the day we spent in trading with them for furs,
which are beavers, lucernes [lynx], martens, otters, wildcat
skins, very large and deep fur, black foxes, cony skins of the
color of our hares but somewhat less, deerskins very large,
sealskins, and other beasts' skins to us unknown."

In addition to furs, there was "great store of copper, some very
red, and some of a paler color; none of them but have chains, earrings or collars of this metal." Asked where the copper came from,
one of the Indians "made a hole with his finger in the ground, and
withal, pointed to the main from whence they came." Another of
their ornaments was "beards of the hair of beasts." A red-bearded
sailor was offered one for his "which, because it was of a red color,
they judged to be none of his own."
These Indians did not make fire by rubbing sticks together.

"They strike fire in this manner: everyone carrieth about him
a purse of thewed leather, a mineral stone (which I take to be

their copper), and with a flat emery stone (wherewith glaziers cut glass and cutlers glaze blades) tied fast to the end of a little stick, gently he striketh upon the mineral stone, and within a stroke or two a spark falleth upon a piece of touchwood (much like our sponge in England) and with the least spark he maketh a fire presently."

Brereton describes them as "exceeding courteous, gentle of disposition, and well conditioned, excelling all others that we have seen." In addition: "for shape of body and lovely favor, I think they excel all the people of America; of stature much higher than we, of complexion or color much like a dark olive, their eyebrows and hair black, which they wear long, tied up behind in knots whereon they prick feathers of fowls in fashion of a coronet."

They appear to have had a good ear for foreign speech.

"One of them one day sitting by me, upon occasion I spake smiling to him these words—

" 'How now, sirrah, are you so saucy with my tobacco?'—which words, without any further repetition, he suddenly spake so plain and distinctly as if he had been a long scholar in the language. Many other such trials we had, which are here needless to repeat."

In all the time they were there the English saw only three Indian women: "low of stature, their eyebrows, hair, apparel and manner of wearing like to the men; fat, and very well favored, and much delighted in our company." The Indians remained on the island three days, retiring each night to the farthest end to sleep, and on the fourth left in their canoes, six or seven remaining behind.

"Being in their canoes a little from the shore they made huge cries and shouts of joy unto us; and we with our trumpet and cornet, and casting up our caps into the air, made them the best farewell we could."

Those who remained helped the Englishmen cut and carry sassafras bark, a sovereign remedy for all ills. It was first planned to leave some men behind and use the fort as a trading post; but there were dissensions. Another "gentleman of the said voyage," one Gabriel Archer, afterward reported:

"The eighth [of June] we divided the victuals, *viz.*, the ship's store for England, and that of the planters, which by Captain Gilbert's allowance could be but six weeks for six months; whereby there fell out a controversy, the rather for that some seemed secretly to understand of a purpose Captain Gilbert had not to return with supply of the issue those goods should make, by him to be carried home."

All, therefore, returned. The *Concord* weighed anchor on Friday, June 18, and reached Exmouth Friday, July 23 ("in all, bare five weeks," as Brereton exultantly put it). The huge amount of sassafras bark put on the market caused the price to drop from twenty shillings a pound to a little over three. Raleigh investigated, knowing where sassafras came from, and having the monopoly. And this was how he learned of the voyage of Gosnold and Gilbert, which had not been made with his permission, the title and dedication of *A Brief and True Relation* notwithstanding, they being a means of placating him. The expedition had been sent, instead, by some high personages, among them the Earl of Southampton.

The sassafras brought back by Gosnold and Gilbert was pounded into powder and taken in water, enlivening the spirits of many, and in particular of those who sold it. The next voyage to northern Virginia (that is, New England) "set out from the City of Bristol at the charge of the chiefest merchants and inhabitants of the said city" to get more of the same. This time the adventurers (backers) had Raleigh's permission.

There were two ships, the *Speedwell* and the *Discoverer*. Contrary winds kept them at Milford Haven, during which time the news reached them of the death of Queen Elizabeth. The "master and chief commander" was Martin Pring, a Devonshire man—young man, really; he was only twenty-three. In addition to the usual arsenal there were two mastiffs named Fool and Gallant; one of them had been trained to carry a half-pike in his mouth.

The ships left Milford Haven April 10, 1603. Landfall in June was "a multitude of small islands" east of Penobscot Bay, Maine. The expedition having set out at the behest of merchants, merchantable items are quickly specified in the narrative (authorship unknown, though ascribed to Pring by Samuel Purchas, who continued Hakluyt's work under the title *Pilgrims*):

> "Here we found an excellent fishing for cod, which are better than those of Newfoundland, and withal we saw good and rocky ground fit to dry them upon. Also, we see no reason to the contrary but that salt may be made in these parts, a matter of no small importance.

KING JAMES I
Successor to Elizabeth, 1603. Saw Virginia colonized, 1607.
Painted by David Mytens, 1621. Reproduced by permission
of the National Portrait Gallery, London.

"We sailed to the southwest end of these islands, and there
rode with our ships under one of the greatest [perhaps North
Haven or Vinalhaven]. One of them we named Fox Island, because we found those kinds of beasts thereon."

Taking the ships' boats, Pring and a party rowed to the mainland, "which lieth for a good space northeast and southwest." Four

inlets were explored, which may have been those of the Saco, Kennebunk, York and Piscataqua rivers. The Englishmen went up one of these for a distance of about five miles, and up another "ten or twelve."

"In all these places we found no people, but signs of fires where they had been. Howbeit, we beheld very goodly groves and woods replenished with tall oaks, beeches, pine trees, fir trees, hazels, witch hazels and maples. We saw here also sundry sorts of beasts, as stags, deer, bears, wolves, foxes, lucernes, and dogs with sharp noses. But meeting with no sassafras, we left these places with all the aforesaid islands, shaping our course for Savage Rock discovered the year before by Captain Gosnold, where going upon the main we found people, with whom we had no long conversation, because here also we could find no sassafras.

"Departing hence, we bore into that great gulf which Captain Gosnold overshot the year before, coasting and finding people on the north side thereof. Not yet satisfied in our expectation, we left them and sailed over and came to an anchor on the south side in the latitude of 41 degrees and odd minute, where we went on land in a certain bay, which we called Whitson Bay by the name of the Worshipful Master John Whitson, then Mayor of the City of Bristol, and one of the chief adventurers, and finding a pleasant hill thereunto adjoining, we called it Mount Aldworth for Master Robert Aldworth's sake, a chief furtherer of the voyage, as well with his purse as with his travail. Here we had sufficient quantity of sassafras."

Various conjectures have been made about this spot; perhaps it was Plymouth Harbor.

"At our going on shore, upon view of the people and sight of the place, we thought it convenient to make a small barricade to keep diligent watch and ward in, for the advertisement and succor of our men, while they should work in the woods. During our abode on shore the people of the country came to our men, sometimes ten, twenty, forty or threescore, and at one time one hundred and twenty at once. We used them kindly, and gave them divers sorts of our meanest [cheapest] merchandise. They did eat peas and beans with our men. Their own victuals were most of fish.

"We had a youth in our company that could play upon a gittern [early form of guitar], in whose homely music they took great delight, and would give him many things, as tobacco, tobacco pipes, snakes' skins of six foot long, which they use for girdles, fawns' skins, and such like, and danced twenty in a ring, and the gittern in the middest of them, using many savage gestures, singing 'Lo, la, lo, la, la, lo.' Him that first broke the ring the rest would knock and cry out upon."

By July 31 the *Discoverer* held as much sassafras as could be conveniently transported and was sent back, "to give some speedy contentment to the adventurers." The men left behind with Pring bestirred themselves to follow.

"On a day about noontide, while our men which used to cut down sassafras in the woods were asleep, as they used to do for two hours in the heat of the day, there came down about seven score savages armed with their bows and arrows, and environed our house or barricade, wherein were four of our men alone with their muskets to keep sentinel, whom they sought to have come down unto them, which they utterly refused and stood upon their guard.

"Our master likewise being very careful and circumspect, having not past two with him in the ship, put the same in the best defense he could, lest they should have invaded the same, and caused a piece of great ordnance to be shot off, to give terror to the Indians and warning to our men which were fast asleep in the woods; at the noise of which piece they were a little awaked and began to call for Fool and Gallant, their great and fearful mastiffs, and full quietly laid themselves down again. But being quickened up eftsoons again with a second shot, they roused up themselves, betook them to their weapons, and with their mastiffs, great Fool with an half-pike in his mouth, drew down to their ship; whom, when the Indians beheld afar off, with the mastiff which they most feared, in dissembling manner they turned all to a jest and sport, and departed away in friendly manner.

"Yet not long after, even the day before our departure, they set fire on the woods where we wrought, which we did behold to burn for a mile space. And the very same day that we weighed anchor they came down to the shore in greater number—to wit, very near two hundred by our estimation, and some of them came in their boats to our ship and would have had us come in again. But we sent them back, and would none of their entertainment."

The *Speedwell* arrived on the Severn October 3, two weeks after the *Discoverer*. Pring brought back, in addition to the shiploads of sassafras, one of the Indians' canoes, which provided a sensation.

"Their boats, whereof we brought one to Bristol, were in proportion like a wherry of the River Thames, seventeen feet long and four foot broad, and made of the bark of a birch tree, far exceeding in bigness those of England. It was sewed together with strong and tough osiers or twigs, and the seams covered over with rosin or turpentine little inferior in sweetness to frankincense, as we made trial by burning a little thereof on the coals at sundry times after our coming home. It was also open like a wherry and sharp at both ends, saving that the beak was a little bending roundly upward. And though it carried nine men standing upright, yet it weighed not at the most above sixty pounds in weight, a thing almost incredible in regard of the largeness and capacity thereof. Their oars were flat at the end like an oven peel [baker's shovel], made of ash or maple very light and strong, about two yards long, wherewith they row very swiftly."

The next to come took two canoes and five of the six Indians who were in them, but set up a cross before leaving. He was George Waymouth, another Devonshire mariner, who was sweeping through northern waters in search of the nonexistent northwest passage when Gosnold was off New England. Three years later, backed by the Protestant Earl of Southampton and the Catholic Thomas Arundell, first Lord Arundell of Wardour, he essayed lower latitudes, Monhegan his landfall. On adjoining Allen's Island was found an excellent harbor, where Waymouth's ship, *Archangel,* anchored: "a most safe berth, defended from all winds, in an excellent depth of water for ships of any burden." Waymouth named it Pentecost Harbor, "we arriving there that day out of our last harbor in England, from whence we set sail upon Easter Day" [1605].

A survey of the islands resulted in the following observations:

"All along the shore, and some space within, where the wood hindereth not, grow plentifully raspberries, gooseberries, strawberries, roses, currants, wild vines, angelica [aromatic plant used in cooking and medicine].

"Within the islands grow wood of sundry sorts, some very great, and all tall: birch, beech, ash, maple, spruce, cherry tree, yew, oak, very great and good, fir tree, out of which issueth turpentine in so marvelous plenty, and so sweet, as our surgeon and others affirmed they never saw so good in England. We pulled off much gum congealed on the outside of the bark, which smelled like frankincense. This would be a great benefit for making tar and pitch."

They also found "abundance of great mussels among the rocks, and in some of them many small pearls. And in one mussel (which we drew up in our net) was found fourteen pearls whereof one of pretty bigness and orient; in another, above fifty small pearls." Another American paradise.

"We stayed the longer in this place, not only because of our good harbor (which is an excellent comfort) but because every day we did more and more discover the pleasant fruitfulness; insomuch as many of our company wished themselves settled here, not expecting any further hopes or better discovery to be made."

But Waymouth had other plans. He had brought on the *Archangel* the parts of a shallop or pinnace, and these were now fitted together for closer inspection of the mainland. On May 29 a cross was erected "on the shore side" of Allen's Island, which was practical as well as pious, and the next day Waymouth and thirteen armed men set out for the Maine coast, leaving fifteen behind to man the ship (James Rosier, the narrator, says fourteen; but as the expedition consisted of twenty-nine persons he, too, must be included since he stayed on board).

The departure of the shallop with half of the crew was observed, and Indians made their appearance on a nearby island.

"They sent one canoe with three men, one of which, when they came near unto us, spoke in his language very loud and very boldly, seeming as though he would know why we were there, and by pointing with his oar toward the sea, we conjectured he meant we should be gone.

"But when we showed them knives and their use—by cutting of sticks—and other trifles, as combs and glasses, they came close aboard our ship as desirous to entertain our friendship. To these we gave such things as we perceived they liked when we showed them the use: bracelets, rings, peacock feathers, which they stuck in their hair, and tobacco pipes."

By the time the shallop returned, on the night of the 31st, friendly relations had been established.

"Our captain had in this small time discovered up a great river, trending along the main about forty miles"—the St. George's, which the Indians called Tahanock; later, Waymouth sailed up it for sixty miles. It was a beautiful river, and a useful one: "subject by shipping to bring in all traffics of merchandise, a benefit always accounted the richest treasury to any land, for which cause our Thames hath that due denomination." Some of the sailors had seen the Orinoco: they "gave reasons why it was not to be compared with this." Others had been in the West Indies, France, Wales: their rivers were "inferior to this."

Meanwhile, trade with the natives, now eager for more of the white man's baubles, was brisk and profitable. Rosier wrote:

> "The next day, being Saturday and the first of June, I traded with the savages all the forenoon upon the shore, where were eight and twenty of them, and because our ship rode nigh, we were but five or six; where for knives, glasses [mirrors], combs and other trifles to the value of four or five shillings, we had forty good beavers' skins, otters' skins, sables and other small skins, which we knew not how to call. Our trade being ended, many of them came aboard us and did eat by our fire, and would be very merry and bold, in regard of our kind usage of them."

The kind usage was repaid:

> "When we came on shore they gave us the best welcome they could, spreading fallow deer's skins for us to sit on the ground by their fire, and gave us of their tobacco in our pipes, which was excellent, and so generally commended of us all to be as good as any we ever took, being the simple leaf without any composition, strong and of sweet taste. They gave us some to carry to our Captain."

Nevertheless, suspicion between the red man and the white man grew, and Rosier remarks:

> "We began to join them in the rank of other savages, who have been by travelers in most discoveries found very treacherous, never attempting mischief until by some remissness fit opportunity affordeth them certain ability to execute the same. Wherefore, after good advice taken, we determined so soon as we could to take some of them, lest (being suspicious we had discovered their plots) they should absent themselves from us.
>
> "Tuesday, the fourth of June, our men took cod and haddock with hooks by our ship's side, and lobsters, very great, which before we had not tried.

"About eight o'clock this day we went on shore with our boats to fetch aboard water and wood, our Captain leaving word with the gunner in the ship, by discharging a musket, to give notice if they espied any canoe coming; which they did about ten o'clock. He therefore being careful they should be kindly entreated, requested me to go aboard, intending with dispatch to make what haste after he possibly could.

"When I came to the ship there were two canoes, and in either of them three savages, of whom two were below at the fire; the others stayed in their canoes about the ship. And because we could not entice them aboard we gave them a can of pease [pudding] and bread, which they carried to the shore to eat. But one of them brought back our can presently and stayed aboard with the other two; for he, being young, of a ready capacity, and one we most desired to bring with us into England, had received exceeding kind usage at our hands, and was therefore much delighted in our company.

"When our Captain was come we consulted how to catch the other three at shore, which we performed thus.

"We manned the light horseman [gig] with seven or eight men; one standing before carried our box of merchandise, as we were wont when I went to traffic with them, and a platter of pease, which meat they loved. But before we were landed one of them (being too suspiciously fearful of his own good) withdrew himself into the wood. The other two met us on the shore side to receive the pease, with whom we went up to the cliff to their fire and sat down with them; and while we were discussing how to catch the third man who was gone, I opened the box and showed them trifles to exchange, thinking thereby to have banished fear from the other and drawn him to return; but when we could not, we used little delay, but suddenly laid hands upon them. And it was as much as five or six of us could do to get them into the light horseman. For they were strong and so naked as our best hold was by their long hair on their heads, and we would have been very loath to have done them any hurt, which of necessity we had been constrained to have done if we had attempted them in a multitude, which we must and would rather than have wanted them, being a matter of great importance for the full accomplishment of our voyage.

"Thus we shipped five savages, two canoes, with all their bows and arrows."

News of the abduction was brought to a French exploring and

trading party on the Kennebec by an Indian who "trafficked a little in furs."

"He told us that there was a ship, ten leagues off the harbor, which was engaged in fishing, and that those on her had killed five savages of this river, under cover of friendship. From his description of the men on the vessel, we concluded that they were English, and we named the island where they were La Nef; for, at a distance, it had the appearance of a ship."

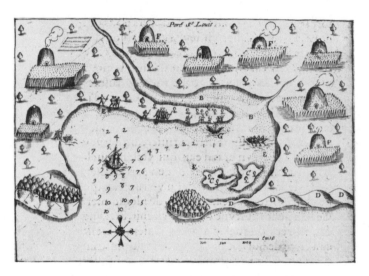

CHAMPLAIN AT CAPE COD, JULY 19, 1605
"We saw some land which seemed to us to be islands, but as we came nearer we found it to be the mainland, lying to the north-north-west of us, and that it was the cape of a large bay, containing more than eighteen or nineteen leagues in circuit, into which we had run so far that we had to wear off [nautical: come about, put up helm] on the other tack in order to double the cape which we had seen. The latter we named Cap Blanc, since it contained sands and downs which had a white appearance." Port St. Louis on this map is Plymouth Harbor. The huts of Indians are surrounded by stands of corn. Numerals indicate depths in fathoms. Picture and text by Champlain from *Les Voyages*, 1613. Courtesy of the Rare Book Division, The New York Public Library.

The author of these lines was Samuel de Champlain, a native of Brouage, France, and the future founder of Quebec. For the present he was under the command of the Sieur de Monts, the King's Lieutenant General in Acadia (which appears to have comprised everything from the Philadelphia-Trenton area to Newfoundland—40 to 46 degrees of latitude). An experienced soldier, sailor and navigator, thirty-eight years old in 1605, Champlain was engaged in charting and colonizing the coast of Norumbega (as New England was termed). Three settlements had already been made—at Port Royal, Nova Scotia, the present-day Annapolis; and Mt. Desert and St. Croix in Maine.

La Nef was Monhegan.

The Indians abducted by Waymouth were not killed. Four of them will reappear.

On April 10, 1606, James I, "by the grace of God, King of England, Scotland, France and Ireland, Defender of the Faith, etc.," signed a license, or charter, authorizing "certain knights, gentlemen, merchants and other adventurers of our City of London" and "sundry knights, gentlemen, merchants and other adventurers of our Cities of Bristol and Exeter and of our Town of Plymouth" to establish two colonies in America—the first between 34 and 41 degrees of latitude, the second between 38 and 45 degrees (or from Cape Fear, North Carolina, to Nova Scotia).

In the light of future events it may be useful to see, once more, the new charter's guarantees:

> "All and every the persons, being our subjects, which shall dwell and inhabit within every or any of the said several colonies and plantations, and every of their children, which shall happen to be born within any of the limits and precincts of the said several colonies and plantations, shall have and enjoy all liberties, franchises and immunities within any of our other dominions, to all intents and purposes as if they had been abiding and born within this our realm of England, or any of our said dominions."

James reserved the usual rights to the fifth part of any gold or silver found and, additionally, the fifteenth part of any copper.

Those named for the establishment of the first colony were Sir Thomas Gates, Sir George Somers, Richard Hakluyt, and Edward

Maria Wingfield; and for the second, Thomas Hanham, Raleigh Gilbert (another son of the famous Sir Humphrey Gilbert), William Parker and George Popham, a nephew of Sir John Popham, Lord Chief Justice of England. The companies formed by them, in association with others, were the Virginia Company of London and the Virginia Company of Plymouth. Prominent in the affairs of the latter was Sir Ferdinando Gorges, governor of the fort at Plymouth and a veteran of the Low Countries and the Armada. Three of the Indians brought back by Waymouth were taken into his household, the other two by Sir John Popham. They were taught English, and in return supplied information.

The Plymouth Company was the first to send out ships for a reconnaissance of the Maine coast, one of them captained by Thomas Hanham, with Martin Pring as navigator. They took one of the Indians back. Two more sailed with Captain Henry Challoung, or Challons, whose ship was captured by Spaniards. A fourth returned with Popham and Gilbert. The fifth appears to be unaccounted for.

The London Company was the first to establish a colony. There were three ships, replicas of which may be seen moored at Jamestown: *Susan Constant,* 100 tons, with 71 persons aboard, Christopher Newport captain; *Goodspeed* or *Godspeed* (actually the same word), 40 tons, 52 aboard, Bartholomew Gosnold captain; and *Discovery,* 20 tons, 21 persons aboard, John Ratcliffe captain. They sailed from London December 20, 1606, anchoring in the Downs on January 5. Contrary winds kept them there six weeks, and it was not until March 23 that they reached the West Indies, where the usual procedures were followed to obtain fresh water and provisions, and wood for the ships' fires.

On the island of Nevis the Englishmen discovered a hot spring, where they refreshed themselves. They liked the climate so well that they remained six days hunting, fowling and fishing, and did not have to draw on their ships' stores the entire time. Nevis was left behind April 3. On the island of Mona more fresh water was taken on, and on a march inland two wild boars were killed. A gentleman named Edward Brookes, "whose fat melted within him by the great heat," died.

On Monica, four leagues from Mona, birds and eggs were so thick on the ground that the men could not take a step, but managed to fill two ships' boats in three hours. This was on April 9; on the 10th the ships "disembogued out of the West Indies and bore our course northerly," and on April 26,

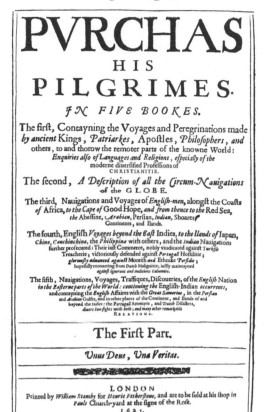

THE OVERFLOW
Title page of Purchas' *Pilgrims*, a continuation of the great
work by Richard Hakluyt. From the Rare Book Division,
The New York Public Library.

"about four o'clock in the morning we descried the land of
Virginia. The same day we entered into the Bay of Chesupioc
directly, without any let or hindrance. There we landed and
discovered [explored] a little way, but we could find nothing
worth the speaking of but fair meadows and goodly tall trees,
with such fresh waters running through the woods as I was
almost ravished at the first sight thereof.

"At night, when we were going aboard, there came the savages creeping upon all fours from the hills, like bears, with
their bows in their mouths, [and] charged us very desperately
in the faces, hurt Captain Gabriel Archer in both his hands, and

a sailor in two places of the body, very dangerous. After they had spent their arrows, and felt the sharpness of our shot, they retired into the woods with a great noise, and so left us."

The author of these lines was George Percy, a son of the Earl of Northumberland, "the wizard Earl," so called from his scientific experiments, made chiefly in the Tower of London where he was a fellow prisoner with Raleigh. He was assisted by Hariot. Percy's *Observations* was abridged by Purchas in the belief that "the rest is more fully set down in Captain Smith's *Relations*." He appears also to have rewritten portions of it, for the style varies. It is, nevertheless, a vivid narrative of Virginia in 1607:

"The seven-and-twentieth we began to build up our shallop [from parts brought over]. The gentlemen and soldiers marched eight miles up into the land. We could not see a savage in all that march. We came to a place where they had made a great fire and had been newly a-roasting oysters. When they perceived our coming they fled away to the mountains and left many of the oysters in the fire. We ate some of the oysters, which were very large and delicate in taste.

"The eight-and-twentieth we launched our shallop. The Captain [Newport] and some gentlemen went in her and discovered up the Bay. We found a river on the south side running into the main; we entered it and found it very shoal water, not for any boats to swim [Lynnhaven River, Princess Anne County]. We went further into the Bay and saw a plain plot of ground where we went on land, and found the place five mile in compass without either bush or tree. We saw nothing there but a canoe which was made out of the whole tree, which was five and forty foot long by the rule. Upon this plot of ground we got good store of mussels and oysters, which lay on the ground as thick as stones. We opened some, and found in many of them pearls.

"We marched some three or four miles further into the woods, where we saw great smokes of fire. We marched to those smokes and found that the savages had been there burning down the grass—as we thought, either to make their plantation there, or else to give signs to bring their forces together and so to give us battle [but perhaps to drive game out of the woods]. We passed through excellent ground full of flowers of divers kinds and colors, and as goodly trees as I have seen, as cedar, cypress, and other kinds. Going a little further we came into a little plot of ground full of fine and beautiful strawberries, four times bigger and better than ours in England.

"All this march we could neither see savage nor town. When it grew to be toward night, we stood back to our ships. We sounded and found it shallow water for a great way, which put us out of all hopes for getting any higher with our ships, which rode at the mouth of the river. We rowed over to a point of land where we found a channel and sounded six, eight, ten or twelve fathom, which put us in good comfort. Therefore we named that point of land Cape Comfort.

"The nine-and-twentieth day we set up a cross at Chesupioc Bay and named that place Cape Henry [for the Prince of Wales]. Thirtieth day, we came with our ships to Cape Comfort, where we saw five savages running on the shore. Presently the Captain caused the shallop to be manned; so rowing to the shore, the Captain called to them in sign of friendship, but they were at first very timersome [timorous], until they saw the captain lay his hand on his heart. Upon that they laid down their bows and arrows and came very boldly to us, making signs to come ashore to their town, which is called by the savages Kecoughtan. We coasted to their town, rowing over a river running into the main, where these savages swam over with their bows and arrows in their mouths.

"When we came over to the other side there was a many of other savages which directed us to their town, where we were entertained by them very kindly. When we came first aland they made a doleful noise, laying their faces to the ground, scratching the earth with their nails. We did think they had been at their idolatry. When they had ended their ceremonies they went into their houses and brought out mats and laid [them] upon the ground. The chiefest of them sat all in a rank; the meanest sort brought us such dainties as they had, and of their bread which they make of their maize or Guinea wheat [Indian corn]. They would not suffer us to eat unless we sat down, which we did on a mat right against them. After we were well satisfied they gave us of their tobacco, which they took in a pipe made artificially of earth as ours are, but far bigger, with the bowl fashioned together with a piece of fine copper.

"After they had feasted us, they showed us, in welcome, their manner of dancing, which was in this fashion. One of the savages standing in the midst singing, beating one hand against another, all the rest dancing about him, shouting, howling and stamping against the ground, with many antic tricks and faces, making noise like so many wolves or devils. One thing of them I observed: when they were in their dance they kept stroke with their feet just one with another; but with their hands, heads, faces and bodies every one of them had a several gesture. So they continued for the space of half an hour. When they had ended their dance the captain gave them beads and other trifling jewels.

"They hang through their ears fowls' legs. They shave the right side of their heads with a shell; the left side they wear of an ell long [45 inches] tied up with an artificial knot with many of the fowls' feathers sticking in it. They go altogether naked, but their privities are covered with beasts' skins beset commonly with little bones or beasts' teeth. Some paint their bodies black, some red, with artificial knots of sundry lively colors, very beautiful and pleasing to the eye, in a braver fashion than they in the West Indies."

The Indians of Virginia were Algonquins.

The ships next proceeded up Powhatan's river (the James) seeking a site for the colony. On May 4 they reached the territory of the Paspihes (or Paspaheghs, as Smith terms them) on the north side of the river.

"They entertained us with much welcome. An old savage made a long oration, making a foul noise, uttering his speech with a vehement action; but we knew little what they meant. Whilst we were in company with the Paspihes, the werowance of Rapahanna came from the other side of the river in his canoe. He seemed to take displeasure of our being with the Paspihes. He would fain have had us come to his town. The Captain was unwilling. Seeing that the day was so far spent, he returned back to his ships for that night.

"The next day, being the fifth of May, the werowance of Rapahanna sent a messenger to have us come to him. We entertained the said messenger and gave him trifles, which pleased him. We manned our shallop with muskets and targeteers sufficiently [and] this said messenger guided us where our determination was to go. When we landed, the werowance of Rapahanna came down to the waterside with all his train, as goodly men as any I have seen of savages or Christians, the werowance coming before them playing on a flute made of a reed, with a crown of deer's hair colored red, in fashion of a rose, fastened about his knot of hair, and a great plate of copper on the other side of his head, with two long feathers in fashion of a pair of horns placed in the midst of his crown. His body was painted all with crimson, with a chain of beads about his neck, his face painted blue, besprinkled with silver ore, as we thought, his ears all behung with bracelets of pearls, and in either ear a bird's claw through it, beset with fine copper or gold.

"He entertained us in so modest a proud fashion, as though he had been a prince of civil government, holding his countenance without laughter or any such ill behavior. He caused his mat to be spread on the ground, where he sat down with a great majesty, taking a pipe of tobacco, the rest of his company standing about him. After he had rested a while he rose and made signs to us to come to his town. He went foremost, and all the rest of his people and ourselves followed him up a steep hill where his palace was settled. We passed through the woods in fine paths having most pleasant springs which issued from the mountains. We also went through the goodliest corn fields that ever was seen in any country. When we came to Rapahanna's town, he entertained us in good humanity.

"The eighth day of May we discovered [explored] up the river. We landed in the country of Apamatica. At our landing, there came many stout and able savages to resist us with their bows and arrows in a most warlike manner, with the swords [clubs] at their backs beset with sharp stones and pieces of iron able to cleave a man in sunder. Among the rest, one of the chiefest, standing before them cross-legged, with his arrow ready in his bow in one hand, and taking a pipe of tobacco in the other, with a bold uttering of his speech demanded of us our being there, willing us to be gone. We made signs of peace, which they perceived in the end and let us land in quietness."

It was while the ships were anchored off Cape Henry that a sealed box, or chest, was opened by Captain Newport in the presence of the other officers and chief men of the enterprise. In it were the Virginia Company's nominees for membership in the council which was to govern the settlement. They were Edward Maria Wingfield, Captain Gosnold, Captain John Smith, Captain Ratcliffe, Captain John Martin, Captain George Kendall, and the Reverend Robert Hunt, the expedition's preacher, afterward vicar of Jamestown. All were present, save Smith, who was under confinement and in danger of summary punishment or of being sent back with Newport to face charges in London. He was, in his own words, "restrained as a prisoner, upon the scandalous suggestions of some

SMITH'S MAP OF VIRGINIA, WITH INDIAN PLACE NAMES
Inset shows Powhatan in state (for description by Smith when a pris-
oner, see text). Below, the first places reached by the Jamestown colonists.
Right, a Susquehanna Indian: "The Sasquesahanougs are a Giant-like
people & thus attired." Bottom right, Smith's coat of arms, showing three
Turks' heads.

of the chief (envying his repute), who feigned he intended to
usurp the government, murder the council, and make himself king."

Smith's reputation was indeed great. He had been a soldier of
fortune from youth, had served in Europe wherever there was
fighting and had done high deeds in Hungary. His coat of arms was
adorned with three Turks' heads, he having slain, while with a
prince of Transylvania, three Turkish champions, one after the
other, in single combat, and cut off their heads in sight of the
opposing armies. He was also a braggart, and he may have alarmed
some of those with him in the long watches at sea. His bravery—
or audacity—cannot be questioned; nor can the leadership he
afterward displayed.

This is the first instance of dissension among the colonists; it was
not the last.

Chesapeake Bay . . . Rappahannock . . . Appomattox . . . the old

American names are beginning to appear in their Indian form as the search for a site continued. There was a creek at a point of land they called Archer's Hope, which was almost chosen; Captain Archer was for it, the soil was good, there was excellent timber, and there were many squirrels, rabbits, and numerous birds, among them "black birds with crimson wings"—the red-winged blackbird. But ships could not ride close enough to the shore.

A few miles higher up, however, there was six fathom of water and the ships were "moored to the trees." It seemed just right; but here, too, there was difference of opinion, particularly between Wingfield and Gosnold. Wingfield won; he had been elected president of the council.

The site which was chosen was on the western end of a little peninsula, now an island, where the James bends and flows softly, majestically past flat earth, marshes and creeks. There were no springs, and little arable land. Perhaps the trees were decisive.

"The fourteenth day we landed all our men which were set to work about the fortification, and others, some to watch and ward as it was convenient.

"The first night of our landing, about midnight, there came some savages sailing close to our quarter. Presently there was an alarum given; upon that the savages ran away, and we [were] not troubled any more by them that night.

"Not long after there came two savages that seemed to be commanders, bravely dressed, with crowns of colored hair upon their heads, which came as messengers from the werowance of Paspihes, telling us that their werowance was coming and would be merry with us with a fat deer.

"The eighteenth day the werowance of Paspihes came himself to our quarter with one hundred savages armed, which guarded him in a very warlike manner with bows and arrows, thinking at that time to execute their villainy. Paspihes made great signs to us to lay our arms away; but we would not trust him so far. He, seeing he could not have convenient time to work his will, at length made signs that he would give us as much land as we would desire to take.

"As the savages were in a throng in the fort, one of them stole a hatchet from one of our company, which spied him doing the deed; whereupon he took it from him by force, and also struck him over the arm. Presently, another savage seeing that, came fiercely at our man with a wooden sword [club], thinking to beat out his brains. The werowance of Paspihes saw us take to our arms [and] went suddenly away with all his company in great anger.

"The nineteenth day, myself and three or four more walking into the wood, by chance we espied a pathway like to an Irish pace [narrow lane, or passage]. We were desirous to know whither it would bring us. We traced along some four miles, all the way as we went having the pleasantest suckles, the ground all flowing over with fair flowers of sundry colors and kinds, as though it had been in any garden or orchard in England. There be many strawberries, and other fruits unknown. We saw the woods full of cedar and cypress trees, with other trees which issue out sweet gums like to balsam.

"We kept on our way in this paradise. At length we came to a savage town, where we found but few people. They told us the rest were gone a-hunting with the werowance of Paspihes. We stayed there a while and had of them strawberries and other things.

"In the meantime, one of the savages came running out of his house with a bow and arrows and ran mainly [hard] through the woods. Then I began to mistrust some villainy, that he went to call some company, and so betray us. We made all haste away we could. One of the savages brought us on the way to the woodside where there was a garden of tobacco and other fruits and herbs. He gathered tobacco and distributed to every one of us. So we departed.

"The twentieth day the werowance of Paspihes sent forty of his men with a deer to our quarters; but they came more in villainy than any love they bore us. They fain would have lain in our fort all night, but we would not suffer them for fear of their treachery.

"One of our gentlemen having a target [shield] which he trusted in, thinking it would bear out a slight shot, he set it up against a tree, willing one of the savages to shoot; who took from his back an arrow of an ell long, drew it strongly in his bow, shoots the target a foot through or better—which was strange, being that a pistol would not pierce it. We, seeing the force of his bow, afterward set him up a steel target; he shot again, and burst his arrow all to pieces. He presently pulled out another arrow and bit it in his teeth and seemed to be in a great rage; so he went away, in great anger.

"Their bows are made of tough hazel, their strings of leather, their arrows of canes or hazel, headed with very sharp stones,

and are made artificially [artistically] like a broad arrow. Some
other of their arrows are headed with the ends of deers' horns
and are feathered very artificially.

"Paspiha was as good as his word, for he sent venison; but
the sauce came within a few days after."

The sauce was a furious Indian attack on the uncompleted fort
while Captain Newport and about twenty others, Smith and Percy
among them, were once more exploring the river, going as far as
the falls below present-day Richmond. (It was on this journey that
the Englishmen saw an Indian boy, aged about ten, "which had a
head of hair of a perfect yellow and a reasonable white skin," Percy
wrote.) Smith's *True Relation* gives details of the battle in soldierly
syntax:

"Captain Newport intended to have visited Paspahegh and
Rappahanocke, but the instant change of the wind being fair
for our return we repaired to the fort with all speed, where
the first we heard was that 400 Indians the day before [May
26] had assaulted the fort and surprised it; had not God (beyond all their expectations) by means of the ships, at whom
they shot with their ordnances and muskets, caused them to
retire, they had entered the fort with our own men, which were
then busied in setting corn, their arms being then in dryfats
and few ready but certain gentlemen of their own; in which
conflict most of the council was hurt, a boy slain in the pinnace [the *Discovery*] and thirteen or fourteen more hurt.

"With all speed we palisadoed our fort. Each [every] other
day for six or seven days we had alarums by ambuscadoes, and
four or five cruelly wounded by being abroad. The Indians' loss
we know not, but as they report, three were slain and divers
hurt."

The fort was completed June 15. Percy says it was built "trianglewise, having three bulwarks, [one] at each corner, like a half
moon, and four or five pieces of artillery mounted in them. We had
made ourselves sufficiently strong for those savages." The riverside
wall, or "curtain," was 420 feet long, while the sides measured 300
feet to the apex. Inside were hastily constructed buildings for
stores, living quarters, and church services. On June 21, the third
Sunday after Trinity, the first Anglican communion of record in
America was celebrated by Mr. Hunt.

It was the eve of Captain Newport's departure for England; on
Monday, the 22nd, he sailed with the *Susan Constant* and *Good-*

speed, "leaving us (one hundred and four persons) very bare and scanty of victuals," Percy wrote; Smith says "leaving provision for 13 or 14 weeks." But the corn they had planted on two nearby hills, which were probably mounds, although Percy calls them "mountains"—the highest elevation of the Jamestown peninsula is not more than ten feet above sea level—was already "a man's height from the ground," and "of sturgeon we had great store, whereon our men would so greedily surfeit as it cost many their lives," according to Smith. They were in a land full of game, which the various narrators never tired of listing; nevertheless, famine as well as sickness killed half the colonists, "our want of sufficient and good victuals, with continual watching, four or five each night at the three bulwarks, being the chief cause," Smith wrote. The melancholy roster appears in Percy's *Observations*:

"The sixth of August there died John Asbie of the bloody flux. The ninth day died George Flower of the swelling. The tenth day died William Brewster, gentleman, of a wound given by the savages, and was buried the eleventh day.

"The fourteenth day, Jerome Alicock, ancient [ensign], died of a wound; the same day, Francis Midwinter, [and] Edward Morris, corporal, died suddenly.

"The fifteenth day, there died Edward Browne and Stephen Galthorpe. The sixteenth day, there died Thomas Gower, gentleman. The seventeenth day, there died Thomas Mounslie. The eighteenth day, there died Robert Pennington, and John Martin, gentleman. The nineteenth day, died Dru (or Drew) Piggase [also spelled Pickhouse], gentleman.

"The two-and-twentieth day of August, there died Captain Bartholomew Gosnold, one of our council. He was honorably buried, having all the ordnance in the fort shot off, with many volleys of small shot. After Captain Gosnold's death, the council could hardly agree by the dissension of Captain Kendall, which [who] was afterward committed about heinous matters, which was proved against him.

"The four-and-twentieth day, died Edward Harrington and George Walker, and were buried the same day. The six-and-twentieth day, died Kenelm Throgmorton. The seven-and-twentieth day died William Roods. The eight-and-twentieth day died Thomas Stoodie, cape merchant [keeper of the stores].

"The fourth day of September died Thomas Jacob, sergeant. The fifth day, there died Benjamin Beast. The eighteenth day, died one Ellis Kingston, which was starved to death with cold.

The same day, at night, died one Richard Simmons. The nineteenth day, there died one Thomas Mouton.

"Our men were destroyed with cruel diseases, as swellings, fluxes, burning fevers, and by wars; and some departed suddenly, but for the most part they died of mere famine. There were never Englishmen left in a foreign country in such misery as we were in this newly discovered Virginia. We watched [stood guard] every three nights, lying on the bare, cold ground, what weather soever came; warded all the next day, which brought our men to be most feeble wretches. Our food was but a small can of barley sod[den] in water, to five men a day; our drink, cold water taken out of the river, which was at a flood very salt, at a low tide full of slime and filth, which was the destruction of many of our men.

"Thus we lived for the space of five months in this miserable distress, not having five able men to man our bulwarks upon any occasion. If it had not pleased God to have put a terror in the savages' hearts, we had all perished by those vile and cruel pagans, being in that weak state as we were, our men night and day groaning in every corner of the fort, most pitiful to hear. If there were any conscience in men, it would make their hearts to bleed to hear the pitiful murmurings and outcries of our sick men without relief, every night and day, for the space of six weeks, some departing out of the world, many times three or four in a night; in the morning, their bodies trailed out of their cabins like dogs to be buried. In this sort did I see the mortality of divers of our people."

The Indians saved them.

"It pleased God (in our extremity) to move the Indians to bring us corn, ere it was half ripe, to refresh us, when we rather expected when they would destroy us," Smith wrote; and Percy, "It pleased God, after a while, to send those people which were our mortal enemies to relieve us with victuals, as bread, corn, fish and flesh in great plenty, which was the setting up of our feeble men, otherwise we had all perished."

There was now a great deal of dissatisfaction with Wingfield's presidency, and he was replaced by Ratcliffe. At the same time, Kendall was dropped from the council. Smith, meanwhile, was going up and down the river by pinnace and barge to trade with the Indians for corn. On his first journey he brought back ten bushels. On his second, there was "such abundance of corn, as having laded our barge, as also I might have laded a ship." On the next, another bargeload: "I unladed again 7 or 8 hogsheads at our fort."

"Having thus by God's assistance gotten good store of corn,
notwithstanding, some bad spirits, not content with God's providence, still grew mutinous; insomuch, that our president, having
occasion to chide the [black]smith for his misdemeanor, he not
only gave him bad language, but also offered to strike him with
some of his tools. For which rebellious act the smith was by a
jury condemned to be hanged.

"But being upon the ladder [to be "turned off"] continuing
very obstinate as hoping upon a rescue, when he saw no other
way but death with him, he became penitent and declared a
dangerous conspiracy. For which Captain Kendall, as principal, was by a jury condemned, and shot to death."

The conspiracy, or plot, was to seize the *Discovery* and take her
to England. The execution of Kendall took place on December 1,
1607. One James Read is listed as blacksmith in the roll of "them
that were the first planters." He appears to have been reprieved,
and is listed as "soldier" in a later roll. These are the first jury
trials recorded in America.

That December, while on a trading mission in the Chickahominy
River area, Smith was captured and taken to the mighty Powhatan.
From *A True Relation*:

"Having two Indians for my guide and two of our own company, I set forward, leaving seven in the barge. Having discovered [explored] 20 miles further in this desert [in the
Indians' canoe], the river still kept his depth and breadth, but
much more cumbered with trees. Here we went ashore (being
some 12 miles higher than the barge had been) to refresh
ourselves during the boiling of our victuals. One of the Indians
I took with me, to see the nature of the soil, and to cross the
bights of the river. The other Indian I left with Master Robinson and Thomas Emry, with their matches lit and order to discharge a piece, for my retreat, at the first sight of any Indian.

"But within a quarter of an hour I heard a loud cry and a
holloing of Indians, but no warning piece. Supposing them
surprised, and that the Indians had betrayed us, presently I
seized him and bound his arm fast to my hand in a garter,
with my pistol ready bent to be revenged on him. He advised
me to fly, and seemed ignorant of what was done. But as we
went discoursing, I was struck with an arrow on the right
thigh, but without harm.

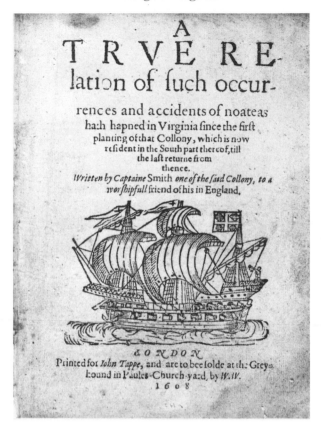

A TRUE RELATION

Title page of *A True Relation* by Captain John Smith, 1608. From the Rare Book Division, The New York Public Library.

"Upon this occasion I espied two Indians drawing their bows, which I prevented in discharging a French pistol. By that I had charged [loaded] again three or four more did the like, for the first fell down and fled. At my discharge they did the like. My hind [the Indian guide; hind: servant or rustic, Scotland and northern England] I made my barricade, who offered not to strive. Twenty or thirty arrows were shot at me, but short. Three or four times I had discharged my pistol ere the king of Pamunky called Opechancanough with 200 men environed me, each drawing their bow; which done, they laid them upon the ground, yet without shot.

"My hind treated betwixt them and me of conditions of

peace. He discovered [revealed] me to be the Captain. My request was to retire to the boat. They demanded my arms; the rest, they said, were slain, only me they would reserve. The Indian importuned me not to shoot. In retiring, being in the midst of a low quagmire, and minding them more than my steps, I stepped fast into the quagmire, and also the Indian in drawing me forth. Thus surprised, I resolved to try their mercies. My arms I cast from me, till which none durst approach me."

The capture is thought to have taken place in White Oak Swamp. Smith was brought back to the canoe where he saw John Robinson lying dead "with 20 or 30 arrows in him. Emry I saw not." Robinson is listed as a gentleman, Emry as a carpenter. He is heard of no more.

Despite some mutterings and threats, Smith was well treated and well fed:

"a quarter of venison and some ten pound of bread I had for supper; what I left was reserved for me, and sent with me to my lodging. Each morning three women presented me with great platters of fine bread; more venison than ten men could devour I had. My gown, points and garters, my compass and my table they gave me again"

(gown: cloak; points: tagged lace, or lacing, with metal point for fastening clothing; table: writing tablet). He appears to have charmed them.

All this time he was being conveyed, with a great host surrounding him, to the dwelling place of Powhatan—werowocomoco, "the house of the werowance"—on the Pamunkey River, now the York. Smith thought the word was a place name—the syntax is his own:

"Arriving at Weramocomoco, their emperor proudly lying upon a bedstead a foot high, upon ten or twelve mats, richly hung with many chains of great pearls about his neck, and covered with a great covering of rahaughcums [Algonquin for "raccoons"]. At head sat a woman, at his feet another. On each side sitting upon a mat upon the ground were ranged his chief men on each side the fire, ten in a rank, and behind them as many young women, each a great chain of white beads over their shoulders, their heads painted in red. And with such a grave and majestical countenance, as drave me into admiration to see such state in a naked savage, he kindly welcomed me

Ætatis suæ 21. Aᵒ. 1616.

Matoaks als Rebecka daughter to the mighty Prince Powhatan Emperour of Attanoughkomouck als Virginia converted and baptized in the Christian faith, and Wife to the worᵗ Mʳ Thoᵇ Rolff.

POCAHONTAS

Painted in England by an unknown portrait artist in 1616, "in the year of her age 21." She is wearing a high-crowned hat (almost the only hats worn by Englishwomen at this time were of a masculine type); earrings, a lace whisk, and a Spanish-influenced coat-dress with gauze over the gown. The legend gives her secret Indian name, Matoaks; her baptismal name, Rebecca; her father's name, Powhattan, "Emperor of Attanoughtkomouck and Virginia"; and the name of her husband—which was John Rolfe, not Thomas; Thomas was the son born to them. From Thomas Rolfe and his wife, Jane Poythress, are descended many Virginia families with memorable names, among them Bolling, Randolph and Eldridge. Courtesy of the National Portrait Gallery, Smithsonian Institution, Washington, D.C.

with good words and great platters of sundry victuals, assuring me his friendship, and my liberty in four days."

There is no mention of Pocahontas. That most charming and enigmatic of Indian princesses was only twelve or thirteen years old, with braided hair hanging down in back. Percy observed: "The maids you shall always see the fore part of their head and sides shaven close, the hinder part very long, which they tie in a pleat [plait] hanging down to their hips." The reader may recall the story of Juan Ortiz, saved by the daughter of Ucita in Florida, which Smith could have read or heard about, although there is nothing inherently improbable about his later claim that Pocahontas saved him from death at this time. Of the strong bonds of affection between them there is much evidence, and it comes from other pens besides his own. That stout fellow with blue eyes and bushy beard must have been utterly charming; he could not have survived so many dangers else.

Powhatan wanted to know what Smith and his countrymen were doing there. The reply is a marvel of lucidity considering Smith's syntax and other embroideries:

> "I told him, being in fight with the Spaniards, our enemy, being overpowered, near put to retreat, and by extreme weather put to this shore where, landing at Chesipiack, the people shot us. But at Kequoughtan they kindly used us. We, by signs, demanded fresh water; they described us up the river was all fresh water. At Paspahegh also they kindly used us. Our pinnace, being leaky, we were enforced to stay to mend her, till Captain Newport, my father [leader], came to conduct us away.
>
> "He demanded why we went further with our boat. I told him, in that I would have occasion to talk of the back Sea, that [which flows] on the other side the main, where was salt water."

Powhatan told Smith what he wished to hear.

> "After good deliberation, he began to describe me the country beyond the Falls, with many of the rest; confirming what not only Opechancanough, and an Indian which had been prisoner to Powhatan had before told me: but some called it five days, some six, some eight, where the said water dashed amongst many stones and rocks each storm."

It had the sound of the sea in it; Smith was eager to hear more.

> "He described also upon the same sea a mighty nation called Pocoughtronack, a fierce nation that did eat men and warred

with the people of Moyaoncer and Patawomecke [Potomac], nations upon the top of the head of the bay, under his territories, where the year before they had slain an hundred. He signified their crowns were shaven, long hair in the neck tied on a knot, swords [clubs] like poleaxes.

"Beyond them, he described people with short coats and sleeves to the elbows that passed that way in ships like ours. Many kingdoms he described to me, to the head of the bay, which seemed to be a mighty river issuing from mighty mountains betwixt the two seas."

Smith's tablet has been mentioned; perhaps, while talking, he drew the map which he later sent to Henry Hudson.

"I requited his discourse," Smith wrote, "seeing what pride he had in his great and spacious dominions, seeing that all he knew were under his territories, in describing to him the territories of Europe, which was subject to our great King, whose subject I was; the innumerable multitude of his ships; I gave him to understand the noise of trumpets, and terrible manner of fighting were under Captain Newport, my father, whom I entitled the werowance, which they call the king of all the waters. At his greatness, he admired; and not a little feared."

Powhatan was as good as his word, and Smith was permitted to return to Jamestown, where he was welcomed by most, but not all.

"Great blame and imputation was laid upon me by them for the loss of our two men which the Indians slew, insomuch as they purposed to depose me. But in the midst of my miseries it pleased God to send Captain Newport, who arriving there the same night, so tripled our joy as for a while these plots against me were deferred."

Captain Newport arrived January 2, 1608, in the *John and Francis,* bringing new settlers and supplies. The joy was short-lived. Smith wrote:

"Within five or six days after the arrival of the ship, by a mischance our fort was burned, and the most of our apparel, lodging and private provision. Many of our old men [the first settlers] deceased, and of our new, for want of lodging, perished."

The fort was rebuilt; in time, there were pretty little streets of two-story houses, some with attics. Among the seventy who disembarked with Newport were two women, "the first gentlewoman and woman servant that arrived in our colony." The servant, Anne Burrows, married John Laydon, a carpenter and laborer who had come over with the first settlers; later, there were shiploads of women—some maids, some widows—whose passage was paid by those who chose them as wives. In the end, of course, tobacco assured the plantation's prosperity.

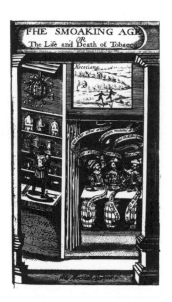

A PURITAN BLAST AT TOBACCO

John Rolfe, who married Pocahontas, showed the Jamestown colonists how to cultivate tobacco profitably, and assured the success of the plantation on Powhatan's river. This is the earliest representation of a tobacco shop in London, with three cavaliers—Captain Whiffe, Captain Pipe and Captain Snuffe—enjoying themselves in a private room. From Richard Braithwait's *The Smoking Age,* 1617. Courtesy of Arents Tobacco Collection in The New York Public Library.

Today, little remains of Jamestown but a little open space thronged with memorials to its past. The trees to which the ship's hawsers were tied are long since gone. So is the shoreline on which they and the fort stood, and where the English first set foot. But in the whole country there is no place quite like it, for it was here that the United States of America was born.

The northern settlement did not fare so well.

Following Pring's latest exploration of the Maine coast the Plymouth Company of Virginia dispatched two ships with colonists on board at May's end, 1607. They were the *Gift of God,* Captain George Popham, and the *Mary and John,* Captain Raleigh Gilbert. At Flores in the Azores they stopped to take on wood and water, and were becalmed. As night fell two other ships were seen approaching. These were also becalmed, as revealed in the morning.

"They sent their boats, being full of men, toward us. And after the orders of the sea, they hailed us, demanding of us whence we were, the which we told them; and found them to be Flemings and the States' ships [that is, from the United Province of the Netherlands].

"One of our company named John Goyett of Plymouth knew the captain of one of the ships, for that he had been at sea with him. Having acquainted Captain Gilbert of this, and being all friends, he desired the captain of the Dutch to come near and take a can of beer, the which he thankfully accepted, we still keeping ourselves in a readiness both of our small shot and great.

"The Dutch captain being come to our ship's side, Captain Gilbert desired him to come aboard, and entertaind him in the best sort he could. This done, they to requite the kind entertainment, desired him that he would go aboard with them. And upon their earnest entreaty he went with them, taking three or four gentlemen with him; but when they had him aboard of them they there kept him perforce, charging him that he was a pirate, and still threatening himself and his gentlemen with him to throw them all overboard and to take our ships from us.

"In this sort they kept them from ten of the clock morning until eight of the clock night, using some of his gentlemen in most wild [perhaps vile] manner, as setting some of them in the bilbows [stocks] and buffeting of others, and other most wild and shameful abuses; but in the end, having seen our commission, the which was proffered unto them at the first but they refused to see it, and the greatest cause, doubting of the Englishmen being of their own company [that is, English sailors on the Dutch ship] who had promised Captain Gilbert that if they proffered to perform that which they still threatened him, that then they all would rise with him and either end their lives in his defense or suppress the ship; the which the Dutch perceiving presently set them at liberty and sent them aboard unto us again, to our no small joy.

"Captain Popham all this time being in the wind of us never would come room unto us [come about before the wind], notwithstanding we making all the signs that possible we might by striking our topsail and hoisting it again three times and making toward him all that ever we possibly could. So here we lost company of him, being the 29th day of June about 8 of the clock at night being 6 leagues from Flores west-northwest, we standing our course for Virginia."

The unknown author of *A Voyage to Sagadahoc* was on board the *Mary and John*—hence his view of things. His manuscript account was found many years later "among the papers of the truly worshipful Sir Ferdinando Gorges, knight," and gives the name of the man who found it; but after the words "written by," there is only a blank. He was probably the navigator, or pilot—the narrative is full of occupational terms. Provision had been made for just such an emergency as the separation of the two ships.

The *Mary and John* proceeded on its westward course without incident. Southwest of Sable Island, on Sable Island Bank, the men "fished three hours and took near to hundred of cods, very great and large fish, bigger and larger fish than that which comes from the bank of the New Found Land.

"From hence, the wind being at southwest, we set our sails and stood by the wind west-northwest toward the land, always sounding for our better knowledge as we ran toward the mainland from this bank."

Off an island "in the latitude of 44 degrees and ½" another Biscayan shallop with Indians aboard hove into view—seagoing traders. There were eight adults and "a little savage boy" in it. They spoke a bit of French. They returned the next day, this time bringing three women along, "proffering their skins to truck with us, but they demanded evermuch for them."

From its anchorage the *Mary and John* sent thirteen men ashore, among them the narrator, who found it to be a "gallant island full of high and mighty trees of sundry sorts. Here we also found abundance of gooseberries, strawberries, raspberries and whorts." The next day the men went a-lobstering, and in a single hour caught "50 great lopsters."

"You shall see them where they lie in shoal water not past a yard deep, and with a great hook made fast to a staff you shall hitch them up. There are great store of them; you may near load a ship with them, and they are of great bigness. I have not seen the like in England. So the boat returned aboard [that is, alongside] and we took our boat in and about midnight the wind came fair at northwest; we set sail and departed from thence, keeping our course southwest, for so the coast lieth."

Thus the solitary ship proceeded. Cape Sable was passed. The Camden Hills were observed. Ragged, Wooden Ball and Seal Islands were seen, "lying together, being low and flat, by the water showing white as if it were sand, but it is white rocks making show afar." The course was west and west by north. August 6 the *Mary and John* reached the St. George's group of islands; on Allen's Island, "we found a cross set up, the which we suppose was set up by George Waymouth." Twelve hours later the *Gift of God* hove into view.

"Friday, being the 7th of August, we weighed our anchor whereby to bring our ship in more better safety howsoever the wind should happen to blow, and about ten of the clock in the morning, as we were standing off a little from the island, we descried a sail standing in toward this island, and we presently made toward her, and found it to be the *Gift*, our consort. So, being all joyful of our happy meeting, we both stood in again for the island we rode under before and there anchored both together."

That night, there was a memorable encounter between two Indians who had been taken to England by Waymouth, one of them a young chief, Tahanedo by name (in Rosier's account), brought back the year before by Pring; and Skicowaros (also Rosier's spelling), brought back by Popham or Gilbert.

"This night following, about midnight, Captain Gilbert caused his ship's boat to be manned and took to himself thirteen other, myself being on, being fourteen persons in all, and took the Indian Skicowaros with us. The weather being fair and the wind calm, we rowed to the west in among many gallant islands and found the river of Pemaquid to be but four leagues west from the island we call St. George's, where our ships remained still at anchor.

"Here we landed in a little cove by Skicowaros' direction

[perhaps New Harbor] and marched over a neck of the land near three miles. So the Indian Skicowaros brought us to the savages' houses where they did inhabit, although much against his will, for that he told us that they were all removed and gone from the place they were wont to inhabit; but we answered him again that we would not return back until such time as we had spoken with some of them.

"At length he brought us where they did inhabit, where we found near a hundred of them—men, women and children. And the chief commander of them is Tahanedo. At our first sight of them, upon a howling or cry that they made, they all presently issued forth toward us with their bows and arrows, and we presently made a stand and suffered them to come near unto us. Then our Indian, Skicowaros, spoke unto them in their language, showing them what we were, which when Tahanedo, their commander, perceived what we were, he caused them all to lay aside their bows and arrows and came unto us and embraced us, and we did the like to them again. So we remained with them near two hours, and were in their houses. Then we took our leave of them and returned, with our Indian Skicowaros with us, toward our ships the 8th day of August, being Saturday in the afternoon.

"Sunday, being the 9th of August, in the morning the most part of our whole company of both our ships landed on this island the which we call St. George's Island, where the cross standeth, and there we heard a sermon delivered unto us by our preacher, giving God thanks for our happy meeting and safe arrival into the country, and so returned aboard again."

The preacher was the Reverend Richard Seymour.

The next time the Englishmen—to the number of fifty—sought to go ashore in Tahanedo's territory they were opposed.

After rounding Pemaquid Point in shallop and ship's boat they arrived right before the Indian encampment; whereupon Tahanedo drew up his warriors on the sand. Skicowaros again served as intermediary. At first, Tahanedo said he did not wish all the Englishmen to land, and then agreed that they all could. But an hour or so later the young chief with all his braves "suddenly withdrew themselves from us into the woods." The Englishmen embarked— "all except Skicowaros, who was not desirous to return with us. We, seeing this, would in no sort proffer any violence unto him by drawing him, perforce suffered him to remain and stay behind us, he promising to return unto us the next day following; but he held not his promise."

The English spent the night encamped across the river, then returned to their ships.

"Tuesday, being the 12th of August, we weighed our anchors and set our sails to go for the river of Sagadahoc. We kept our course from thence due west until 12 of the clock midnight of the same; then we struck our sails and laid a-hull until the morning, doubting for to overshoot it."

The "river of Sagahadoc" was the Kennebec. The *Mary and John* did, in fact, overshoot its mouth and was storm-tossed for a day and a night. At last, on Sunday the 16th, Popham's shallop towed the *Mary and John* into the river, where it anchored alongside the *Gift of God*. The time had come to find a site for the colony.

"We sailed up into this river near fourteen leagues and found it to be a most gallant river, very broad and of a good depth. We never had less water than three fathoms when we had least, and abundance of great fish [sturgeon] in it leaping above the water on each side of us as we sailed."

Again:

"We find this river to be very pleasant, with many goodly islands in it and to be both large and deep water, having many branches in it. That which we took bendeth itself towards the northwest.

"Tuesday, being the 18th, after our return we all went to the shore and there made choice of a place for our plantation, which is at the very mouth or entry of the river of Sagahadoc on the west side of the river, being almost an island of a good bigness. Whilst we were upon the shore there came in three canoes by us, but they would not come near us, but rowed up the river and so past away.

"Wednesday, being the 19th August, we all went to the shore where we made choice for our plantation, and there we had a sermon delivered unto us by our preacher, and after the sermon our patent was read with the orders and laws therein prescribed, and then we returned aboard our ships again.

"Thursday, being the 20th of August, all our companies landed and there began to fortify. Our president, Captain Popham, set the first spit [spade-depth] of ground unto it, and after him all the rest followed and labored hard in the trenches about it."

Work on the fort and essential buildings continued through August and into September. On September 7 the *Mary and John* began to unload provisions for the colonists, sailing away, under the command of a Captain Robert Davies, in October, "to advertise of their safe arrival and forwardness of their plantation within this river of Sagadahoc, with letters to the Chief Justice importuning a supply for the most necessary wants to the subsisting of a colony to be sent unto them betimes the next year."

The *Gift of God* followed soon after.

The fort, when finished, was defended by twelve cannon; and there was now a church (chapel, really) as well as a storehouse and houses for the men. Carpenters under the direction of one Digby of London, a shipwright, "framed a pretty pinnace of thirty ton, which they called the *Virginia.*" Explorations were made; Indians came to visit, among them Tanahedo and Skicowaros. But one New England winter did for them. A number of men, including Popham, died.

The sombre events and the end of the colony are narrated by William Strachey in his *History of Travail in Virginia:*

"Many discoveries likewise had been made both to the main and unto the neighbor rivers and the frontier nations fully discovered by the diligence of Captain Gilbert, had not the winter proved so extreme unseasonable and frosty; for it being in the year 1607, when the extraordinary frost was felt in most parts of Europe, it was here likewise as vehement, by which no boat could stir upon any business.

"Howbeit, as time and occasion gave leave, there was nothing omitted which could add unto the benefit or knowledge of the planters, for which when Captain Davies arrived there in the year following (set out from Topsam, the port town of Exeter, with a ship laden full of victuals, arms, instruments and tools, etc.) albeit he found Master George Popham, the president, and some other dead, yet he found all things in good forwardness, and many kinds of furs obtained from the Indians by way of trade; good store of sarsaparilla gathered, and the new pinnace all finished.

"But by reason that Captain Gilbert received letters that his brother was newly dead [Sir John Gilbert died July 8, 1608], and a fair portion of land fallen unto his share which required his repair home, and no mines discovered, nor hope thereof, being the main intended benefit expected to uphold the charge of this plantation, and the fear that all other winters would prove like the first, the company by no means would stay any longer in the country, especially Captain Gilbert being to leave them, and Mr. Popham as aforesaid dead. Wherefore they all embarked in this new arrived ship and in the new pinnace, the *Virginia,* and set sail for England. And this was the end of that northern colony upon the river Sagahadoc."

The *Virginia* returned to America with a fleet carrying settlers and supplies to Jamestown in 1609.

Raleigh had long been out of it, a prisoner in the Tower on a false charge of treason. His meeting with Elizabeth's successor in 1603 had been a personal disaster.

"O my soul, mon," remarked James, newcome from Scotland, "I have heard rawly of thee."

Aubrey, who relates this, has a fitting commentary:

"He was such a person every way that a Prince would rather be afraid of than ashamed of."

From Hariot, and other visitors, he learned of the successful planting in Virginia, and about the expeditions, led by Captain Ratcliffe and others, seeking the lost colonists of Roanoke. He remained a prisoner until 1618. Young Prince Henry, for whom the cape in Chesapeake Bay had been named, was another constant caller. Raleigh wrote for him a discourse about ships, another about the navy and sea-service, and a monumental *History of the World,* only the first volume of which survives. Henry is said to have remarked: "No man but my father would keep such a bird in such a cage."

VII

$\mathcal{L}$AKE

$\mathcal{C}$HAMPLAIN

From Quebec to Three Rivers, over Lake St. Peter, along the dreaded River of the Iroquois (the Richelieu) and "the lake which is of great extent," and which was about to be named, went Samuel de Champlain and two other Frenchmen with a war party of Hurons, Algonquins and Montagnais, taking with them armor and arquebuses. The Indians numbered sixty. They were transported in twenty-four canoes, which were carried overland from time to time, together with their weapons and baggage.

While on the move, the warriors were divided into three groups—two for hunting and scouting, the third representing the main body, always armed and ready for combat. The hunting was done behind the screen of the main force. There was much feasting; but when within two or three days of the enemy, fires were forbidden and the food was reduced to corn bread soaked in water to make a kind of porridge.

The order of battle was decided in the following manner. Sticks a foot long were taken to a level spot and laid out in a pattern, each stick representing a warrior, longer sticks a chief. At another spot the Indians placed themselves in the same order as the sticks, mingled with each other, then returned to the original order. This exercise was repeated several times at all encampments on their route; and, as Champlain observed, a sergeant was not needed.

Champlain's account, after the arrival of the war party at the juncture of river and lake, follows:

"There are many pretty islands here, low and containing very fine woods and meadows, with abundance of fowl and such animals of the chase as stags, fallow deer, fawns, roebucks, bears, and others, which go from the mainland to these islands. We captured a large number of these animals. There are also many beavers, not only in this river, but also in numerous other little ones that flow into it. These regions, although they are pleasant, are not inhabited by any savages, on account of their wars; but they withdraw as far as possible from the rivers into the interior, in order not to be suddenly surprised.

"The next day we entered the lake, which is of great extent, say eighty or a hundred leagues long [an exaggeration], where I saw four fine islands, ten, twelve, and fifteen leagues long, which were formerly inhabited by the savages, like the River of the Iroquois; but they have been abandoned since the wars with one another prevail. There are also many rivers falling into the lake, bordered by many fine trees of the same kinds as those we have in France, with many vines finer than any I have seen in any other place; also many chestnut trees on the border of this lake, which I had not seen before.

"There is also a great abundance of fish, of many varieties, among others one called by the savages of the country *Chaou-sarou* [the gar pike], which varies in length, the largest being, as the people told me, eight or ten feet long. I saw some five feet long which were as large as my thigh, the head being as big as my two fists, with a snout two feet and a half long, and a double row of very sharp and dangerous teeth. Its body is, in shape, much like that of a pike; but it is armed with scales so strong that a poniard could not pierce them. Its color is silver-gray, the extremity of its snout is like that of swine.

"This fish makes war upon all others in the lakes and rivers. It also possesses remarkable dexterity, as these people informed me, which is exhibited in the following manner. When it wants to capture birds, it swims in among the rushes, or reeds, which are found on the banks of the lake in several places, where it puts its snout out of water and keeps perfectly still, so that when the birds come and light on its snout, supposing it to be only the stump of a tree, it adroitly closes it, which it had kept ajar, and pulls the birds by the feet down under water. The savages gave me the head of one of them, of which they make great account, saying that when they have the headache, they bleed themselves with the teeth of this fish on the spot where they suffer pain, when it suddenly passes away.

"Continuing our course over this lake on the western side, I noticed, while observing the country, some very high mountains on the eastern side, on the top of which there was snow [the Green Mountains of Vermont]. I made inquiry of the savages whether these localities were inhabited, when they told me that the Iroquois dwelt there, and that there were beautiful valleys in these places, with plains productive in grain, such as I had eaten in this country, together with many kinds of fruit without limit.

CHAMPLAIN AT TICONDEROGA, 1609
"I rested my musket against my cheek, and aimed directly at one of the three chiefs. With the same shot, two fell to the ground; and one of their men was so wounded that he died some time after. I had loaded my musket with four balls." Drawing and text by Champlain, *Les Voyages*, 1613. Courtesy of the Rare Book Division, The New York Public Library.

"They said also that the lake extended near mountains, some twenty-five leagues distant from us, as I judge. I saw, on the south, other mountains, no less high than the first, but without any snow [the Adirondacks]. The savages told me that these mountains were thickly settled, and that it was there we were to find their enemies; but that it was necessary to pass a fall [Ticonderoga] in order to go there (which I afterward saw), when we should enter another lake nine or ten leagues long

[Lake George]. After reaching the end of the lake, we should have to go, they said, two leagues by land, and pass through a river [the Hudson] flowing into the sea on the Norumbega coast near that of Florida, whither it took them only two days to go by canoe, as I have since ascertained from some prisoners we captured, who gave me minute information in regard to all they had personal knowledge of, through some Algonquin interpreters who understood the Iroquois language.

"Now, as we began to approach within two or three days' journey of the abode of their enemies, we advanced only at night, resting during the day. But they did not fail to practice constantly their accustomed superstitions, in order to ascertain what was to be the result of their undertaking; and they often asked me if I had had a dream and seen their enemies, to which I replied in the negative. Yet I did not cease to encourage them, and inspire in them hope. When night came, we set out on the journey until the next day, when we withdrew into the interior of the forest, and spent the rest of the day there.

"About ten or eleven o'clock, after taking a little walk about our encampment, I retired. While sleeping, I dreamed that I saw our enemies, the Iroquois, drowning in the lake near a mountain, within sight. When I expressed a wish to help them, our allies, the savages, told me we must let them all die, and that they were of no importance. When I awoke they did not fail to ask me, as usual, if I had had a dream. I told them that I had, in fact, had a dream. This, upon being related, gave them so much confidence that they did not doubt any longer that good was to happen to them.

"When it was evening, we embarked in our canoes to continue our course; and, as we advanced very quietly and without making any noise, we met on the 29th of the month [it was July, 1609] the Iroquois, about ten o'clock at evening, at the extremity of a cape which extends into the lake on the western bank. We both began to utter loud cries, all getting their arms in readiness. We withdrew out on the water, and the Iroquois went on shore, where they drew up all their canoes close to each other and began to fell trees with poor axes, which they acquire in war sometimes, using also others of stone. Thus they barricaded themselves very well.

"Our forces also passed the entire night, their canoes being drawn up close to each other and fastened to poles so that they might not get separated, and that they might be all in readiness to fight, if occasion required. We were out upon the water, within arrow range of their barricades. When they were armed and in array, they dispatched two canoes by themselves to the enemy to inquire if they wished to fight; to which the latter replied that they wanted nothing else. But they said that, at present, there was not much light, and that it would be necessary to wait for daylight, so as to be able to recognize each other, and that, as soon as the sun rose, they would offer us battle.

"This was agreed to by our side.

"Meanwhile, the entire night was spent in dancing and singing, on both sides, with endless insults and other talk: as, how little courage we had, how feeble a resistance we should make against their arms, and that when day came we should realize it to our ruin.

"Ours also were not slow in retorting, telling them they would see such execution of arms as never before, together with an abundance of such talk as is not unusual in the siege of a town.

"After this singing, dancing, and bandying words on both sides to the fill, when day came, my companions and myself continued under cover, for fear that the enemy would see us. We arranged our arms in the best manner possible, being, however, separated, each in one of the canoes of the savage Montagnais. After arming ourselves with light armor, we each took an arquebus and went on shore. I saw the enemy go out of their barricade, nearly two hundred in number, stout and rugged in appearance. They came at a slow pace toward us, with a dignity and assurance which greatly amused me, having three chiefs at their head. Our men also advanced in the same order, telling me that those who had three large plumes were the chiefs, and that they had only these three, and that they could be distinguished by these plumes, which were much larger than those of their companions, and that I should do what I could to kill them.

"I promised to do all in my power, and said that I was very sorry they could not understand me, so that I might give order and shape to their mode of attacking their enemies, and then we should, without doubt, defeat them all; but that this could not now be obviated, and that I should be very glad to show them my courage and good will when we should engage in the fight.

"As soon as we had landed, they began to run for some two

hundred paces toward their enemies, who stood firmly, not having as yet noticed my companions, who went into the woods with some savages. Our men began to call me with loud cries; and, in order to give me a passageway, they opened in two parts and put me at their head, where I marched some twenty paces in advance of the rest, until I was within about thirty paces of the enemy, who at once noticed me and, halting, gazed at me, as I did also at them.

"When I saw them making a move to fire at us, I rested my musket against my cheek and aimed directly at one of the three chiefs. With the same shot, two fell to the ground; and one of their men was so wounded that he died soon after. I had loaded my musket with four balls.

"When our side saw this shot so favorable for them, they began to raise such loud cries that one could not have heard it thunder. Meanwhile, the arrows flew on both sides.

"The Iroquois were greatly astonished that two men had been so quickly killed, although they were equipped with armor woven from cotton thread and with wood which was proof against their arrows. This caused great alarm among them.

"As I was loading again, one of my companions fired a shot from the woods, which astonished them anew to such a degree that, seeing their chiefs dead, they lost courage, and took to flight, abandoning their camp and fort, and fleeing into the woods, whither I pursued them, killing still more of them. Our savages also killed several of them, and took ten or twelve prisoners. The remainder escaped with the wounded. Fifteen or sixteen were wounded on our side with arrow-shots; but they were soon healed.

"After gaining the victory, our men amused themselves by taking a great quantity of Indian corn and some meal from their enemies, also their armor, which they left behind that they might run better. After feasting sumptuously, dancing and singing, we returned three hours after, with the prisoners. The spot where this attack took place is in latitude 43 degrees and some minutes, and the lake was called Lake Champlain."

The spot was Ticonderoga. Champlain drew a picture of the battle to illustrate his text. It is a strange and surprising composition— arms and the man in a wilderness of arrows.

The fate of the prisoners was awesome.

"After going some eight leagues, toward evening they took one of the prisoners, to whom they made an harangue, enumerating the cruelties which he and his men had already practiced toward them without any mercy, and that, in like manner, he ought to make up his mind to receive as much. They commanded him to sing, if he had courage, which he did; but it was a very sad song.

"Meanwhile, our men kindled a fire, and when it was well burning, they each took a brand and burned this poor creature gradually, so as to make him suffer greater torment. Sometimes they stopped and threw water on his back. Then they tore out his nails, and applied fire to the extremities of his fingers and private member. Afterwards they flayed the top of his head, and had a kind of gum poured all hot upon it. Then they pierced his arms near the wrists and, drawing up the sinews with sticks, they tore them out by force; but seeing that they could not get them, they cut them. This poor wretch uttered terrible cries, and it excited my pity to see him treated in this manner, and yet showing such firmness that one would have said, at times, that he suffered hardly any pain at all.

"I remonstrated with them, saying that we practiced no such cruelties, but killed them at once, and that, if they wished me to fire a musket-shot at him, I should be willing to do so. They refused, saying that he would not, in that case, suffer any pain. I went away from them, pained to see such cruelties practiced upon his body. When they saw I was displeased, they called me, and told me to fire a musket-shot at him. This I did without his seeing it, and thus put an end, by a single shot, to all the torments he would have suffered, rather than see him tyrannized over.

"After his death, they were not yet satisfied, but opened him and threw his entrails into the lake. Then they cut off his head, arms, and legs, which they scattered in different directions, keeping the scalp, which they had flayed off, as they had done in the case of all the rest whom they had killed in the contest.

"They were guilty also of another monstrosity in taking his heart, cutting it into several pieces, and giving it to a brother of his to eat, as also to others of his companions who were prisoners. They took it into their mouths, but would not swallow it. Some Algonquin savages, who were guarding them, made some of them spit it out, when they threw it into the water.

"This is the manner in which these people behave toward those whom they capture in war, for whom it would be better to die fighting, or to kill themselves on the spur of the moment, as many do, rather than fall into the hands of their enemies.

"After this execution, we set out on our return with the rest of the prisoners, who kept singing as they went along, with no better hopes for the future than he had had who was so wretchedly treated."

The song sung by the captive Iroquois was expressive of their courage, there being respect on both sides for such bravado. The Hurons had a song of their own which they sang when being transported to their deaths on the River of the Iroquois:

> "If I die, I die valiant!
> I go without fear
> To that land where brave men
> Have gone long before me—
> If I die, I die valiant!"

The short, sharp and successful engagement had enormous consequences. The enmity aroused in the Iroquois nation effectively sealed off New York State from New France, and gave the Dutch and English precious time and the protection needed to establish settlements.

IROQUOIS ART
Pre-Columbian brownware pottery jar, with human figures. From Madison County, New York. Height: 8¾ inches. Photograph courtesy of the Museum of the American Indian, Heye Foundation.

VIII

THE HUDSON

The *Half Moon* was a two-master with topsails, 80 tons burden, outfitted by the Dutch East India Company, Amsterdam branch, to
seek a passage to the Orient, the directors not caring whether it
voyaged northeast or northwest to find it. It was under the command of an Englishman named Henry Hudson, an experienced
mariner who had served with the Muscovy Company of England
on the icy run to Nova Zembla, and it left the Zuyder Zee April 6,
1609, rounded Norway, and headed for the arctic wastes to the
northeast. Its crew was half English, half Dutch, and numbered
about twenty—a Dutch historian of that time, Emanuel van
Meteren, says "eighteen or twenty men, partly English, partly
Dutch, well provided" (*History of the Netherlanders*).

Some of the crew had been in the East Indies, and did not like
the climate now encountered.

"Upon which," says van Meteren, "Captain Hudson laid before
them two propositions. The first of these was to go to the coast
of America, to the latitude of 40 degrees, moved thereto mostly
by letters and maps which a certain Captain Smith had sent
him from Virginia, and by which he indicated to him a sea
leading into the western ocean, by the north of the southern

English colony. Had this information been true (experience goes as yet to the contrary), it would have been of great advantage, as indicating a short way to India. The other proposition was to direct their search through Davis's Straits [named for John Davis who explored it in 1587]. This meeting with general approval, they sailed thitherward on the 14th of May, and arrived on the last day of May with a good wind at the Faroe Islands, where they stopped but twenty-four hours to supply themselves with fresh water. After leaving these islands they sailed on, till the 18th of July they reached the coast of Nova Francia, under 44 degrees, where they were obliged to run in, in order to get a new foremast, having lost theirs. They found one, and set it up.

"They found this a good place for cod-fishing, as also for traffic in good skins and furs, which were to be got there at a very low price. But the crew behaved badly toward the people of the country, taking their property by force, out of which there arose quarrels among themselves. The English, fearing that between the two they would be outnumbered and worsted, were therefore afraid to pursue the matter further. So they left that place on the 26th of July and kept out to sea till the 3rd of August, when they came near the coast in 42 degrees of latitude. Thence they sailed on, till on the 12th of August they again reached the shore, under 37 degrees 45 minutes."

They had come, in fact, to Chesapeake Bay and "the King's River in Virginia, where our Englishmen are," as an English officer on the *Half Moon* noted. But Hudson did not attempt to sail up the river to Jamestown and consult Smith about the sea "leading into the western ocean." Perhaps his crew, or the Dutch members of it, would not let him, fearing reprisals.

Little is known about Henry Hudson. He may have been the grandson of a London alderman who was connected with the Muscovy Company. It is evident, however, that greatly skilled though he was as a navigator, he lacked the art or forceful nature of a commander. He offered "two propositions" to his men at sea, and could not control their behavior on shore. Now, in August, 1609, we find him probing the American coast from Chesapeake Bay northward, and about to make the discovery with which his name is forever associated. Yet he remains a shadowy figure throughout. His own journal of the voyage has disappeared, except for some brief passages incorporated by Johannes de Laet, another Dutch historian, in his *New World*.

The following account is by one Robert Juet [perhaps Jewett or Jowett] "of Limehouse," as he termed himself, the officer on the *Half Moon* previously mentioned. The ship paused briefly in Delaware Bay on August 28, then resumed its run up the New Jersey shoreline. On the night of September 2 "we saw a great fire, but could not see the land," Juet wrote. They were off Sandy Hook, a spit of Jersey coast which looks like a beckoning finger on the map; past it lay the chief prize of the western world, as yet unclaimed of any. When daylight came the exploration of the great bay and harbor of New York began, the ship's boat sounding for depth, and the ship itself following. Fishing with a net, the men in the boat caught ten mullets, each a foot and half long, and a ray "as great as four men could hale into the ship."

By now the *Half Moon* was being observed from the shore by throngs of Indians, who "came aboard" [paddled to the ship's side] in their hollowed-out canoes to barter tobacco for knives and beads. They wore deerskins which were "well dressed." Later, other Indians offered hemp, and dried currants "which were sweet and very good." Some of these wore mantles made of feathers, others "good furs." The men had red copper pipes and were adorned with copper ornaments.

The *Half Moon* was now anchored in the Narrows. The men in the ship's boat, to the number of five, went back and forth, to barter and explore, and possibly getting into mischief. They reported that "the lands were pleasant, with grass and flowers and goodly trees, as ever they had seen, and very sweet smells came from them." Late on September 6, as the boat was returning once more, two canoes—one carrying twelve Indians, the other fourteen—suddenly attacked, killing one man with an arrow through his throat, and wounding two others. The dead man was John Colman, an Englishman. In the darkness the survivors could not find the ship, and there was "so great a stream" that their grapnel could not hold the boat fast. They spent the night rowing back and forth.

The "great stream" was from the tidal Hudson.

The dead man was buried the next day at a spot which Juet says they named Colman's Point in his honor, somewhere on the Jersey shore. Other Indians came out to the ship to barter, and the boat was put over the side "to mark them [observe them] to see if they would make any show of the death of our man; which they did not." On another occasion, two canoes approached, one of them filled with warriors and the other with traders; of these, Juet says, "we took two of them to have kept them, and put red coats on them, and would not suffer the other to come near us."

The war canoe returned to land, and two Indians paddled out: "we took the one and let the other go; but he which we had taken got up and leapt overboard."

Thus the *Half Moon* proceeded slowly, cautiously, taking soundings and anchoring,

> "the wind at south-southwest, little wind. Our soundings were seven, six, five, six, seven, eight, nine, ten, twelve, thirteen, and fourteen fathoms. Then we anchored, and saw that it was a very good harbor for all winds, and rode all night. The people of the country came aboard of us, making show of love, and gave us tobacco and Indian wheat [corn], and departed for that night; but we durst not trust them."

This was on September 11; on the 12th the *Half Moon* entered the river that bears the name of its English commander. "It floweth southeast by south within." Canoes kept coming—here, twenty-eight of them, filled with men, women and children, appeared with offerings of oysters and beans. Although Juet does not mention it, Hudson went ashore on Manhattan Island. From the lost journal, as quoted by de Laet.

> "When I came on shore the swarthy natives all stood and sang in their fashion. Their clothing consists of the skins of foxes and other animals, which they dress and make the garments from skins of various sorts. Their food is Turkish wheat [Indian corn], which they cook by baking, and it is excellent eating. They soon came on board, one after another, in their canoes, which are made of a single piece of wood. Their weapons are bows and arrows, pointed with sharp stones, which they fasten with hard resin. They had no houses but slept under the blue heavens, some on mats of bulrushes interwoven, and some on the leaves of trees. They always carry with them all their goods, as well as their food and green tobacco, which is strong and good for use. They appear to be a friendly people, but are much inclined to steal, and are adroit in carrying away whatever they take a fancy to."

Later:

> "It is as pleasant a land as one can tread upon, very abundant in all kinds of timber suitable for shipbuilding, and for making large casks. The people had copper tobacco pipes, from which I inferred that copper must exist there; and iron likewise, according to the testimony of the natives who, however, do not understand preparing it for use."

The decision was made to explore the tidal river. The following account of the journey from Manna-hata to Albany is from the day-by-day journal or log kept by Robert Juet:

"The thirteenth, fair weather, the wind northerly. At seven of the clock in the morning, as the flood came, we weighed and turned four miles into the river. The tide being done, we anchored. Then there came four canoes aboard; but we suffered none of them to come into our ship. They brought great store of very good oysters aboard, which we bought for trifles. In the night I set the variation of the compass, and found it to be 13 degrees [from true north]. In the afternoon we weighed, and turned in with the flood two leagues and a half further, and anchored all night, and had five fathoms soft oozy ground; and had an high point of land which showed out to us, bearing north by east five leagues off us.

"The fourteenth, in the morning, being very fair weather, the wind southeast, we sailed up the river twelve leagues, and had five fathoms, and five fathoms and a quarter less, and came to a strait between two points [in the region of West Point], and had eight, nine, and ten fathoms; and it trended northeast by north one league. And we had twelve, thirteen, and fourteen fathoms.

"The river is a mile broad. There is very high land on both sides.

"Then we went up northwest a league and an half deep water. Then northeast by north five miles, then northwest by north two leagues, and anchored. The land grew very high and mountainous.

"The river is full of fish.

"The fifteenth, in the morning, was misty, until the sun arose; then it cleared. So we weighed with the wind at south and ran up into the river twenty leagues, passing by high mountains [the upper Highlands]. We had a very good depth, as six, seven, eight, nine, ten, twelve, and thirteen fathoms, and great store of salmons in the river.

"This morning our two savages got out of a port and swam away. After we were under sail they called to us in scorn.

"At night we came to other mountains, which lie from the river's side [the Catskills]. There we found very loving people, and very old men, where we were well used. Our boat went to fish, and caught great store of very good fish.

"The sixteenth, fair and very hot summer. In the morning

our boat went again to fishing, but could catch but few, by
reason their canoes had been there all night.

"This morning the people came aboard and brought us ears
of Indian corn, and pumpkins and tobacco, which we bought
for trifles. We rode all day and filled fresh water; at night we
weighed and went two leagues higher, and had shoal water. So
we anchored till day.

"The seventeenth, fair, sun-shining weather, and very hot. In
the morning, as soon as the sun was up, we set sail and ran up
six leagues higher, and found shoals in the middle of the channel, and small islands, but seven fathoms water on both sides.
Toward night we borrowed [nautical: approach close] so near
the shore that we grounded. So we laid out our small anchor
and heaved off again. Then we borrowed on the bank in the
channel, and came aground again. While the flood ran, we
heaved off again and anchored all night.

"The eighteenth in the morning was fair weather, and we
rode still [at anchor]. In the afternoon our master's mate went
on land with an old savage, a governor of the country, who
carried him to his house and made him good cheer."

According to de Laet, it was Hudson who went ashore, and
quotes from the lost journal—the last of the surviving passages:

"I sailed to the shore in one of their canoes with an old man
who was the chief of a tribe consisting of forty men and seventeen women; these I saw there in a house well constructed of
oak bark and circular in shape, with the appearance of having
a vaulted ceiling. It contained a great quantity of maize, and
beans of last year's growth, and there lay near the house for
the purpose of drying enough to load three ships, besides what
was growing in the fields.

"On our coming near the house, two mats were spread out to
sit upon, and immediately some food was served in well-made
red wooden bowls. Two men were also dispatched at once with
bows and arrows in quest of game, who soon after brought in a
pair of pigeons which they had just shot. They likewise killed
at once a fat dog, and skinned it in great haste with shells
which they get out of the water. They supposed that I would
remain with them for the night, but I returned after a short
time on board the ship.

"The land is the finest for cultivation that I ever in my life
set foot upon, and it also abounds in trees of every description.
The natives are a very good people; for, when they saw that I

would not remain, they supposed that I was afraid of their bows, and taking the arrows, they broke them in pieces and threw them into the fire."

The *Half Moon* was in the territory of the Mohawks. Juet says:

"The nineteenth was fair, and hot weather. At the flood, being near eleven of the clock, we weighed and ran higher up, two leagues above the shoals, and had no less water than five fathoms. We anchored and rode in eight fathoms. The people of the country came flocking aboard, and brought us grapes and pumpkins, which we bought for trifles. And many brought us beavers' skins and otters' skins, which we bought for beads, knives and hatchets. So we rode there all night.

"The twentieth, in the morning, was fair weather. Our master's mate with four men more went up with our boat to sound the river, and found two leagues above us but two fathoms water and the channel very narrow, and above that place seven or eight fathoms. Toward night they returned, and we rode still all night.

"The one-and-twentieth was fair weather and the wind all southerly. We determined yet once more to go farther up into the river, to try what depth and breadth it did bear; but much people resorted aboard, so we went not this day. Our carpenter went on land and made a foreyard. And our master and his mate determined to try some of the chief men of the country whether they had any treachery in them. So they took them down into the cabin and gave them so much wine and *aqua vitae* [brandy] that they were all merry. And one of them had his wife with him, which sat so modestly, as any of our country-women would do in a strange place. In the end, one of them was drunk, which had been aboard of our ship all the time that we had been there; and that was strange to them, they could not tell how to take it. The canoes and folk went all on shore, but some of them came again and brought stropes of beads [wampum]; some had six, seven, eight, nine, ten, and gave him. So he slept all night quietly. [The offerings of wampum were intended to show respect to their chief, and perhaps to be used to purchase his freedom, if need be. They also stood by.]

"The two-and-twentieth was fair weather. In the morning our master's mate and four more of the company went up with our boat to sound the river higher up. The people of the country came not aboard till noon, but when they came and saw the savages well, they were glad. So at three of the clock in the afternoon they came aboard and brought tobacco and more beads, and gave them to our master and made an oration, and showed him all the country round about. Then they sent one of their company on land, who presently returned and brought a great platter full of venison, dressed by themselves; and they caused him to eat with them. Then they made him reverence and departed, all save the old man that lay aboard. This night, at ten of the clock, our boat returned in a shower of rain from sounding of the river, and found it to be at an end for shipping to go in, for they had been up eight or nine leagues and found but seven foot water and unconstant soundings."

The ship's boat may have gone above the mouth of the Mohawk River. It was the end of exploration by the *Half Moon*. On September 23 it turned back; from time to time, while it rode at anchor, men went ashore on the west bank, gathering nuts and fishing, all the while noting "good ground for corn and other garden herbs, with great store of goodly oaks, and walnut trees, and chestnut trees, yew trees, and trees of sweet wood in great abundance." They saw "great store of slate for houses, and other good stones." In the neighborhood of present-day Newburgh—"this is a very pleasant place to build a town on," Juet wrote—it was observed that "the mountains look as if some metal or mineral were in them. For the trees that grow on them were all blasted, and some of them barren, with few or no trees on them."

Thus far, the Indians had all been friendly, paddling to the ship with produce to barter or give; but on October 1, near Stony Point, "the people of the mountains came aboard us," and it happened. Juet says:

"This afternoon, one canoe kept hanging under our stern with one man in it, which we could not keep from thence, who got up by our rudder to the cabin window and stole out my pillow and two shirts and two bandoleers. Our master's mate shot at him, and struck him on the breast, and killed him. Whereupon all the rest fled away, some in their canoes, and so leapt out of them into the water. We manned our boat and got our things again. Then one of them that swam got hold of our boat, thinking to overthrow it. But our cook took a sword and cut off one of his hands, and he was drowned."

There was a sequel, or repeat performance, the next day.

"Two canoes full of men, with their bows and arrows, shot at us after our stern; in recompense whereof we discharged six muskets and killed two or three of them. Then above an hundred of them came to a point of land to shoot at us. There I shot a falcon [small cannon] at them, and killed two of them, whereupon the rest fled into the woods. Yet they manned off another canoe with nine or ten men, which came to meet us. So I shot at it also a falcon and shot it through, and killed one of them. Then our men with their muskets killed three or four more of them."

The running battle took place at the upper end of Manhattan Island. The attacking Indians came from the New Jersey shore. The mouth of the river was reached on October 4. "Then we took in our boat and set our mainsail and spritsail and our topsails and steered away east-southeast and southeast by east off into the main sea" (from *The Third Voyage of Master Henry Hudson*).

Juet says their course was for England, where the *Half Moon* arrived, "in the Range of Dartmouth in Devonshire," November 7. Emanuel van Meteren wrote:

"While at sea, they held counsel together, but were of different opinions. The mate, a Dutchman, advised to winter in Newfoundland, and to search the northwestern passage of Davis throughout. This was opposed by Skipper Hudson. He was afraid of his mutinous crew, who had sometimes savagely threatened him; and he feared that during the cold season they would entirely consume their provisions, and would then be obliged to return, many of the crew ill and sickly. Nobody, however, spoke of returning home to Holland, which circumstance made the captain still more suspicious. He proposed therefore to sail to Ireland and winter there, which they all agreed to. At last they arrived at Dartmouth, in England, the 7th of November, whence they informed their employers, the directors in Holland, of their voyage.

"They proposed to them to go out again for a search in the northwest, and that, besides the pay, and what they already had in the ship, 1500 florins should be laid out for an additional supply of provisions. He [Captain Hudson] also wanted six or seven of his crew exchanged for others."

He may have failed in this.

Henry Hudson sailed to northern latitudes the following year. In the icy bay named for him he was set adrift in an open boat by his mutinous crew.

IX

ℕEW
ℰNGLAND

From Holland in 1613 came Captain Adrian Block, for whom Block Island was named. He was followed by Captain Cornelius May, who left a sprinkling of names, one of them Cape May, and Captain Hendrick Christianzen, who named an island in the Martha's Vineyard group for himself, but could not make it stick. Soon the Dutch were claiming everything in sight, and their trading posts were strung from the Great North River of the Mountains (the Hudson) to the South River (the Delaware). They were, as yet, unnoticed.

From Spain came a caravel to observe the doings at Jamestown. Three of its crew were seized at Point Comfort (as it was now called). Two were gentlemen—a captain and an ensign; the third was a sailor, Francisco Lembri by name. They were, of course, closely examined. They were also held. The sole survivor, Don Diego de Molina, for all that he was a gentleman, was also a spy, as a letter in which he relates his experiences reveals. He appears to have been kept in a fort at Point Comfort—Fort Algernon. He also mentions Fort Charles on Strawberry Bank (Elizabeth City); Fort Henry on the east side of Hampton River, and the new settlement of Henrico, both named for Prince Henry. Molina believed that all these places could be taken by Spain without much difficulty, and that if it were not done, the king would be confronted

A PORTION OF SMITH'S MAP OF NEW ENGLAND, 1616
First issue, with "Plimouth" at lower left. Later printings have "New Plymouth," the name chosen by the Pilgrims. The legend on the engraving of Smith's portrait states that he was 37 years old. From the Rare Book Division, The New York Public Library.

with "this new Algiers of America"—that is, a resort of pirates and a threat to the West Indies and Mexico. The English were also in possession of Bermuda, which made it that much worse, he cautioned.

The ensign died in captivity—Molina says

"more from hunger than illness, but assuredly with the patience of a saint and the spirit of a good soldier. I have not fared very ill, but tolerably so, because since I arrived I have been in favor with these people and they have shown me friendship as far as their own wretchedness would allow, but with genuine good will. The sailor who came with me is said to be English and a pilot."

When he wrote this, Lembri was dead—hanged at sea.

Molina and Lembri were taken back to England by Sir Thomas Dale, deputy governor of Virginia. During the voyage the questioning of Lembri went on, and it was discovered that he was, in fact, English. Dale ordered him executed as a traitor. Smith's *General History of Virginia, New England and the Summer Isles*, states that Lembri "had been the Spaniards' pilot for England in '88"—that is, for the Armada.

From England came Smith himself, to explore and chart the upper part of Virginia for the Plymouth Company. He gave New England its name, and a particular place on his map was designated Plymouth. One of the ships in his expedition was commanded by a Captain Thomas Hunt, who saw an opportunity for personal profit and seized a number of Indians. All were sold as slaves in Malaga, but were released through the intercession of friars. One of them made his way back, via England.

The French settlements on the coast posed a more immediate threat than spies. From Jamestown went Captain Samuel Argall and burned them all—Mt. Desert and St. Croix (Maine), and for good measure, Port Royal (maps after 1614 term the Bay of Funday "Argall's Bay").

On July 30, 1619, the first representative assembly ever convened on the American continent met at Jamestown. It sat until August 4. In that month, a Dutch man-of-war arrived with a cargo of African slaves, twenty of whom were sold to the settlers—another first instance of its kind.

There were about a thousand persons in the colony. Their chief exports were tobacco and sassafras. Tobacco, in particular, was making many of them rich—those with servants or slaves, richer. John Pory, speaker of the assembly, in a letter sent back by the Dutch ship to Sir Dudley Carleton, his Majesty's ambassador at The Hague, states:

"Now, that your Lordship may know that we are not the veriest beggars in the world, our cow keeper here of James City on Sunday goes accoutered all in flesh flaming silk; and a wife of one that in England had professed the black art, not of a scholar, but of a collier of Croydon, wears her rough beaver hat with a fair pearl hat band, and a silken suit thereto correspondent."

There appear to have been many dogs about. One of the acts passed by the assembly reads:

"That no man do sell or give any of the greater hounds to the Indians, or any English dog of quality, as a mastiff, greyhound, bloodhound, land or water spaniel, or any dog or bitch whatsoever of the English race, upon pain of forfeiting five shillings sterling to the public uses of the Incorporation where he dwelleth."

Another foreshadows the doom that overtook many settlements, north and south, when the public good was sacrificed for private profit:

"That no man do sell or give any Indians any piece, shot or powder, or any other arms, offensive or defensive, upon pain of being held a traitor to the Colony, and of being hanged as soon as the fact is proved, without all redemption."

The last phrase may mean without appeal, or what is more likely, without absolution.

The assembly, which met in the church at Jamestown, was presided over by Sir George Yeardley, the newly arrived governor and captain general of Virginia. There were two delegates each from James City (Jamestown and vicinity); Charles City (City Point); Henricus (Henrico); Kecoughtan (Elizabeth City); Martin Brandon (Captain John Martin's plantation at Brandon, on the south side of the James River); Smith's Hundred (on the north side of the James; afterward Southampton Hundred. Hundred: English, subdivision of county or shire); Martin's Hundred (below Jamestown); Argall's Gift (north of Jamestown); Flowerdew Hundred (between Brandon and City Point); Lawne's Plantation (named for Captain Christopher Lawne; at Lawne's Creek, Isle of Wight County); Ward's Plantation (for Captain William Ward; above Brandon). Martin's delegates were barred because a clause in his patent exempted him from colonial authority.

The meeting was opened by a prayer by the Reverend Richard Buck, an Oxford divine who, in 1614, married John Rolfe and Pocahontas. From the proceedings of the Virginia Assembly (or House of Burgesses as it came to be called):

"All the Burgesses took their places in the choir till a prayer was said by Mr. Buck, the minister, that it would please God to guide and sanctify all our proceedings to His own glory and the good of the Plantation. Prayer being ended, to the intent that as we had begun at God Almighty, so we might proceed with awful and due respect toward the Lieutenant [of God], our most gracious and dread Sovereign, all the Burgesses were entreated to retire themselves into the body of the church; which being done, before they were fully admitted, they were called in order and by name, and so every man (none staggering at it) took the Oath of Supremacy, and entered the Assembly."

"None staggering at it"—they were all loyal subjects, and acknowledged the ecclesiastical supremacy of the king. The Act of Supremacy was originally intended to exclude the authority of the Pope, but could be, and had been, used against Englishmen who were neither Catholic nor Anglican. Such were those who came next to the shores of America.

They came by way of Holland.

There were living in Leyden, not far from the famous university which attracted students and scholars from all Europe, a number of English families from Scrooby, Nottinghamshire. In contradistinction to some in England who merely sought to purify their churches from remaining Catholic influence, ornament and ceremony— whence Puritans—others had rebelled completely and formed congregations of their own. They were called Separatists. One such group had been in Amsterdam since 1593, when Nonconformists were ordered to abjure the realm—that is, depart or die (the law was afterward repealed).

The good people of Leyden admired the sober, industrious English in their midst, and wept when they departed. Their occupations varied. William Brewster taught English at the university, and afterward published some books proscribed in England, chiefly of religious controversy. Edward Winslow was a printer, Robert Cushman a wool-carder, Samuel Fuller, a silk maker, and William Bradford, a fustian maker (fustian: thick twilled short-napped cotton cloth, usually dyed dark, hence applied also to turgid prose; Bradford's prose, however, ranks with the greatest writing ever produced in America and is, in fact, a wellspring of its literature as it is of its historical sources. In its vivid speech and imagery, it is as often Elizabethan as Jacobean). Like Brewster's, Bradford's learning was great, his life pious. The entire English community was praised in public:

> "The magistrates of the city, about the time of their coming away, or a little before, in the public place of justice, gave this commendable testimony of them, in the reproof of the Walloons, who were of the French church in that city. Those English, said they, have lived among us now this twelve years, and yet we never had any suit or accusations came against any of them; but your strifes and quarrels are continual."

These Walloons were Protestant, likewise refugees from religious persecution. Some of them joined the English Separatists when they left Leyden, and it is possible that William Mullins (Moulins? Mollines?) was one of them (his daughter Priscilla is the heroine of Longfellow's *The Courtship of Miles Standish*). Bradford, in his *History of Plymouth Plantation*, just quoted, does not tell what the suits and accusations were about. He adds, however: "In these times also were the great troubles raised by the Arminians who, as they greatly molested the whole state, so this city in particular, in which was the chief university, so as there were daily and hot disputes in the schools thereabouts." And what were these "hot disputes" about? Arminius (in the Latinized form of his name) was a Dutch theologian who opposed the views of Calvin, particularly on predestination, proffering instead, a doctrine of grace. Neither theologian, it may be thought, came out second best, as the issue is yet to be decided.

Bradford was seventeen when he decided to accompany the Scrooby congregation to Holland. He was now a vigorous thirty or thirty-one. In writing about the departure for England, and thence for America, the dilemma of the Separatists is presented with clarity:

> "For Virginia it was objected, that if they lived among the English which were there planted, or so near them as to be under their government, they should be in as great danger to be troubled and persecuted for the cause of religion, as if they lived in England; and it might be, worse. And if they lived too far off, they should neither have succor nor defense from them [against the Spaniards].
>
> "But at length the conclusion was, to live as a distinct body by themselves, under the general government of Virginia; and by their friends to sue to his Majesty that he would be pleased to grant them freedom of religion; and that this might be obtained, they were put in good hope by some great persons, of good rank and quality, that were made their friends. Where-

upon two were chosen and sent into England (at the charge of the rest) to solicit this matter, who found the Virginia Company very desirous to have them go thither, and willing to grant them a patent with as ample privileges as they had or could grant to any, and to give them the best furtherance they could. And some of the chief of that company doubted not to obtain their suit of the King for liberty in religion, and to have it confirmed under the King's broad seal, according to their desires.

"But it proved a harder piece of work than they took it for; for though many means were used to bring it about, yet it could not be effected; for there were divers of good worth labored with the King to obtain it (among whom was one of his chief secretaries), and some other wrought with the archbishop to give way thereunto; but it all proved in vain."

The secretary referred to here was Sir Robert Naunton, Secretary of State for James, who had served Elizabeth as well, and whose portraits of Elizabeth and Raleigh from his pen were given earlier. The archbishop was George Abbot, Archbishop of Canterbury.

James appears to have been inclined to let them go but not "tolerate them by his public authority," since he was Defender of the Faith. Bradford says: "Thus far they prevailed, in sounding His Majesty's mind, that he would connive at them, and not molest them, provided they carried themselves peaceably."

BUILDERS OF THE NEW JERUSALEM
Detail from frontispiece to *Purchas his Pilgrims.*

Next came negotiations with the Council for New England, as it was now called. And to New England they went. Of the departure from Holland in a small ship which was bought for that purpose— the *Speedwell*, 60 tons—and which was to be used in fishing and other profitable ventures in America, Bradford wrote: "They knew they were pilgrims" (from Middle English *pelegrim* from Old French *pelegrin* from the Latin *peregrinus:* stranger. For an extended exegesis on Bradford's tiny text, see Hebrews 11, New Testament). Waiting for them at Southampton was another ship, of 180 tons burden and with two decks, hired for the Atlantic crossing. It was the *Mayflower,* Christopher Jones, captain. The contract brought from the Council for New England by one of the merchant adventurers was not acceptable to the Pilgrim leaders. He, on his part, refused to disburse any money, which was in short supply.

> "And whereas there wanted well near 100 pounds to clear things at their going away, he would not take order to disburse a penny, but let them shift as they could. So they were forced to sell off some of their provisions to stop this gap, which was some three or four score firkins of butter, which commodity they might best spare, having provided too large a quantity of that kind."

(Firkin: small cask. As measure: half of a kilderkin. Kilderkin: cask containing 16 or 18 gallons.)

The two ships left Southampton "about the 5. of August," 1620. The *Speedwell* was found to be aleak, and both ships put into Dartmouth. Again the ships put out to sea, and again the *Speedwell* was forced to return, accompanied by the *Mayflower,* this time to Plymouth; here, it was found that the smaller ship "would not prove sufficient for the voyage. Upon which it was resolved to dismiss her and part of the company, and proceed with the other ship. The which (though it was grievous, and caused great discouragement) was put into execution." Supplies were transferred from the smaller ship to the larger. On September 6 the *Mayflower* set forth by itself on the historic voyage. There were 103 Separatists—or Pilgrims— aboard. John Carver was designated Governor.

It was a rough crossing they had of it. The Pilgrims prayed, and the sailors cursed. They cursed and muttered because the ship was overcrowded, and because in stormy weather, of which there was a great deal, "the ship was shrewdly shaken, and her upper works made very leaky; and one of the main beams in the midship was bowed and cracked." The Pilgrims were just as apprehensive as the sailors and "entered into serious consultation with the master and other officers of the ship, to consider in time of the danger, and rather to return than to cast themselves into a desperate and inevitable peril." It was concluded, however, that the ship was "strong and firm under water; and for the buckling of the main beam, there was a great iron screw the passengers brought out of Holland which would raise the beam into his place; the which being done, the carpenter and master affirmed that with a post put under it, set firm in the lower deck, and other ways bound, he would make it sufficient. And as for the decks and upper works, they would caulk them as well as they could."

And so they proceeded. Some of the storms were so fierce that the ship was "forced to hull divers days together," adrift with sails down. It was November when they neared the coast.

"After long beating at sea they fell with that land which is called Cape Cod; the which being made and certainly known to be it, they were not a little joyful. After some deliberation had among themselves and with the master of the ship, they tacked about and resolved to stand for the southward (the wind and weather being fair) to find some place about Hudson's river for their habitation. But after they had sailed that course about half a day, they fell among dangerous shoals and roaring breakers, and they were so far entangled therewith, as they conceived themselves in great danger; and the wind shrinking upon them withal, they resolved to bear up again for the Cape, and thought themselves happy to get out of those dangers before night overtook them, as by God's providence they did. And the next day they got into the Cape harbor, where they rode in safety."

The date was November 11, 1620 (Old Style, November 21, New Style). The harbor was at Provincetown, on the very tip of the cape, where the monument to the Pilgrims stands; here, sixteen of them went ashore under the leadership of Captain Miles Standish, a Lancashire man and a veteran of the wars in Holland. They were "well armed," Bradford says, and carried provisions. Presumably they went ashore in the ship's boat, or longboat; the shallop brought in the *Mayflower* had received such a battering in the crossing that it could not be used.

"They set forth the 15th of November, and when they had marched about the space of a mile by the seaside, they espied five or six persons with a dog coming toward them, who were savages; but they fled from them and ran up into the woods, and the English followed them, partly to see if they could speak with them, and partly to discover if there might not be more of them lying in ambush. But the Indians seeing themselves thus followed, they again forsook the woods and ran away on the sands as hard as they could, so as they could not come near them, but followed them by the track of their feet sundry miles, and saw that they had come the same way.

"So, night coming on, they made their rendezvous and set out their sentinels, and rested in quiet that night; and the next morning followed their tracks till they had headed a great creek and so left the sands and turned another way into the woods. But they still followed them by guess, hoping to find their dwellings; but they soon lost both them and themselves, falling into such thickets as were ready to tear their clothes and armor in pieces, but were most distressed for want of drink. But at length they found water and refreshed themselves, being the first New England water they drunk of, and was now in their great thirst as pleasant unto them as wine or beer had been in foretimes.

"Afterward they directed their course to come to the other shore, for they knew it was a neck of land they were to cross over, and so at length got to the seaside, and marched to the supposed river, and by the way found a pond of fresh water, and shortly after a good quantity of clear ground where the Indians had formerly set corn, and some of their graves. And proceeding further they saw new stubble where corn had been set the same year, also they found where lately a house had been, where some planks and a great kettle was remaining, and heaps of sand newly paddled with their hands, which they, digging up, found in them divers fair Indian baskets filled with corn of divers colors, which seemed to them a goodly sight (having never seen any such before).

"This was near the place of that supposed river they came to seek, unto which they went and found it to open itself into two arms, with a high cliff of sand in the entrance, but more like to be creeks of salt water than any fresh, for ought they saw."

They had come as far as Truro. The river was the Pamet. The expedition returned to the ship, taking part of the corn and burying the rest.

"After this, the shallop being got ready, they set out again for the better discovery of this place, and the master of the ship desired to go himself, so there went some thirty men, but found it to be no harbor for ships but only for boats. There was also found two of their houses covered with mats, and sundry of their implements in them, but the people were run away and could not be seen; also there was found more of the corn and of their beans, of various colors. The corn and beans they brought away, purposing to give them full satisfaction when they should meet with any of them (as about some six months afterward they did, to their good content).

"And here is to be noted a special providence of God, and a great mercy to this poor people, that here they got seed to plant them corn the next year, or else they might have starved, for they had none, nor any likelihood to get any till the season had been past (as the sequel did manifest). Neither is it likely they had had this if the first voyage had not been made, for the ground was now all covered with snow and hard-frozen. But the Lord is never wanting unto his in their greatest needs; let his holy name have all the praise."

The snow, meanwhile, fell impartially on the anointed of the Lord and the unanointed alike. Those who had buried provisions returned to find other hands had paddled in the sand.

"The month of November being spent in these affairs, and much foul weather falling in, the 6th of December they sent out their shallop again with ten of their principal men and some seamen upon further discovery, intending to circulate that deep bay of Cape Cod. The weather was very cold, and it froze so hard as the spray of the sea lighting on their coats, they were as if they had been glassed. Yet that night betimes they got down into the bottom of the bay, and as they drew near the shore they saw some ten or twelve Indians very busy about something.

"They landed about a league or two from them, and had much ado to put ashore anywhere, it lay so full of flats. Being landed, it grew late, and they made themselves a barricade with logs and boughs as well as they could in the time, and set out their sentinels and betook them to rest, and saw the smoke of the fire the savages made that night.

"When morning was come they divided their company, some to coast along the shore in the boat, and the rest marched through the woods to see the land, if any fit place might be for their dwelling. They came also to the place where they saw the Indians the night before, and found they had been cutting up a great fish like a grampus [dolphinlike cetacean], being some two inches thick of fat like a hog, some pieces whereof they had left by the way; and the shallop found two more of these fishes dead on the sands, a thing usual after storms in that place, by reason of the great flats of sand that lie off.

"So they ranged up and down all that day, but found no people, nor any place they liked. When the sun grew low, they hasted out of the woods to meet with their shallop, to whom they made signs to come to them into a creek hard by, the which they did at high water; of which they were very glad, for they had not seen each other all that day since the morning. So they made them a barricade (as usually they did every night) with logs, stakes and thick pine boughs the height of a man, leaving it open to leeward, partly to shelter them from the cold and wind (making their fire in the middle and lying round about it) and partly to defend them from any sudden assaults of the savages, if they should surround them.

"So, being very weary, they betook them to rest. But about midnight they heard a hideous and great cry, and their sentinel called, 'Arm! Arm!' So they bestirred them and stood to their arms, and shot a couple of muskets, and then the noise ceased. They concluded it was a company of wolves, or suchlike wild beasts, for one of the seamen told them he had often heard such a noise in Newfoundland.

"So they rested till about five of the clock in the morning, for the tide, and their purpose to go from thence, made them be stirring betimes. So after prayer they prepared for breakfast, and it being day dawning, it was thought best to be carrying things down to the boat. But some said it was not best to carry the arms down; others said they would be the readier, for they had lapped them up in their coats from the dew. But some three or four would not carry theirs till they went themselves; yet, as it fell out, the water being not high enough, they laid them down on the bankside, and came up to breakfast.

"But presently, all on the sudden, they heard a great and strange cry, which they knew to be the same voices they heard in the night, though they varied their notes, and one of the company being abroad came running in and cried: 'Men! Indians! Indians!' And withal their arrows came flying among them.

"Their men ran with all speed to recover their arms, as by the good providence of God they did. In the meantime, of those that were there ready, two muskets were discharged at them, and two more stood ready in the entrance of their rendezvous, but were commanded not to shoot till they could take full aim at them; and the other two charged [loaded] again with all speed, for there were only four had arms there and defended the barricade, which was first assaulted.

"The cry of the Indians was dreadful, especially when they saw their men run out of the rendezvous toward the shallop to recover their arms, the Indians wheeling about upon them. But some running with coats of mail on, and cutlasses in their hands, they soon got their arms, and let fly among them, and quickly stopped their violence. Yet there was a lusty man, and no less valiant, stood behind a tree within half a musket shot, and let his arrows fly at them. He was seen shoot three arrows, which were all avoided. He stood three shot of a musket, till one taking full aim at him, and made the bark or splinters of the tree to fly about his ears, after which he gave an extraordinary shriek, and away they went all of them.

"They left some to keep the shallop, and followed them about a quarter of a mile, and shouted once or twice and shot off two or three pieces, and so returned. This they did, that they might conceive that they were not afraid of them or any way discouraged.

"Thus it pleased God to vanquish their enemies and give them deliverance, and by his special providence so to dispose that not any one of them were either hurt or hit, though their arrows came close by them, and on every side them, and sundry of their coats which hung up in the barricade were shot through and through.

"Afterward they gave God solemn thanks and praise for their deliverance, and gathered up a bundle of their arrows, and sent them into England afterward by the master of the ship, and called that place the 'First Encounter.'"

The shallop put off. With sail up it began to coast along the half circle formed by Cape Cod Bay, the Pilgrims still intent to find a site for a settlement. With them was the second mate of the *Mayflower,* one Robert Coppin, "who had been in the country before." He knew of a harbor, he said, which he had been in, "and they might fetch it before night; of which they were glad, for it began to be foul weather.

"After some hours' sailing it began to snow and rain, and about the middle of the afternoon the wind increased and the sea became very rough, and they broke their rudder, and it was as much as two men could do to steer her with a couple of oars. But their pilot bade them be of good cheer, for he saw the harbor; but the storm increasing, and night drawing on, they bore what sail they could to get in while they could see.

"But herewith they broke their mast in three pieces, and their sail fell overboard, in a very grown sea, so as they had like to have been cast away; yet by God's mercy they recovered themselves, and having the flood with them, struck into the harbor. But when it came to, the pilot was deceived in the place, and said, 'The Lord be merciful unto them, for his eyes never saw that place before'; and he and the master's mate would have run her ashore, in a cove full of breakers, before the wind. But a lusty seaman which steered bade those which rowed 'if they were men, about with her, or else they were all cast away'; the which they did with speed. So he bid them be of good cheer and row lustily, for there was a fair sound before them, and he doubted not but they should find one place or other where they might ride in safety. And though it was very dark, and rained sore, yet in the end they got under the lee of a small island, and remained there all that night in safety. But they knew not this to be an island till morning, but were divided in their minds. Some would keep the boat for fear they might be amongst the Indians; others were so weak and cold, they could not endure, but got ashore, and with much ado got fire (all things being so wet), and the rest were glad to come to them, for after midnight the wind shifted to the northwest, and it froze hard.

"But though this had been a day and night of much trouble and danger unto them, yet God gave them a morning of comfort and refreshing (as usually he doth to his children), for the next day was a fair sun-shining day, and they found themselves to be on an island secure from the Indians, where they might dry their stuff, fix their pieces, and rest themselves, and gave God thanks for his mercies in their manifold deliverances. And this being the last day of the week, they prepared there to keep the Sabbath.

"On Monday they sounded the harbor and found it fit for shipping; and marched into the land and found divers cornfields, and little running brooks, a place (as they supposed) fit for situation; at least it was the best they could find, and the season and their present necessity made them glad to accept of it."

The spot where they landed was Plymouth Rock, in Plymouth Harbor. It took place on December 11 (Old Style; December 21, New Style), and is generally termed "the historic landing," which seems unfair to Provincetown. What took place at Jamestown in the first summer months of the plantation was now repeated at New Plymouth, as it was called, in the winter season. The first building erected was a storehouse. A few makeshift "cottages" followed. Bradford wrote:

"In two or three months' time half of their company died, especially in January and February, being the depth of winter and wanting houses and other comforts; being infected with the scurvy and other diseases which this long voyage and their in-accommodate condition had brought upon them; so as there died sometimes two or three of a day in the foresaid time, that of 100 and odd persons scarce fifty remained. And of these in the time of most distress there was but six or seven sound persons who, to their great commendation be it spoken, spared no pains, night nor day; but with abundance of toil, and hazard of their own health, fetched them wood, made them fires, dressed their meat, made their beds, washed their loathsome clothes, clothed and unclothed them—in a word, did all the homely and necessary offices for them which dainty and queasy stomachs cannot endure to hear named."

Construction of shelters and the work of unloading the *Mayflower* proceeded slowly, which is not surprising, the general sickness and the weather considered. The Pilgrims had also to be on their guard. "All this while the Indians came skulking about them." But one day —it was March 16, 1621—"a certain Indian came boldly among them, and spoke to them in broken English, which they could well understand, but marveled at it."

He was Samoset, an Indian from Monhegan Island.

"They understood by discourse with him that he was not of these parts, but belonged to the eastern parts, where some English ships came to fish, with whom he was acquainted, and could name sundry of them by their names, among whom he had got his language."

The marvel grew—Samoset named another Indian who spoke better English than himself; this one had been in England.

"He was carried away with divers others by one Hunt, a master of a ship, who thought to sell them for slaves in Spain; but he got away for England, and was entertained by a merchant in London, and employed to Newfoundland and other parts, and lastly brought hither into these parts by one Mr. Dermer, gentleman employed by Sir Ferdinando Gorges and others, for discovery and other designs in these parts."

Captain Thomas Dermer had gone from Plymouth, England, to the New England coast, and thence to Jamestown by way of Cape Cod.

The Indian's name was Tisquantum or, as the Pilgrims called him, Squanto. Bradford termed him "a special instrument of God." He taught the Pilgrims how to plant corn, with this caution—"except they got fish and set with it (in these old grounds) it would come to nothing, and he showed them that in the middle of April they should have store enough come up the brook." He was referring to "alewives" (perhaps a corruption of his name for them), a herringlike fish that each spring poured into the brooks, streams and rivers of New England like a tide, until the Pilgrims' descendants put a stop to it.

Squanto liked the English so well that he stayed with them. He was their interpreter, "pilot" on explorations of the coast, guide into the interior, and instrumental in bringing about the treaty of peace between the Pilgrims and the great sachem Massasoit, who came to call. The visit was afterward returned by Edward Winslow and Stephen Hoskins, led by Squanto. They brought a "gratuity" to the chief—"a suit of clothes and a horseman's coat, with some other small things, which were kindly accepted." The courtesy call masked a serious purpose—to "view the country, and see in what manner he lived, what strength he had about him, and how the ways were to his place, if at any time they should have occasion." The domain of Massasoit was at Sowams, the present-day Warren, Rhode Island, and across the bay from him dwelt the powerful Narragansetts.

The April of the alewives was memorable on other accounts. Governor Carver died, and Bradford was elected to succeed him. The first marriage occurred.

> "May 12 was the first marriage in this place, which, according to the laudable custom of the Low Countries, in which they had lived, was thought most requisite to be performed by the magistrate, as being a civil thing, upon which many questions about inheritance do depend, with other things most proper to their cognizance, and most consonant to the Scriptures, Ruth 4, and nowhere found in the gospel to be laid on the ministers as a part of their office."

The marriage was between Winslow, whose wife had died in March, and Susanna White, whose husband had died in February, leaving two sons, one an infant born on shipboard and who was named Peregrine, an old meaning of the word being foreign or imported from abroad; but perhaps wanderer or traveler was in-

tended, from "peregrinate." The name of the other son was Resolved, which is strictly Puritan. The Book of Ruth, Chapter Four,
deals not only with the marriage of Boaz and Ruth, but with other
relations, real estate, and inheritance. It concludes joyfully with a
spurt of begats.

In July the Indians of Nauset were compensated for their corn.
It was rather roundabout.

> "One John Billington lost himself in the woods, and wan-
> dered up and down some five days, living on berries and what
> he could find. At length he lit on an Indian plantation, twenty
> miles south of this place, called Manamet. They conveyed him
> further off, to Nauset, among those people that had before set
> upon the English when they were coasting, while the ship lay
> at the Cape, as is before noted. But the Governor caused him
> to be enquired for among the Indians, and at length Massasoit
> sent word where he was, and the Governor sent a shallop for
> him, and had him delivered. Those people also came and made
> their peace; and they [the Pilgrims] gave full satisfaction to
> those whose corn they had found and taken when they were
> at Cape Cod."

A man born to be hanged need not fear scalping; Billington was
later executed for murder.

More ships came, bringing new settlers—the first was the *Fortune*, with thirty-five. (It returned with a cargo of clapboards and
beaver and otter skins.) There is a curious passage in Bradford's
History about the newcomers which foreshadows what was to come
on the spiritual side, not only for the Plymouth colony, but all of
New England:

> "On the day called Christmas Day, the Governor called them
> out to work (as was used), but the most of this new company
> excused themselves and said it went against their consciences
> to work on that day. So the Governor told them that if they
> made it matter of conscience, he would spare them till they
> were better informed. So he led away the rest and left them;
> but when they came home at noon from their work, he found
> them in the street at play, openly—some pitching the bar and
> some at a stool-ball and suchlike sports [stool-ball: game re-
> sembling cricket, still played in Sussex, usually by girls, the
> ball being driven from stool to stool].
>
> "So he went to them, and took away their implements, and
> told them that was against his conscience that they should play

and others work; if they made the keeping of it matter of devotion, let them keep their houses, but there should be no gaming or reveling in the streets. Since which time nothing hath been attempted that way, at least openly."

After the Pilgrims came the Puritans—not to seek religious freedom or even separation of church and state, but to establish a church-state; and this they did. In England they were much derided —those odd first names, their sober dress, and their holier-than-thou preachments. They hated Christmas and May Day and Maypoles, which meant ribbons and dancing, and all that made for jollity, and jollity itself. But they triumphed at home as the army of the Lord, and they triumphed in the wilderness of Massachusetts, stringing the shoreline and the land itself with place names brought over, with their Bibles and muskets, like a phantom cargo.

THE WORLD IN 1625

Detail from frontispiece to Purchas' *Pilgrims*, published when the author was 48 years old. The globe on the left shows Tartary, "Rusia" "Calicut" and the beginning of the word "America," with Drake's Albion above California. The right-hand globe depicts Newfoundland, Virginia, Florida, New Spain, Guiana and Brazil. Courtesy of the Rare Book Division, The New York Public Library.

X

NEW NETHERLAND

To the Great North River of the Mountains in the summer of 1624 came Captain—or as the Dutch liked to term it, Skipper—Cornelius May on a vessel of 260 tons called the *Nieu Nederlandt*, with thirty families on board, mostly Walloons. At the mouth of the river, to his and everyone's surprise, there was a French ship; asked what it was doing there, the French captain replied that he had come to erect the arms of the King of France and take possession.

Skipper May forbade it. He showed his credentials—a commission from "the Lords States General and the Directors of the West India Company." At the same time, a Dutch yacht plying the river brought her guns to bear, and the French ship was convoyed out of the harbor. The Walloons were then transported up the river to Fort Orange, on the site of present-day Albany.

The Amsterdam *Historische Verhael* (Historical Account), a semi-annual newspaper, which reported the incident, says the French ship proceeded to the South River (the Delaware) for another try, but was prevented by settlers there.

The *Nieu Nederlandt* returned with a cargo of 500 otter skins, 1,500 beavers, "and a few other skins," which were sold in Amsterdam in four parcels for something over 28,000 guilders, the guilder (from "gold") being worth approximately forty cents. Ten years

FORT NEW AMSTERDAM

The earliest representation of Manhattan, *circa* 1628, with Dutch ships at
the mouth of the Hudson River, a pinnace and longboat off the Battery,
and Indians paddling in canoes. Engraving on copper, Amsterdam, 1651.
Courtesy of The New-York Historical Society, New York City.

later, in the most famous real estate transaction in history, Manhattan Island was purchased for sixty guilders' worth of gaudy merchandise—roughly, $24. By then the tip of the island was a bustling spot. From the *Historische Verhael* for November, 1626:

"The colony is now established on the Manhates, where a fort has been staked out by Master Kryn Frederycks, an engineer. It is planned to be of large dimensions. The ship which has returned home this month brings samples of all sorts of produce growing there, the cargo being 7,246 beaver skins, 675 otter skins, 48 mink, 36 wildcat, and various other sorts; many pieces of oak timber and hickory.

"The countinghouse there is kept in a stone building, thatched with reed; the other houses are of the bark of trees. Each has his own house. The Director and *Koopman* [commercial agent] live together; there are thirty ordinary houses on the east side of the river, which runs nearly north and south. The Honorable Peter Minuit is Director there at present; Jan Lempou *schout* [a combination sheriff and public prosecutor]; Sebastiaen Jansz. Crol and Jan Huych, comforters of the sick [officers of the Reformed Church] who, while awaiting a clergyman, read to the commonalty there, on Sundays, texts of Scripture and the commentaries. François Molemaecker is busy building a horse-mill, over which shall be constructed a spacious room sufficient to accommodate a large congregation, and then a tower is to be erected where the bells brought from Puerto Rico will be hung."

The mill became the first Christian house of worship on Manhattan Island. The bells—there were nine of them—were part of the booty seized when a Dutch West India Company fleet shelled and sacked San Juan de Porto Rico the year before.

There had already been two governors or directors general of New Netherland. The first was Cornelius May, the second Willem Verhulst. Sebastian Jansen Krol (Crol in the newspaper account), comforter of the sick, was to be the fourth.

The third was Peter Minuit, who had arrived in May on the *Meeuwken* (Sea Mew) and lost no time in clearing title. The *koopman* was Isaac de Rasiere, who came in July on board the *Wapen van Amsterdam* (Arms of Amsterdam). This was the ship mentioned by the *Historische Verhael;* its cargo of skins and timber fetched 45,000 guilders.

Rasiere, chief commercial agent of the company, was also secretary of the province of New Netherland, and ranked next to Minuit. The same issue of the newspaper reports activities which followed their arrival:

"Those of the South River will abandon their fort and come hither [that is, to Fort Amsterdam]. At Fort Orange, the most northerly point at which the Hollanders traded, no more than fifteen or sixteen men will remain; the remainder will come down."

This was ordered to strengthen the settlement on Manhattan. Trading on the South River was continued by ship. A social note of sorts:

"It happened this year that the Maykans [Mohicans], going to war with the Maquaes [Mohawks], requested to be assisted by the commander of Fort Orange and six others. Commander [Daniel van] Krieckebeeck went up with them; a league from the fort they met the Maquaes who fell so boldly upon them with a discharge of arrows, that they were forced to fly, and many were killed, among whom were the commander and three of his men. Among the latter was Tymen Bouqenszen, whom they devoured, after having well roasted him."

Also mentioned are the Sequin Indians on the Connecticut River, and the Pilgrims at New Plymouth.

To Rasiere, the Pilgrim settlement represented a potential market of vast proportions, not only as an additional source of furs, but for the sale of Holland goods, whose quality was well known to the English. A ceremonial visit on a well-appointed ship, a cargo of selected merchandise, and the rest would follow. There was not even a language barrier. The ceremonial visit was preceded by a ceremonious letter.

"Noble, worshipful, wise and prudent Lords, the Governor and Councilors residing in New Plymouth, our very good friends. The Director and Council of New Netherland wish to your Lordships

ENGLISH ARMS OVER "NEW JARSEY"

A transitional map, with Indian, Dutch and English names. Inset, top right: a Dutch view of New Amsterdam. Upper left: Cape May, Delaware Bay, and the "South River" (the Delaware). Lower right: "Manhattans," "Brucklen," and part of Long Island (numbers show depth of water in fathoms). An otter hastens toward Staten Island with a catch. Other fauna are beaver, buck deer or elk, squirrel, rabbits, and a turkey. From the I. N. Phelps Stokes Collection of American Historical Prints, Prints Division, The New York Public Library.

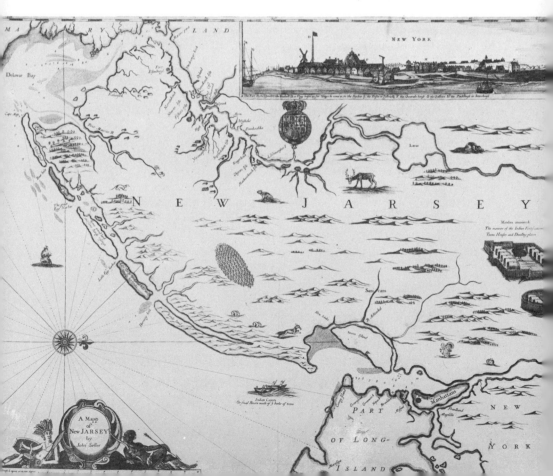

worshipful, wise and prudent happiness in Christ Jesus our Lord, with prosperity and health, in soul and body. Amen"—"it being their manner to be full of complimental titles," Bradford commented in his *History*, where he gave the salutation in the original Dutch, adding: "The rest I shall render in English, leaving out the repetition of superfluous titles." Rasiere's letter was dated "From the Manhatas, in the fort Amsterdam, March 9, Anno 1627." It was written after confirmation had come of the Treaty of Southampton between Charles I (his brother Henry, Prince of Wales, died at eighteen) and the States General, which was not only an encouragement to the Dutch in America caught, as it were, in a vise between Virginia and Massachusetts; it was also useful in the present effort to establish trade relations. Bradford took cognizance of it when he replied, but, added a caution, which was a portent of things to come:

> "But you may please to understand that we are but one particular colony or plantation in this land, there being divers others besides, unto whom it hath pleased those Honorable Lords of His Majesty's Council for New England to grant the like commission and ample privileges to them (as to us) for their better profit and subsistence—namely, to expulse, or make prize of any, either strangers or other English, which shall attempt either to trade or plant within their limits (without their special license and commission) which extend to 40 degrees. Yet for our parts, we shall not go about to molest or trouble you in anything, but continue all good neighborhood and correspondence as far as we may; only we desire that you would forbear to trade with the natives in this bay, and river of Naragansett and Sowames, which is (as it were) at our doors. The which if you do, we think no other English will go about any way to trouble or hinder you; which otherwise are resolved to solicit His Majesty for redress, if otherwise they cannot help themselves."

As for the offer of goods, "for this year we are fully supplied with all necessaries, both for clothing and other things; but hereafter it is like we shall deal with you, if your rates be reasonable." As for trade, Bradford wrote, "we desire to know how you will take beaver, by the pound, and otters, by the skin, and how you will deal per centage for other commodities."

There was more correspondence. In October, de Rasiere made his visit, bringing sugar, linen and Holland cloth, both coarse and fine. He stepped ashore to a flourish of trumpets by his own trumpeters. "And after some few days' entertainment, he returned to his bark, and some of them went with him, and bought sundry of his goods," Bradford wrote. The trade thus begun continued for many years.

"But that which turned most to their profit, in time, was an entrance into the trade of Wampampeake [wampum]; for they now bought about 50 pounds worth of it of them; and they told them how vendable it was at their Fort Orania [Fort Orange], and did persuade them they would find it so at Kennebec; and so it came to pass in time, though at first it stuck, and it was two years before they could put off this small quantity, till the inland people knew of it; and afterward they could scarce ever get enough for them."

Rasiere has left a description of the town the Pilgrims built, together with observations on their strict deportment, which they appear to have imposed on the Indians as well:

"New Plymouth lies on the slope of a hill stretching east toward the seacoast, with a broad street about a cannon shot of 800 feet long [actually over 1,000] leading down the hill; with a crossing in the middle, northward to the rivulet and southward to the land [actually the other way around].

"The houses are constructed of hewn planks, with gardens also enclosed behind and at the sides with hewn planks, so that their houses and courtyards are arranged in very good order, with a stockade against a sudden attack; and at the ends of the streets there are three wooden gates.

"In the center, on the cross street, stands the Governor's house, before which is a square stockade upon which four patereros [pedreros, ordnance for scatter-shot] are mounted, so as to enfilade the streets.

"Upon the hill they have a large square house, with a flat roof, made of thick sawn plank, stayed with oak beams, upon the top of which they have six cannon, which shoot iron balls of four and five pounds, and command the surrounding country.

"The lower part they use for their church, where they preach on Sundays and the usual holidays. They assemble by beat of drum, each with his musket or firelock, in front of the captain's door; they have their cloaks on, and place themselves in order, three abreast, and are led by a sergeant without beat of drum. Behind comes the Governor, in a long robe; beside him, on the right hand, comes the preacher with his cloak on, and on the left hand the captain with his side arms, and cloak on, and with

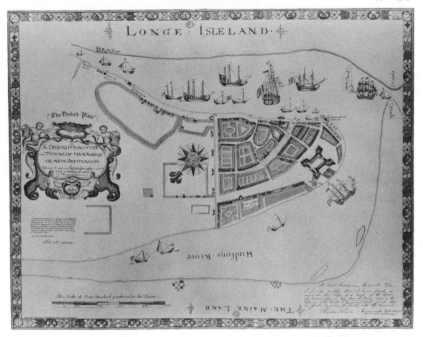

BRITISH FLAG OVER NEW AMSTERDAM

This map depicts the "Towne of Mannados or New Amsterdam" as it was in September 1661, three years before it fell to Charles II's men-of-war. An English artist later added the flag and types of English ships which crowd the Narrows, the East River and the Hudson. The duke of the legend (left), for whom the city was renamed, was the Duke of York, Charles's brother, afterward James II. Courtesy of The New-York Historical Society, New York City.

a small cane in his hand; and so they march in good order, and each sets his arms down near him. Thus they are constantly on their guard night and day.

"Their government is after the English form. The Governor has his council, which is chosen every year by the entire community, by election or prolongation of term. In inheritance they place all children in one degree, only the eldest son has an acknowledgment for his seniority of birth [a double portion].

"They have made stringent laws and ordinances upon the subject of fornication and adultery, which laws they maintain and enforce very strictly indeed, even among the tribes which live among them."

The first confrontation between the English and Dutch came on the South River, and is related by a Captain Thomas Yong, or

Young, of London, gentleman, who arrived on the Delaware with two ships, July 24, 1634, after a stopover at Jamestown. Like others before him he was enchanted by the beauty and fruitfulness of the land—here, portions of Pennsylvania, Delaware and New Jersey:

"This river dischargeth itself into a great bay in the north part of Virginia, in 39 and almost a half of latitude. The river is broad and deep, and is not inferior to any in the North of America, and a ship of 300 tons may sail up within three leagues of the rocks [the Falls at Trenton]. The river aboundeth with beavers, otters, and other meaner furs, which are not only taken upon the banks of the main river, but likewise in other lesser rivers which discharge themselves into the greater, whereof I think few rivers of America have more or pleasant.

"The people are for the most part very well proportioned, well featured, gentle, tractable and docible. The land is very good and fruitful, and withal very healthful. The soil is sandy and produceth divers sorts of fruits, especially grapes, which grow wild in great quantity, of which I have eaten six several sorts, some of them as good as they are ordinarily in Italy or Spain; and were they replanted I think they would be far better. Here also grows the fruit which in Italy they call lazarroli [medlar], plums, divers sorts of berries and divers other fruits not known in Europe. The climate is much like that of Italy, and all sorts of fruits of that country will thrive here exceedingly.

"The earth, being fruitful, is covered over with woods and stately timber, except only in those places where the Indians had planted their corn. The country is very well replenished with deer, and in some places store of elks. The low grounds, of which there is great quantity, excellent for meadows and full of beaver and otter. The quantity of fowl is so great as can hardly be believed; we took at one time 48 partridges together as they crossed the river, chased by wild hawks. I myself sprang, in two hours, five or six coveys in walking of a mile. There are infinite number of wild pigeons, blackbirds, turkeys, swans, wild geese, ducks, teals, widgeons, brants, herons, cranes, etc. of which there is so great abundance as that the rivers and creeks are covered with them in winter.

"Of fish here is plenty, but especially sturgeon all the summertime, which are in such abundance in the upper parts of the river, as that great benefit might be raised by setting up a fishing for them, for in the spring and beginning of summer the weather is so temperate that they will keep very well. Here are also great store of wild hops, yet excellent good and as fair as those in England. Here are also divers other things which with industry will prove excellent good commodities, and for my part, I am confident that this river is the most healthful, fruitful and commodious river in all the North of America to be planted [i.e., colonized]."

Far up the river, between the Schuylkill and the falls at Trenton, he was overtaken by two Dutch ships with traders aboard, including a *koopman,* or head merchant; Yong thought that word of his presence had been carried to Fort Amsterdam by Indians. He sent a boat to ask who they were and what they were doing there, with orders to bring the master back. The master and his *koopman* were rowed to Captain Yong's ship in their own boat. He received them in his cabin.

"I asked them if they had any commission from his Majesty to trade in the river or no. They answered they had none from the King of England, but from the Governor of New Netherland they had. To which I replied that I knew of no such governor, nor no such place as New Netherland.

"I told them that this country did belong to the crown of England, as well by ancient discovery as likewise by possession lawfully taken, and that his Majesty was now pleased to make more ample discovery of this river, and of other places also, where he would erect colonies, and that I was therefore sent hither with a royal commission under the Great Seal to take possession hereof.

"I perceived by their countenance that this news struck them cold at heart, and after a little pause they answered me that they had traded in this river heretofore.

"I then replied that therein they had done his Majesty and his subjects the greater injury, for supposing, as some of the Dutch pretended, that they had by his Majesty's leave traded and planted in Hudson's River, yet ought they not to usurp upon other trades and countries of his Majesty without his leave, and since that he is now pleased to make use of this river, either for himself or his subjects, it would be good manners in them to desist.

"Then they desired to see my commission, which I showed them, and after they had read it, and considered well thereof, apprehending the power I had, if they should trade without license, to make them prize, they desired me to give them a copy thereof.

"I answered them that it was not the custom of England for his Majesty's ministers to give copies of their commissions. They then desired to know how I would proceed with them, which they hoped would be the better in regard they knew not of my commission. I told them I would let them know that hereafter."

Captain Yong had sent his lieutenant in a shallop to explore the falls that very day, and thought it best to have him back should force be necessary. The shallop returned on September 2, and Yong invited the Hollanders to dine with him. One of them—perhaps the master—raised his glass and made a toast.

"Herr Governor of the South River, I drink to you, and indeed confess your commission is much better than ours. How say you, Koopman, is it not?"

"Yes, indeed, I have not seen a larger commission," said the head merchant.

Captain Yong's decision was to let them depart peacefully "in regard they were subjects to so ancient allies of my Prince, and that they were neighbors here." He sent his lieutenant in a pinnace to see that they left.

SUBJECTS OF THE KING

A final commentary. From the Eno Collection, Prints Division, The New York Public Library, Astor, Lenox and Tilden Foundations.

NEW YORK *a City in* N America *inhabited by* English *and* Dutch *subject to the* K. *of* England.

The vise began to close in March, 1664, when Charles II presented his brother, the Duke of York, with all the territory from the Connecticut River to the Delaware. Four frigates proceeded to New Amsterdam, after a stopover in Boston. They were under the command of Colonel Richard Nicolls; with him were three other commissioners of the King. After anchoring off Gravesend Bay, not far from Coney Island, Nicolls dispatched a letter to Peter Stuyvesant, Director General, which called on him to surrender the fort and the colony.

Stuyvesant asked for three days' delay for consultation with his burgomasters. This was granted; meanwhile, however, the frigates moved closer, two of them taking positions in front of the fort, and a third dropping anchor off Nut Island (now Governor's Island), where five companies of soldiers encamped. These were soon joined by a company of horse as well as foot soldiers from Connecticut and Long Island.

The surrender followed.

A report sent to the Lords Directors of the Honorable West India Company, Department of Amsterdam, by the town council is subscribed: "Done in York, heretofore named Amsterdam in New Netherland Anno 1664 the 16th of September."

New Netherland was now New York, and Fort Orange was renamed Albany, from another title belonging to the Duke of York, afterward James II.

ℰPILOGUE:
𝒯HE 𝒻RONTIER

"Virginia is a country in America that lieth between the degrees of 34 and 44 [actually 45 in the original charter] of the north latitude. The bounds thereof on the East side are the great Ocean. On the South lieth Florida; on the North, Nova Francia. As for the West thereof, the limits are unknown." (Captain John Smith, *A Map of Virginia*.)

From Nova Francia, New France, came the explorers and missionaries, the trappers and traders—past Lake Superior, into the upper Mississippi Valley, and down the Mississippi to its mouth, leaving behind a string of forts and trading posts from the shores of Lake Erie to New Orleans. By the middle of the eighteenth century the heartland of this vast empire in being was the Ohio Valley, on Virginia's frontier. The French flag flew at Venango (Franklin, Pa.), hitherto an English trading post on the Allegheny, and English settlers in the wilderness were being abducted and taken north for questioning, or slain in their homes by Indians from Canada.

In the fall of 1753 it became clear to the Delawares, who had already been pushed westward by the settlers of Pennsylvania, and to the Shawnees and Mingos (the local name for Senecas) that the French intended to take possession of the Ohio. Tanacharison, a Seneca chief, whom the English called "the Half-King" because of his dependence on the Iroquois confederacy of New York, set out for Fort Le Boeuf on French Creek (now Waterford, Pa.) to remonstrate with the commander, Pierre Paul, Sieur de Marin. He spoke as follows:

"Fathers, we kindled a fire a long time ago, at a place called Montreal, where we desired you to stay, and not to come and intrude upon our land.

"I now desire you may dispatch to that place, for be it known to you, Fathers, that this is our land, and not yours."

He then laid down a wampum belt, signifying eviction.

The commander replied, Tanacharison afterward reported, "in a very stern manner." Said the Sieur de Marin:

"I am not afraid of flies, or mosquitoes, for Indians are such as those. I tell you, down that river I will go, and will build upon it, according to my command. If the river was blocked up, I have forces sufficient to burst it open, and tread under my feet all that stand in opposition, together with their alliances, for my force is as the sand upon the seashore. Therefore, here is your wampum, I fling it at you.

"Child, you talk foolish. You say this land belongs to you but there is not the black of my nail yours. I saw that land sooner than you did, before the Shawnees and you were at war. Lead was the man that went down and took possession of that river." (*Monsieur Plomb*—in real life, Céloron de Blainville, who had buried lead plates engraved with the arms of France in the Ohio Valley.)

The French designs were a provocation to the English—more correctly, British, since the union of England and Scotland in 1706, whence Great Britain—and on October 31, 1753, from his palace on Duke of Gloucester Street, Williamsburg, Governor Robert Dinwiddie addressed a letter "to the Commandant of the French Forces on the Ohio."

"Sir," he wrote.

"The lands upon the River Ohio, in the western parts of the Colony of Virginia, are so notoriously known to be the property of the Crown of Great Britain, that it is a matter of equal concern and surprise to me to hear that a body of French forces are erecting fortresses and making settlements upon that river, within his Majesty's dominions.

"The many and repeated complaints I have received of these acts of hostility lay me under the necessity of sending, in the name of the King, my master, the bearer hereof, George Washington, Esq., one of the Adjutants General of the forces of this Dominion, to complain to you of the encroachment thus made."

The conclusion was a request for "your peaceable departure," which was as good as an ultimatum. "I persuade myself," Dinwiddie wrote, "you will receive and entertain Major Washington with the candor and politeness natural to your nation."

Washington left Williamsburg the same day. He was twenty-one years old. In Fredericksburg he "engaged" a Hollander, Jacob Van Braam, who taught French, to be his interpreter. At Alexandria they picked up "necessaries," at Winchester "baggage, horses, etc." They arrived at Wills Creek (Cumberland, Maryland) on November 14 by the "new road" and were joined by Christopher Gist, frontiersman and agent of the Ohio Company. Four men were hired as "servitors."

The next stop was Turtle Creek on the Monongahela River, where one James Frazier, or Fraser, had a trading post—store, and blacksmith shop where he repaired guns and tools for frontiersmen and Indians. He had previously operated at Venango.

> "We were informed here," Washington wrote in his journal, "that expresses were sent a few days ago to the traders down the river, to acquaint them with the French general's death, and the return of the major part of the French army into winter quarters.
>
> "The waters were quite impassable, without swimming our horses; which obliged us to get the loan of a canoe from Frazier, and to send Barnaby Currin and Henry Steward down Monongahela with our baggage, to meet us at the Forks of Ohio, about 10 miles, to cross Allegheny."

The Forks were the site of present-day Pittsburgh. From there Washington descended the Ohio about eighteen miles to a place called Logstown (near present-day Economy, Pa.), an important Indian settlement, the abode of several tribes, including the Half-King's. His purpose was to call a council of sachems to confirm English friendship, and to request assistance on the journey that still lay ahead. For this, he had the help of John Davison, a trader familiar with the dialects of the region.

The council was held "at the long house" on November 26. The tall, young soldier spoke as follows:

> "Brothers, I have called you together in council by order of your brother, the Governor of Virginia, to acquaint you that I

am sent, with all possible dispatch, to visit and deliver a letter
to the French commandant, of very great importance to your
brothers, the English; and I dare say, to you their friends and
allies.

"I was desired, brothers, by your brother the Governor, to
call upon you, the Sachems of the Nations, to inform you of it,
and to ask your advice and assistance to proceed to the nearest
and best road to the French. You see, brothers, I have got thus
far on my journey.

"His Honor likewise desired me to apply to you for some of
your young men, to conduct and provide provisions for us on
our way, and be a safeguard against those French Indians who
have taken up the hatchet against us. I have spoke[n] this particularly to you, brothers, because his Honor our Governor
treats you as good friends and allies, and holds you in great
esteem.

"To confirm what I have said, I give you this string of
wampum."

As usual, there was a long pause while the chiefs sat in con-
templation. The reply was finally made by Tanacharison.

"I return you this answer," he said. "I rely upon you as a brother
ought to do, as you say we are brothers and one people. We shall
put heart in hand, and speak to our fathers the French concerning
the speech they made to me, and you may depend that we will
endeavor to be your guard."

From Washington's journal, from which the foregoing has been
taken, under the date November 30:

"Last night the great men assembled to their council house,
to consult further about this journey, and who were to go; the
result of which was, that only three of their chiefs, with one of
their best hunters, should be our convoy. The reason which
they gave for not sending more, after what had been proposed
at council the 26th, was that a greater number might give
the French suspicions of some bad design, and cause them to
be treated rudely. But I rather think they could not get their
hunters in.

"We set out about 9 o'clock with the Half-King, Jeskakake,
White Thunder, and the hunter, and traveled on the road to
Venango, where we arrived the 4th of December, without any-
thing remarkable happening but a continued series of bad
weather. This is an old Indian town, situated at the mouth of
French Creek on Ohio, and lies near north about 60 miles from

the Logstown, but more than 70 the way we were obliged to go.

"We found the French colors hoisted at a house which they drove Mr. John Frazier, an English subject, from. I immediately repaired to it, to know where the commander resided. There were three officers, one of whom, Capt. Joncaire, informed me that he had command of the Ohio, but that there was a general officer at the near fort, which he advised me to for an answer. He invited us to sup with them, and treated us with the greatest complaisance. The wine, as they dosed themselves pretty plentifully with it, soon banished the restraint which at first appeared in their conversation, and gave a license to their tongues to reveal their sentiments more freely.

"They told me that it was their absolute design to take possession of the Ohio, and by G— they would do it."

The "near fort," previously mentioned, was Fort Le Boeuf; just beyond it, on Lake Erie, was Fort Presqu' Isle. The French at Venango attempted to keep the Indians accompanying Washington and his party, using liquor and presents, but at last all set out, December 7. On December 11 they reached the fort; on the 12th Washington was conducted into the presence of the new commander, Legardeur de St. Pierre, knight of the Military Order of St. Louis, "an elderly gentleman [who] has much the air of a soldier." Washington delivered his letter, and "the chief officers retired, to hold a council of war, which gave me an opportunity of taking the dimensions of the fort, and making what observations I could."

At Fort Le Boeuf, as at Venango, efforts were made to persuade the Indians with Washington to stay behind; these included the promise of guns. He wrote: "I can't say that ever in my life I suffered so much anxiety as I did in this affair." He confronted the commander "and desired him to do their business, and complained of ill treatment; for keeping them, as they were part of my company, was detaining me, which he promised not to do."

The return journey was grim.

"As the snow increased very fast, and our horses daily became weaker, I sent them off unloaded, under the care of Barnaby Currin and two others, to make all convenient dispatch to Venango, and there wait our arrival if there was a prospect of the river's freezing; if not, then to continue down to Shanapin's Town [a Delaware village on the Allegheny] at the Forks of Ohio, and there to wait till we came to cross Allegheny, intend-

ing myself to go down by water, as I had the offer of a canoe
or two."

Venango was reached on December 22.

"Our horses were now so weak and feeble, and the baggage
heavy, as we were obliged to provide all the necessaries that
the journey would require, that we doubted much their per-
forming it. Therefore, myself and others (except the drivers
which were obliged to ride) gave up our horses for packs, to
assist along with the baggage.

"I put myself in an Indian walking dress, and continued with
them three days, till I found there was no probability of their
getting in, in any reasonable time. The horses grew less able
to travel every day. The cold increased very fast, and the roads
were becoming much worse by a deep snow, continually freezing; and as I was uneasy to get back, to make report of my
proceedings to his Honor the Governor, I determined to prose-
cute my journey the nearest way through the woods, on foot.

"Accordingly, I left Mr. Van Braam in charge of our baggage, with money and directions, to provide necessaries from
place to place for themselves and horses, and to make the most
convenient dispatch in.

"I took my necessary papers, pulled off my clothes, tied myself up in a matchcoat [from "matchcore," a Virginia Indian
word meaning skins or garments, here probably a wrapper of
furs sewed together]; and with my pack at my back with my
papers and provisions in it, and a gun, set out with Mr. Gist,
fitted in the same manner, on Wednesday the 26th.

"The day following, just after we had passed a place called
the Murdering Town [location unknown, but west of the Alle-
gheny], where we intended to quit the path and steer across
the country for Shanapin's Town, we fell in with a party of
French Indians, who had lain in wait for us. One of them fired
at Mr. Gist or me, not 15 steps, but fortunately missed.

"We took this fellow into custody, and kept him till about
9 o'clock at night, and then let him go, and walked all the
remaining part of the night without making any stop, that we
might get the start, so far, as to be out of the reach of their
pursuit the next day, as we were well assured they would follow our track as soon as it was light."

When Washington and Gist got to the Allegheny, they found the
river was not frozen over, "only about 50 yards from each shore,"
and it was necessary to build a raft. This was done "with but one

poor hatchet," and took all day. Halfway over it became jammed in the ice, and while attempting to get it loose with a setting pole, "the rapidity of the stream threw it with so much violence against the pole," Washington wrote, "that it jerked me out into ten feet water, but I fortunately saved myself by catching hold of one of the raft logs."

The raft itself did not budge.

"We could not get the raft to either shore, but were obliged, as we were near an island, to quit our raft and make to it. The cold was so extremely severe that Mr. Gist had all his fingers and some of his toes frozen."

In the morning they were able to walk across the packed ice and proceeded to Turtle Creek.

"We met here with 20 warriors who were going to the southward to war, but coming to a place upon the head of the great Cunnaway [the Kanawha River], where they found seven people killed and scalped, all but one woman with very light hair, they turned about and ran back, for fear the inhabitants should rise and take them as the authors of the murder. They report that the people were lying about the house, and some of them much torn and eaten by hogs. By the marks that were left, they say they were French Indians of the Ottawa nation that did it."

From Turtle Creek, Washington went to pay a courtesy visit to Queen Alliquippa at the mouth of the Youghiogheny River, where McKeesport, Pa., now stands.

"I made her a present of a matchcoat and a bottle of rum, which latter was thought much the best present of the two."

On January 1 "we left Mr. Frazier's house, and arrived at Mr. Gist's at Monongahela the 2nd, where I bought horse, saddle, etc. The 6th we met 17 horses loaded with materials and stores for a fort at the Forks of Ohio, and the day after some families going out to settle."

Wills Creek was left behind; on the 11th Washington reached Belvoir, the home of Colonel William Fairfax on the Potomac, where he rested a day. He arrived in Williamsburg the 16th, and "waited upon his Honor the Governor with the letter I had brought from the French commandant." It read as follows:

"Sir,

"As I have the honor of commanding here in chief, Mr. Washington delivered me the letter which you writ to the Commandant of the French troops.

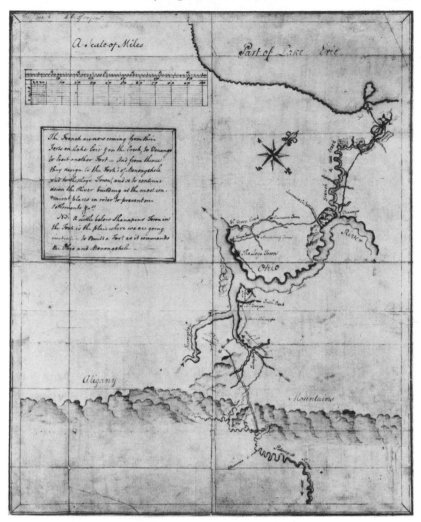

WASHINGTON MAPS THE FRONTIER

The territory of the Ohio Valley, drawn by Major George Washington on his mission to Fort Le Boeuf (upper right) with an ultimatum. The race between the French and Virginians to build forts on the Ohio (detailed in legend at left) led to the opening clashes of the French and Indian War. Courtesy of the Public Record Office, London. Crown copyright. Reproduced by permission of the Controller of H. M. Stationery Office.

"I should have been glad that you had given him orders, or that he had been inclined to proceed to Canada, to see our General, to whom it better belongs than to me to set forth the evidence and reality of the rights of the King, my master, upon the lands situated along the River Ohio, and to contest the pretensions of the King of Great Britain thereto.

"I shall transmit your letter to the Marquis Duquesne; his answer will be a law to me, and if he shall order me to communicate it to you, Sir, you may be assured I shall not fail to dispatch it to you forthwith.

"As to the summons you send me to retire, I do not think myself obliged to obey it; whatever may be your instructions, I am here by virtue of the orders of my General; and I entreat you, Sir, not to doubt one moment but that I am determined to conform myself to them with all the exactness and resolutions which can be expected from the best officer."

Legardeur de St. Pierre praised Washington's "quality and great merit," and assured Dinwiddie of his "profound respect."

Three months later—in May, 1754—the French and Indian War began, with a volley from Washington's militiamen. It lasted nine years. When it was over, the British flag flew from Quebec to Florida, and over Florida as well.

$\mathcal{S}$ELECTED $\mathcal{B}$IBLIOGRAPHY

PROLOGUE. *American Heritage Pictorial Atlas of United States History, The,* Hilde Heun Kagan, editor; chapter texts by Roger Butterfield, Bruce Catton, John A. Garraty, Alvin M. Josephy, Jr., and Stephen W. Sears; American Heritage Publishing Co., Inc., New York, 1966. Bakeless, John, *The Eyes of Discovery;* Dover Publications, Inc., New York, 1961. Blacker, Irwin R., and Harry M. Rosen, *Conquest: Dispatches of Cortes From the New World;* The Universal Library, Grosset & Dunlap, New York, 1962. Bourne, Edward Gaylord, *Spain in America 1450–1580,* with new introduction and supplementary bibliography by Benjamin Keen; Barnes & Noble, Inc., New York, 1962. Brown, Lloyd A., *The Story of Maps;* Little, Brown and Company, Boston, 1949. Columbus, Christopher, *Four Voyages to the New World: Letters and Selected Documents,* translated by R. H. Major; bilingual edition, introduction by James E. Fagg; Corinth Books, New York, 1961. Harrisse, Henry, *The Discovery of North America. A Critical, Documentary, and Historic Investigation;* Henry Stevens and Son, London, and H. Welter, Paris, 1892. Gibson, Charles, *Spain in America;* Harper & Row, New York, 1966. Landström, Björn, *Columbus;* The Macmillan Company, New York, 1967. Mahn-Lot, Marianne, *Columbus,* Evergreen Profile Book, Grove Press, Inc., New York, 1961. Taylor, E. G. R., *Tudor Geography, 1485–1583;* Methuen, London, 1930.

I. *The Voyage of John de Verazzano, Along the Coast of North America, From Carolina to Newfoundland,* A.D. *1524,* translated from the original Italian by Joseph G. Cogswell; The New-York Historical Society Collections, 2nd series, Vol. I, New York, 1841.

II. Burpee, Lawrence J., *An Historical Atlas of Canada;* Thomas Nelson & Sons, Ltd., Toronto, 1927. Burrage, Henry S., *Early English and French Voyages (Chiefly From Hakluyt) 1534–1608;* Barnes & Noble, Inc., New York, 1959.

III. Bourne, E. G., *Narratives of the career of Hernando de Soto in the conquest of Florida, as told by a knight of Elvas, and in a relation by Luys Hernandez de Biedma, factor of the expedition; translated by Buckingham Smith, with an account of de Soto's expedition based on a diary of Rodrigo Ranjel, his private secretary, translated from Oviedo's Historia general y natural de las Indias;* Allerton Book Company, New York, 1922. Cumming, W. P., *The Southeast in Early Maps,* University of North Carolina Press, Chapel Hill, 1963. Hodge, Frederick W., and Theodore H. Lewis, *Spanish Explorers in the Southern United States, 1528–1543;* Barnes & Noble, Inc., New York, 1965. Lowery, Woodbury, *The Spanish Settlements Within the Present Limits of the United States, 1513–1561;* Russell & Russell, Inc., New York, 1959. (Vol. I; for Vol. II, see below.) Smith, Buckingham, *The Narrative of Alvar Nuñez Cabeza de Vaca;* Washington, 1851. (The first appearance of this work in English, privately printed "for presentation . . . to a few friends.") Winship, George Parker, *The Journey of Coronado 1540–1542, from the City of Mexico to the Grand Canyon of the Colorado and the Buffalo Plains of Texas, Kansas, and Nebraska as told by himself and his followers;* A. S. Barnes & Company, New York, 1904. (Contains Coronado's dispatches from the field.)

IV & V. Adams, Thomas R., *A Notable History, Containing Four Voyages Made By Certain French Captains Unto Florida, By René Laudonnière, Edited by Martin Basanier and Translated into English by Richard Hakluyt. A Facsimile of the Edition Printed in London in 1587, With A Survey of the Sixteenth-Century Printed French Accounts of the Attempt to Establish a French Colony in Florida;* Henry Stevens, Son & Stiles, 4 Upper Church Lane, Farnham, Surrey, England, and at Albee Court, Larchmont, N. Y., 1964. Lowery, Vol. II, *The Spanish Settlements Within the Present Limits of the United States, Florida 1562–1574.* (For Vol. I, see above.)

VI. Aubrey, John, *Brief Lives, edited from the Original Manuscripts and with an Introduction* by Oliver Lawson Dick; Secker and Warburg, London, 1950. Bigges, Walter, *A Summary and True Discourse of Sir Francis Drake's West Indian Voyage;* London, 1589. Commager, Henry Steele, *Documents of American History.* Appleton-Century-Crofts, New York, 1963. De Bry, Theodor, *Collectiones Peregrinationum in Indiam Orientalem et Indiam Occidentalem* (Voyages to the East and West Indies), Part I, Virginia, Part II, Florida; Frankfurt-on-Main, 1590, 1591. (With De Bry's engravings after White and Le Moyne.) Fletcher, Francis, *The World Encompassed by Sir Francis Drake, carefully Collected out of the notes of Master Francis Fletcher, Preacher in this Imployment, and divers others his followers;* London, 1628. Hakluyt, Richard, *The Principall Navigations, Voiages and Discoveries of the English Nation;* London, 1598–1600. Hulton, Paul Hope, and David Beers Quinn, *The American Drawings of John White, 1577–1590, With Drawings of European and Oriental Subjects;* London (Trustees of the British Museum), Chapel Hill (University of North Carolina Press), 1964. Lewis, Michael, *The Spanish Armada;* Thomas Y. Crowell Company, New York, 1968. Naunton, Sir Robert, *Fragmenta Regalia,* edited by Edward Arber; A. Constable and Co.,

Westminster, 1895. Purchas, Samuel, *Hakluytus Posthumus or Purchas his Pilgrimes;* London, 1625. Tyler, Lyon Gardiner, *Narratives of Early Virginia 1606–1625;* Barnes & Noble, Inc., New York, 1966. Waters, David W., *The Art of Navigation in Elizabethan and Early Stuart Times;* Hollis and Coates, London, 1958.

VII. Biggar, H. P., general editor, *The Works of Samuel de Champlain in six volumes . . . with a portfolio of plates and maps;* The Champlain Society, Toronto, 1922–36. Grant, W. L., *Voyages of Samuel de Champlain 1604–1618, With a map and two plans;* Charles Scribner's Sons, New York, 1907.

VIII. Juet, Robert, *Juet's Journal of Hudson's Voyage;* The New-York Historical Society Collections, 2nd series, Vol. I, New York, 1841.

IX & X. Bradford, William, *Correspondence between the colonies of New Netherlands and New-Plymouth,* A.D. *1627. From the letter-book of William Bradford, Governor of New-Plymouth, &c;* The New-York Historical Society Collections, 2nd series, Vol. I, New York, 1841. Doyle, John A., *History of the Plimoth plantation containing an account of the voyage of the 'Mayflower' written by William Bradford . . . Now reproduced in facsimile from the original manuscript;* London (Ward and Downey, Ltd.), Boston (Houghton, Mifflin Co.), 1896. Jameson, J. Franklin, *Narratives of New Netherland 1609–1664;* Barnes & Noble, Inc., New York, 1959. Morison, Samuel Eliot, *Of Plymouth Plantation, 1620–1647. The Complete Text, With Notes and an Introduction;* new edition, Modern Library, New York, 1967.

EPILOGUE. Washington, George, *The Journal of Major George Washington, sent by the Hon. Robert Dinwiddie, Esq., His Majesty's Lieutenant-Governor, and Commander-in-Chief of Virginia, to the Commandant of the French Forces on Ohio, Williamsburg, 1754;* facsimile edition, Dominion Books, A Division of The University of Virginia, Charlottesville, 1963.

INDEX

DAT